FAIRY TALE BATTLE ROYALE

2

STORY & ART BY
Soraho Ina

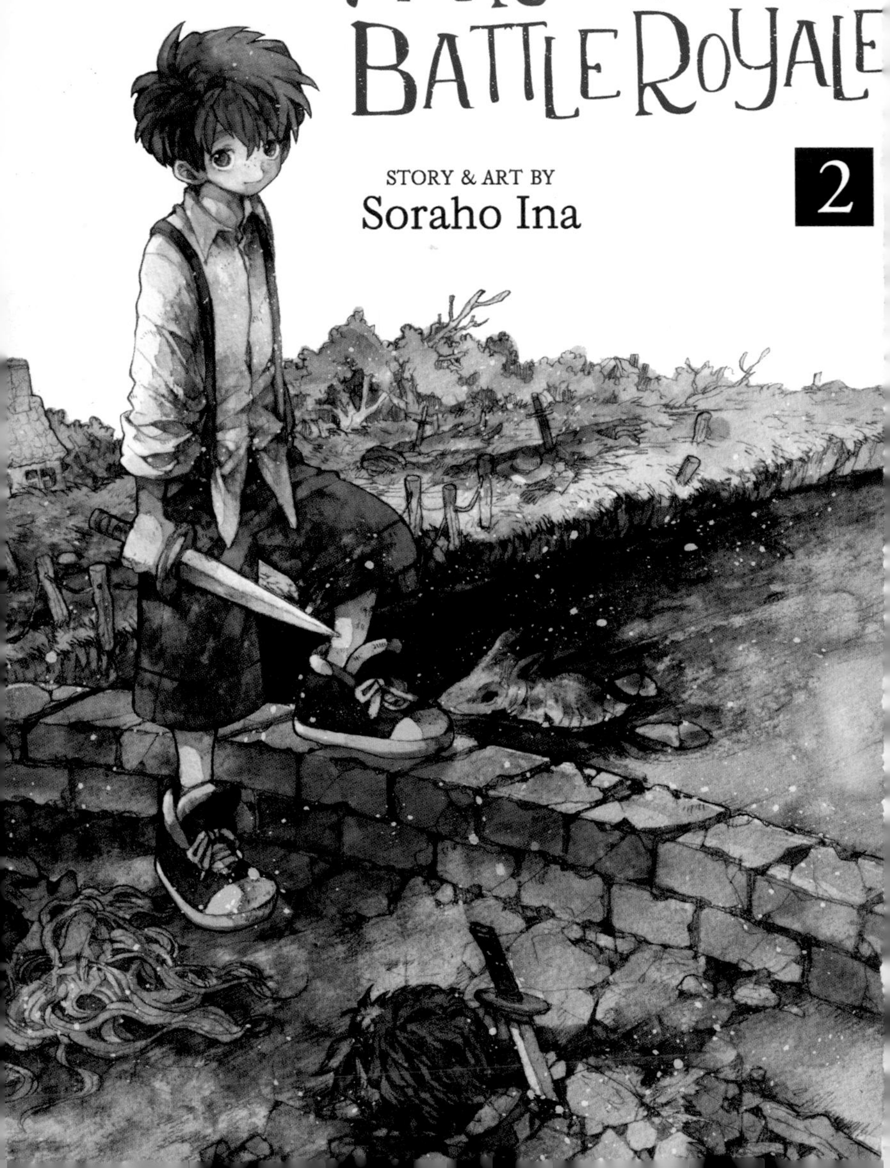

Contents

Chapter 5: Weapons

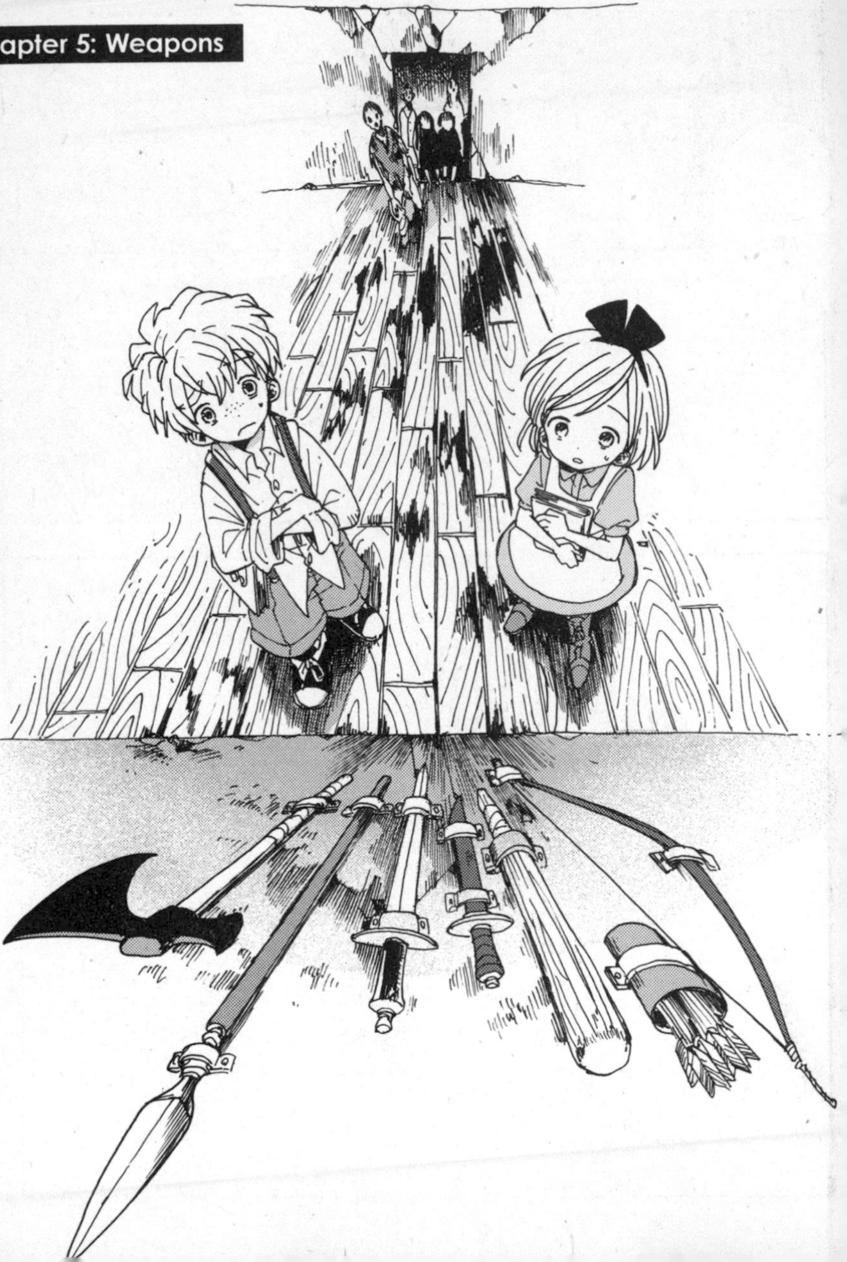

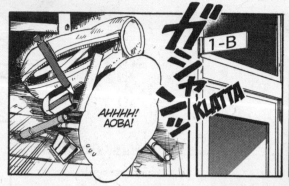

1-B
ガシャーンッ
KLATTA
AHHHH! AOBA!
WHAT IN THE WORLD ARE YOU DOING?
I... I'M SORRY!
OH, KUNINAKA. DID I WAKE YOU?
SORRY ABOUT THAT.
HEY! DON'T YOU TEASE AOBA LIKE THAT!
I found a way back into the Story World. Think we can meet up?

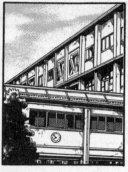

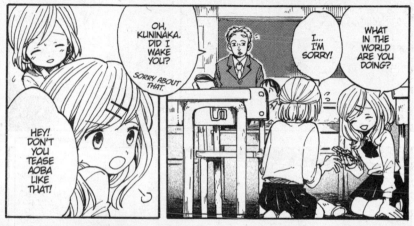

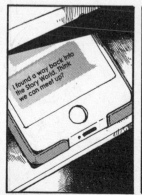

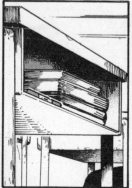

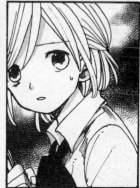

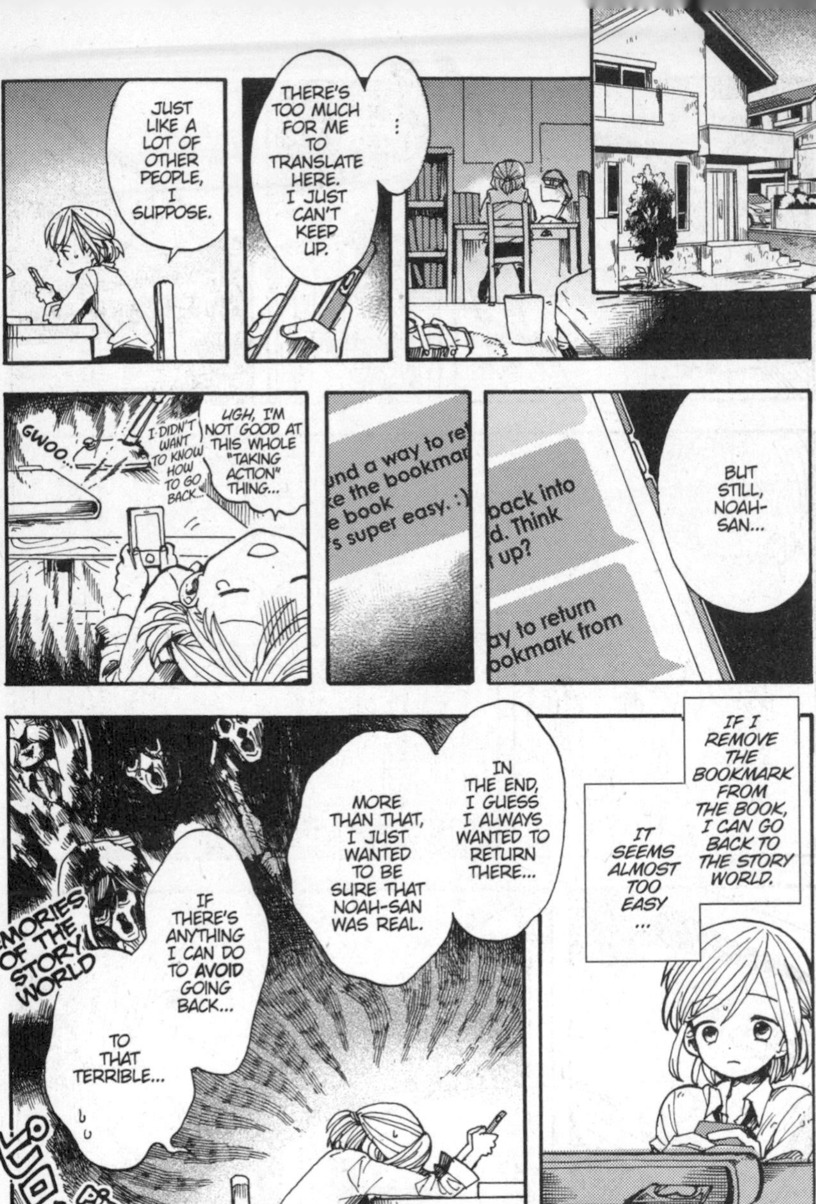
THERE'S TOO MUCH FOR ME TO TRANSLATE HERE. I JUST CAN'T KEEP UP.
...
JUST LIKE A LOT OF OTHER PEOPLE, I SUPPOSE.
BUT STILL, NOAH-SAN...
back into
d. Think
up?
ay to return
bookmark from
nd a way to re
e the bookmar
e book
's super easy. :)
UGH, I'M NOT GOOD AT THIS WHOLE "TAKING ACTION" THING...
I DIDN'T WANT TO KNOW HOW TO GO BACK...
GWOO...
IF I REMOVE THE BOOKMARK FROM THE BOOK, I CAN GO BACK TO THE STORY WORLD.
IT SEEMS ALMOST TOO EASY...
IN THE END, I GUESS I ALWAYS WANTED TO RETURN THERE...
MORE THAN THAT, I JUST WANTED TO BE SURE THAT NOAH-SAN WAS REAL.
IF THERE'S ANYTHING I CAN DO TO AVOID GOING BACK...
TO THAT TERRIBLE...
MEMORIES OF THE STORY WORLD
pirorin

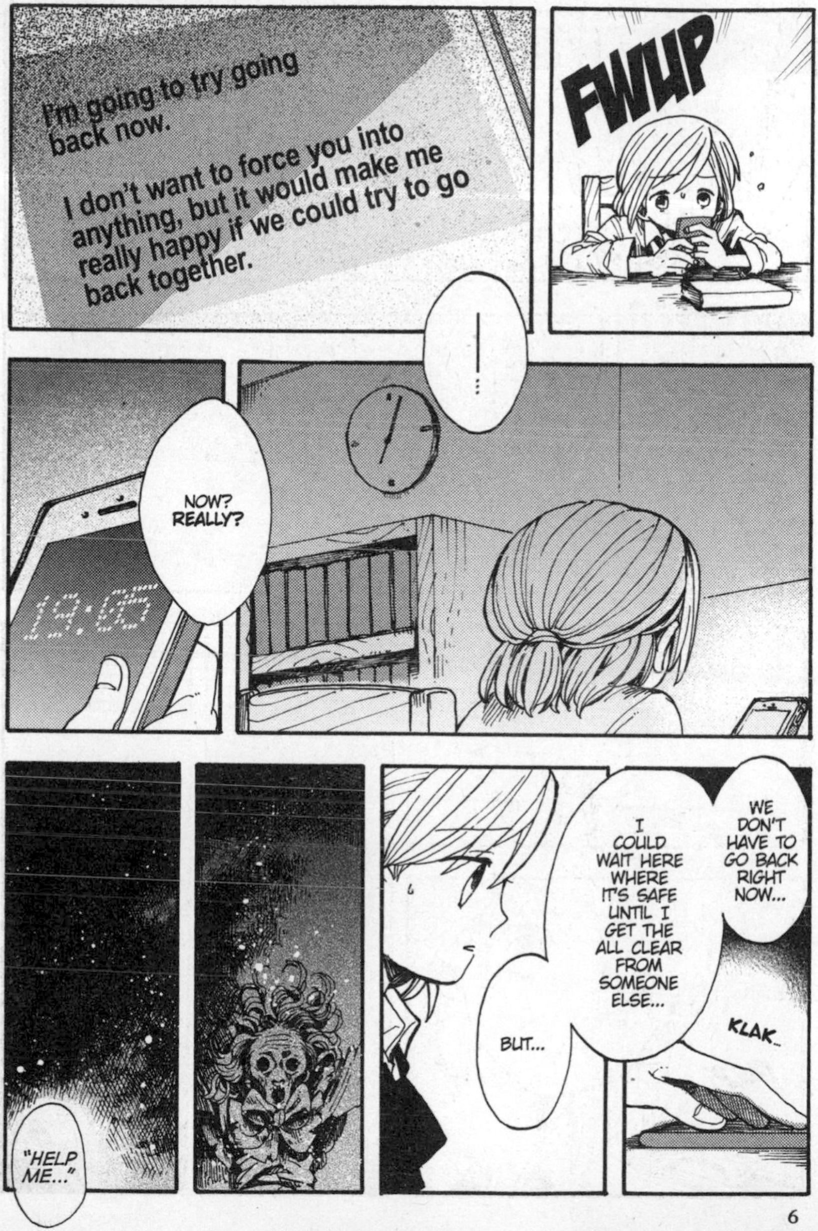
FWUP
I'm going to try going back now.
I don't want to force you into anything, but it would make me really happy if we could try to go back together.
—...
NOW? REALLY?
19:05
WE DON'T HAVE TO GO BACK RIGHT NOW...
I COULD WAIT HERE WHERE IT'S SAFE UNTIL I GET THE ALL CLEAR FROM SOMEONE ELSE...
BUT...
KLAK
"HELP ME..."

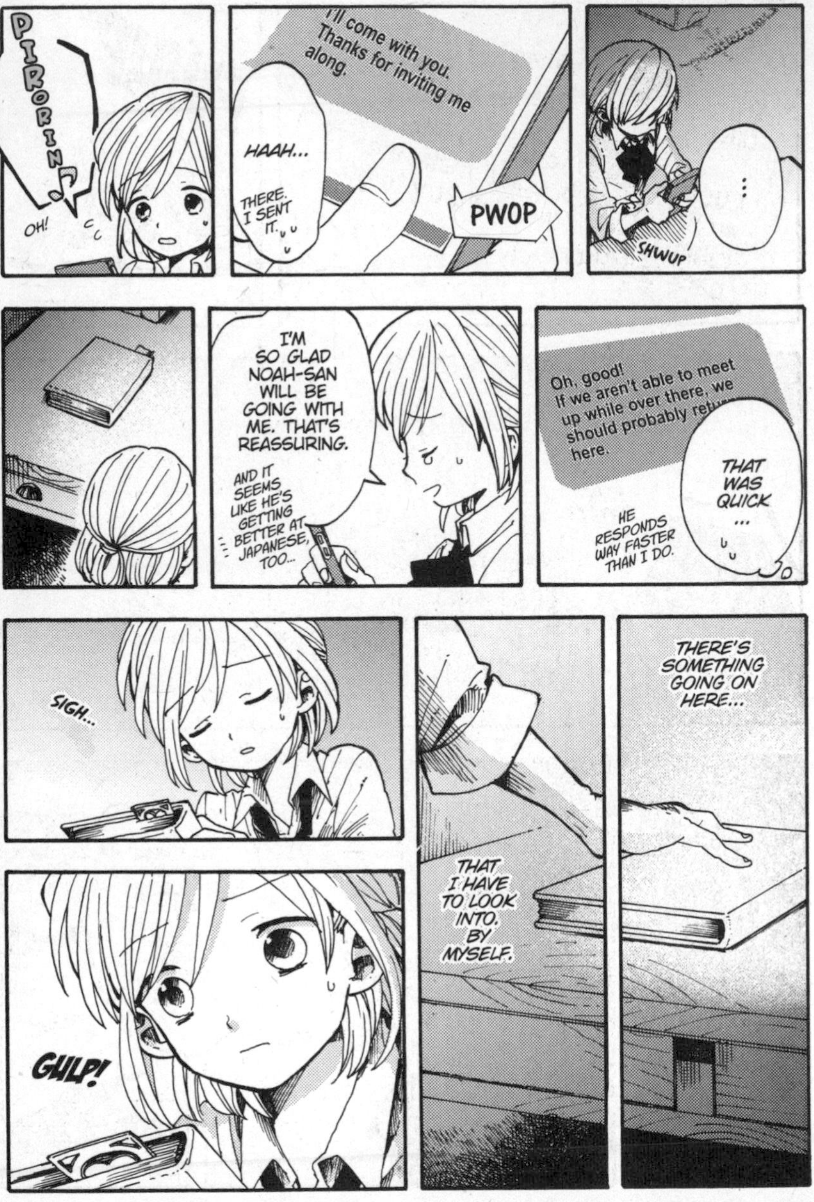
SHWUP
...
I'll come with you. Thanks for inviting me along.
HAAH...
THERE. I SENT IT.
PWOP
PIRORIN♪
OH!
Oh, good! If we aren't able to meet up while over there, we should probably retu
here.
THAT WAS QUICK...
HE RESPONDS WAY FASTER THAN I DO.
I'M SO GLAD NOAH-SAN WILL BE GOING WITH ME. THAT'S REASSURING.
AND IT SEEMS LIKE HE'S GETTING BETTER AT JAPANESE, TOO...
THERE'S SOMETHING GOING ON HERE...
THAT I HAVE TO LOOK INTO. BY MYSELF.
SIGH...
GULP!

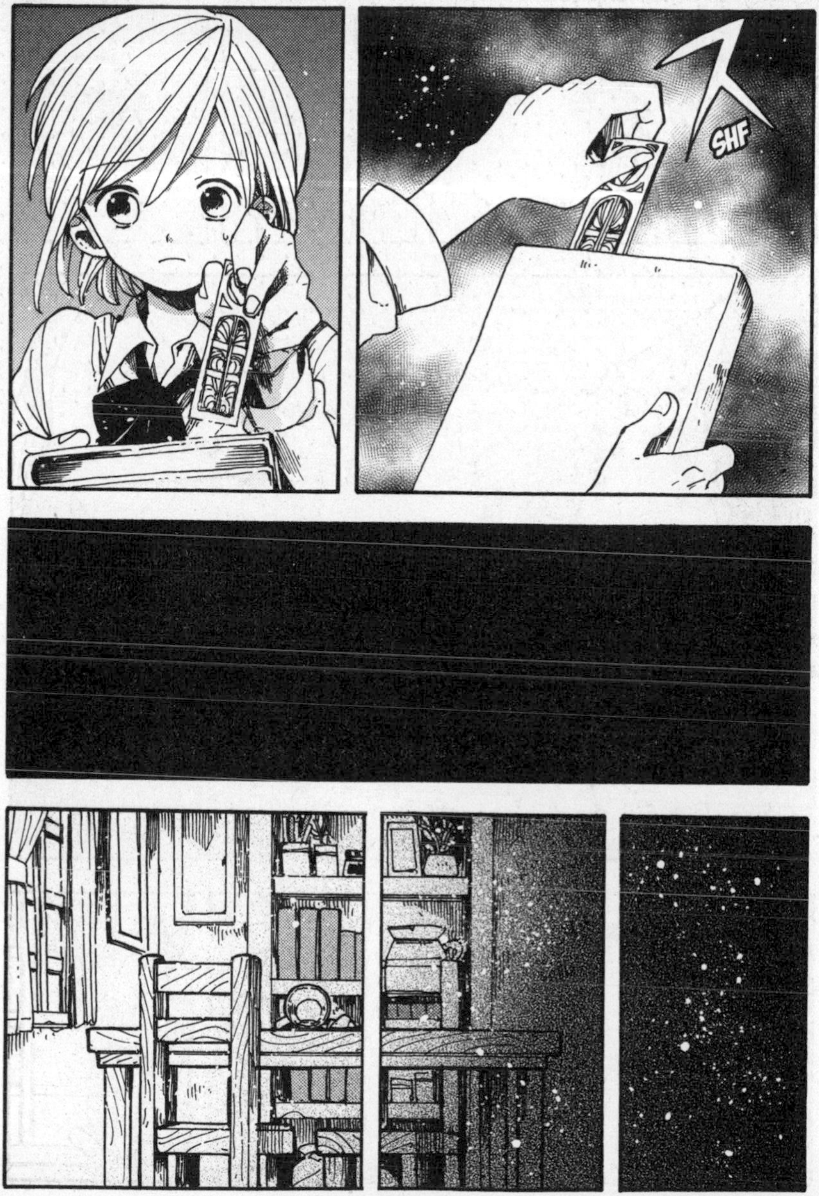
ス
SHF

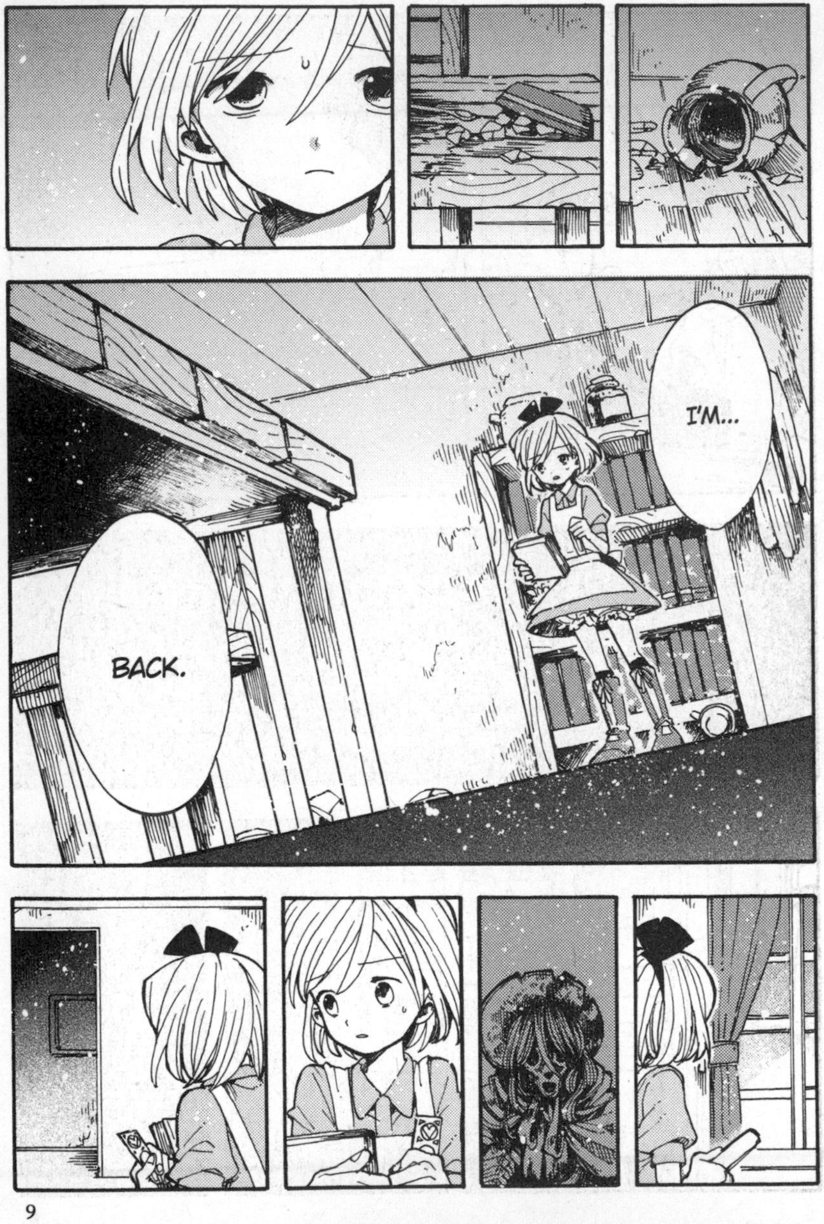
I'M...
BACK.

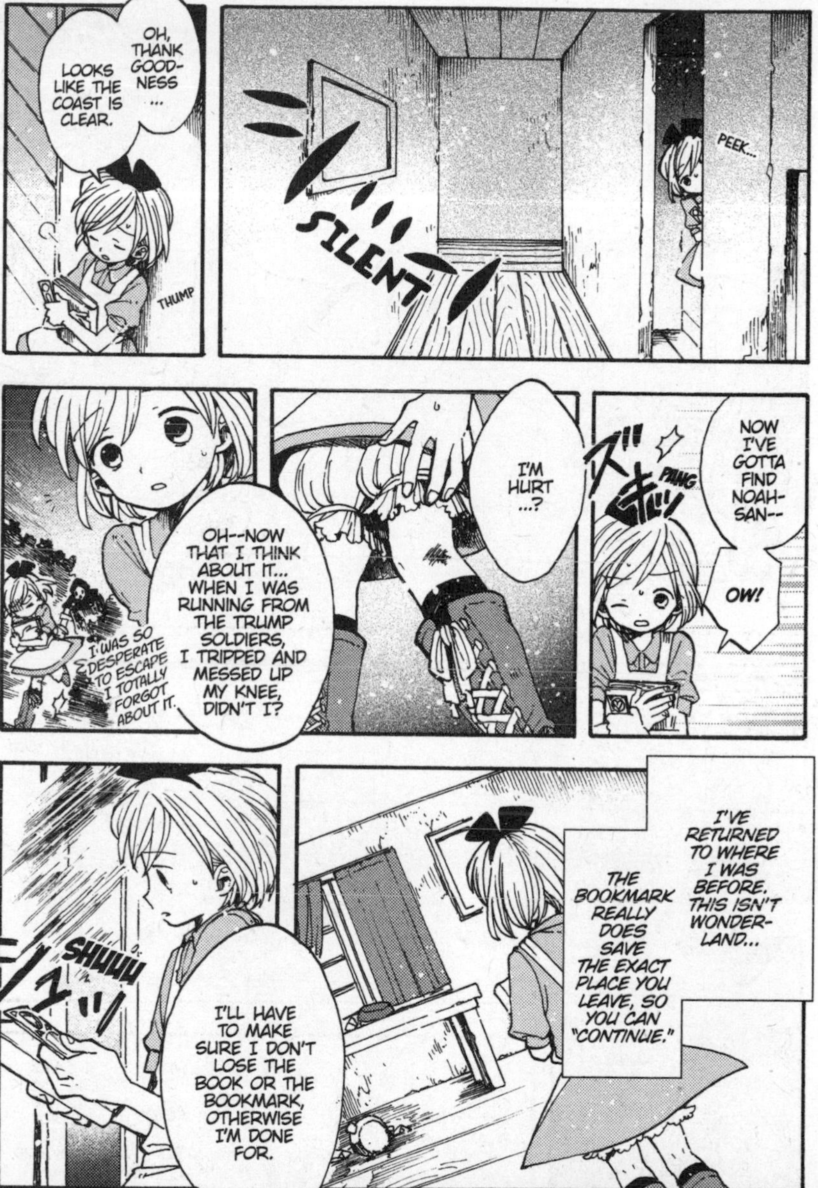
PEEK...
SILENT
OH, THANK GOODNESS...
LOOKS LIKE THE COAST IS CLEAR.
THUMP
NOW I'VE GOTTA FIND NOAH-SAN--
PANG
OW!
I'M HURT...?
OH--NOW THAT I THINK ABOUT IT... WHEN I WAS RUNNING FROM THE TRUMP SOLDIERS, I TRIPPED AND MESSED UP MY KNEE, DIDN'T I?
I WAS SO DESPERATE TO ESCAPE I TOTALLY FORGOT ABOUT IT.
I'VE RETURNED TO WHERE I WAS BEFORE. THIS ISN'T WONDERLAND...
THE BOOKMARK REALLY DOES SAVE THE EXACT PLACE YOU LEAVE, SO YOU CAN "CONTINUE."
SHUUU
I'LL HAVE TO MAKE SURE I DON'T LOSE THE BOOK OR THE BOOKMARK, OTHERWISE I'M DONE FOR.

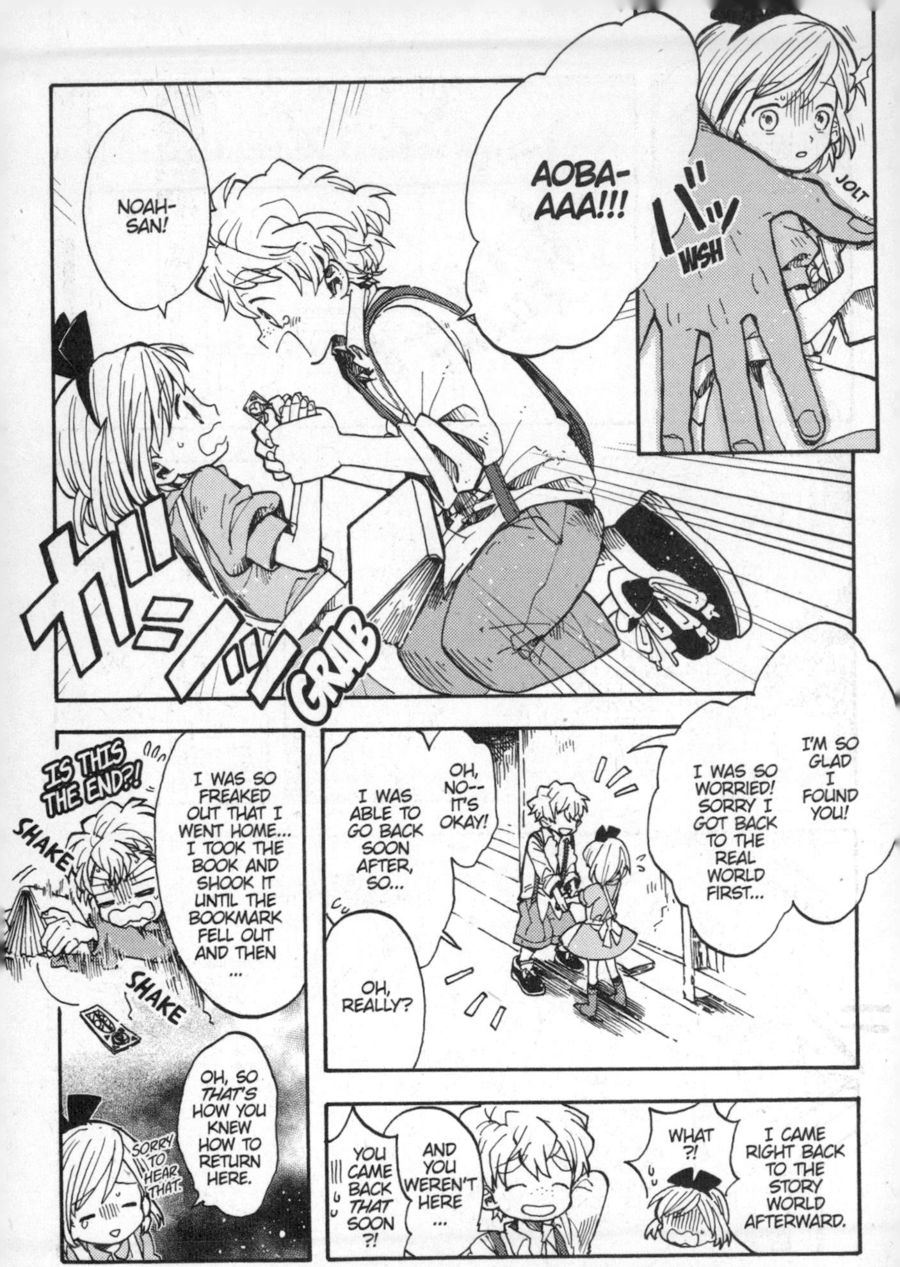
JOLT
WSH
AOBA-AAA!!!
NOAH-SAN!
GRAB
I'M SO GLAD I FOUND YOU!
I WAS SO WORRIED! SORRY I GOT BACK TO THE REAL WORLD FIRST...
OH, NO-- IT'S OKAY!
I WAS ABLE TO GO BACK SOON AFTER, SO...
OH, REALLY?
I CAME RIGHT BACK TO THE STORY WORLD AFTERWARD.
WHAT?!
AND YOU WEREN'T HERE...
YOU CAME BACK THAT SOON?!
IS THIS THE END?!
SHAKE
I WAS SO FREAKED OUT THAT I WENT HOME... I TOOK THE BOOK AND SHOOK IT UNTIL THE BOOKMARK FELL OUT AND THEN...
SHAKE
OH, SO *THAT'S* HOW YOU KNEW HOW TO RETURN HERE.
SORRY TO HEAR THAT.

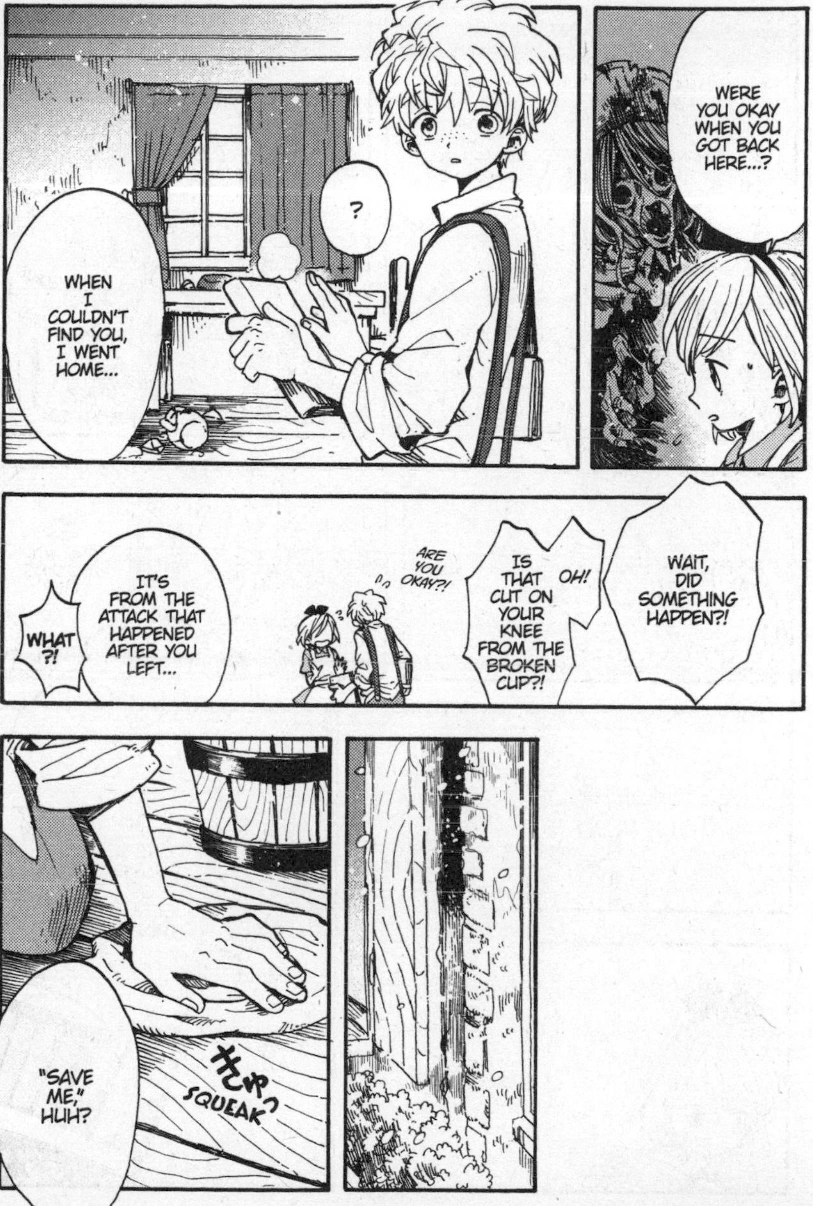
WERE YOU OKAY WHEN YOU GOT BACK HERE...?
?
WHEN I COULDN'T FIND YOU, I WENT HOME...
WAIT, DID SOMETHING HAPPEN?!
OH!
IS THAT CUT ON YOUR KNEE FROM THE BROKEN CUP?!
ARE YOU OKAY?!
IT'S FROM THE ATTACK THAT HAPPENED AFTER YOU LEFT...
WHAT?!
きゅっ
SQUEAK
"SAVE ME," HUH?

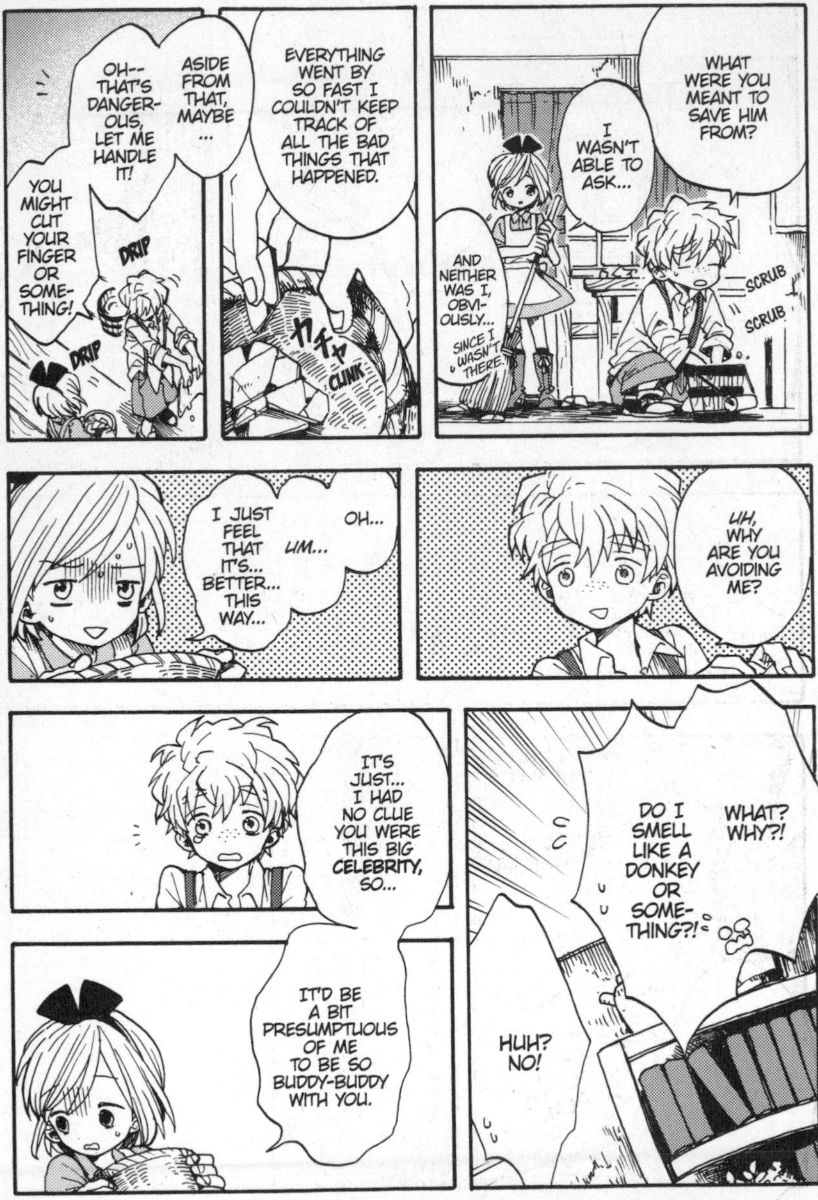
WHAT WERE YOU MEANT TO SAVE HIM FROM?
I WASN'T ABLE TO ASK...
AND NEITHER WAS I, OBVIOUSLY...
SINCE I WASN'T THERE.
SCRUB
SCRUB
EVERYTHING WENT BY SO FAST I COULDN'T KEEP TRACK OF ALL THE BAD THINGS THAT HAPPENED.
CLINK
ASIDE FROM THAT, MAYBE ...
OH-- THAT'S DANGEROUS, LET ME HANDLE IT!
YOU MIGHT CUT YOUR FINGER OR SOMETHING!
DRIP
DRIP
UH, WHY ARE YOU AVOIDING ME?
OH...
UM...
I JUST FEEL THAT IT'S... BETTER... THIS WAY...
WHAT? WHY?!
DO I SMELL LIKE A DONKEY OR SOMETHING?!
HUH? NO!
IT'S JUST... I HAD NO CLUE YOU WERE THIS BIG CELEBRITY, SO...
IT'D BE A BIT PRESUMPTUOUS OF ME TO BE SO BUDDY-BUDDY WITH YOU.

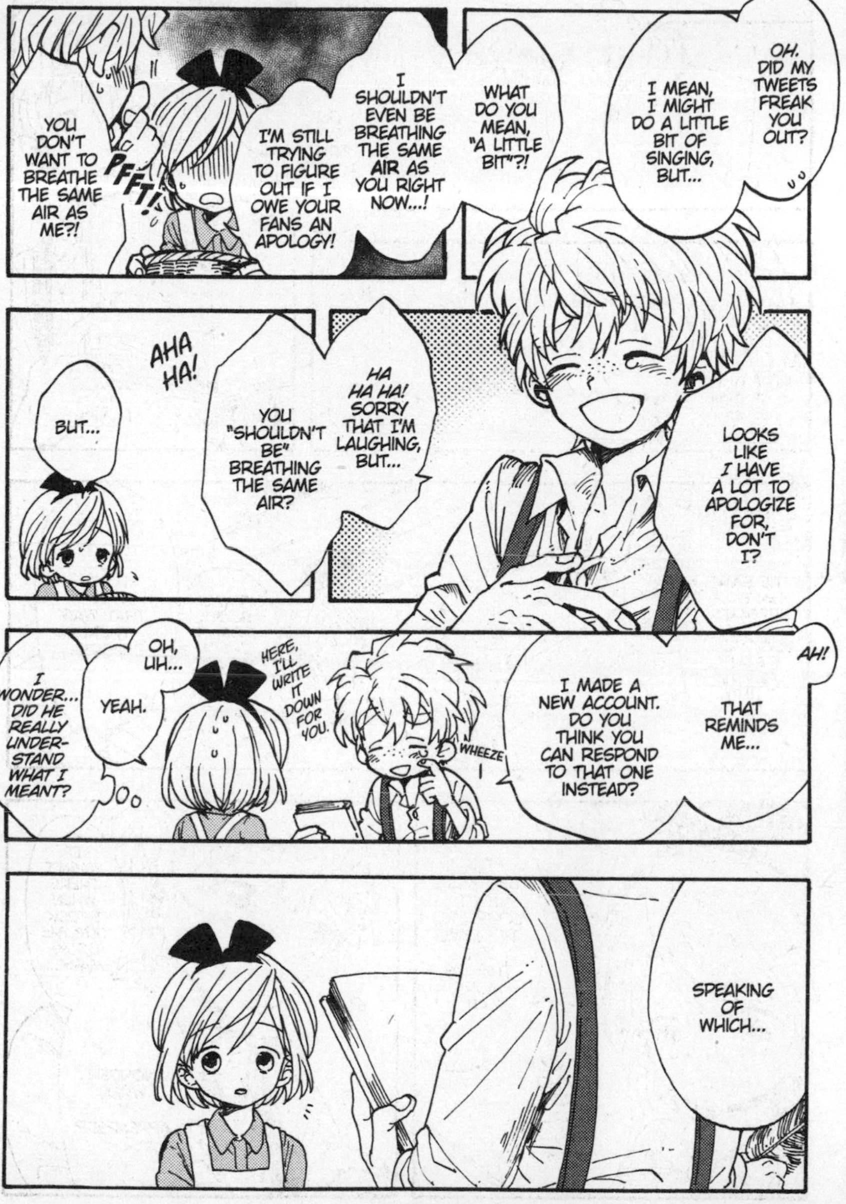
OH. DID MY TWEETS FREAK YOU OUT?
I MEAN, I MIGHT DO A LITTLE BIT OF SINGING, BUT...
WHAT DO YOU MEAN, "A LITTLE BIT"?!
I SHOULDN'T EVEN BE BREATHING THE SAME AIR AS YOU RIGHT NOW...!
I'M STILL TRYING TO FIGURE OUT IF I OWE YOUR FANS AN APOLOGY!
PFFT!
YOU DON'T WANT TO BREATHE THE SAME AIR AS ME?!
LOOKS LIKE I HAVE A LOT TO APOLOGIZE FOR, DON'T I?
HA HA HA! SORRY THAT I'M LAUGHING, BUT...
YOU "SHOULDN'T BE" BREATHING THE SAME AIR?
AHA HA!
BUT...
AH!
THAT REMINDS ME...
I MADE A NEW ACCOUNT. DO YOU THINK YOU CAN RESPOND TO THAT ONE INSTEAD?
WHEEZE
HERE, I'LL WRITE IT DOWN FOR YOU.
OH, UH...
YEAH.
I WONDER... DID HE REALLY UNDERSTAND WHAT I MEANT?
SPEAKING OF WHICH...

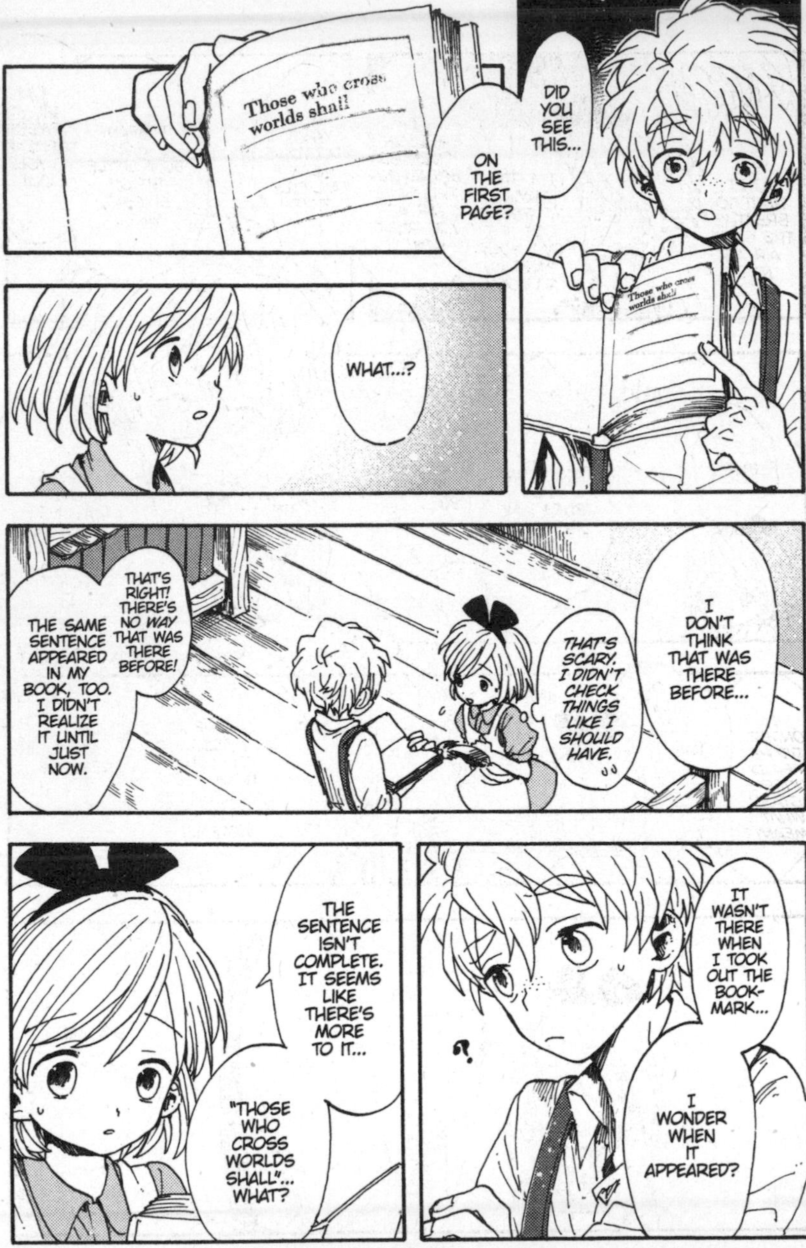
DID YOU SEE THIS...
ON THE FIRST PAGE?
Those who cross worlds shall
Those who cross worlds shall
WHAT...?
I DON'T THINK THAT WAS THERE BEFORE...
THAT'S SCARY. I DIDN'T CHECK THINGS LIKE I SHOULD HAVE.
THAT'S RIGHT! THERE'S NO WAY THAT WAS THERE BEFORE!
THE SAME SENTENCE APPEARED IN MY BOOK, TOO. I DIDN'T REALIZE IT UNTIL JUST NOW.
IT WASN'T THERE WHEN I TOOK OUT THE BOOK-MARK...
?
I WONDER WHEN IT APPEARED?
THE SENTENCE ISN'T COMPLETE. IT SEEMS LIKE THERE'S MORE TO IT...
"THOSE WHO CROSS WORLDS SHALL"... WHAT?

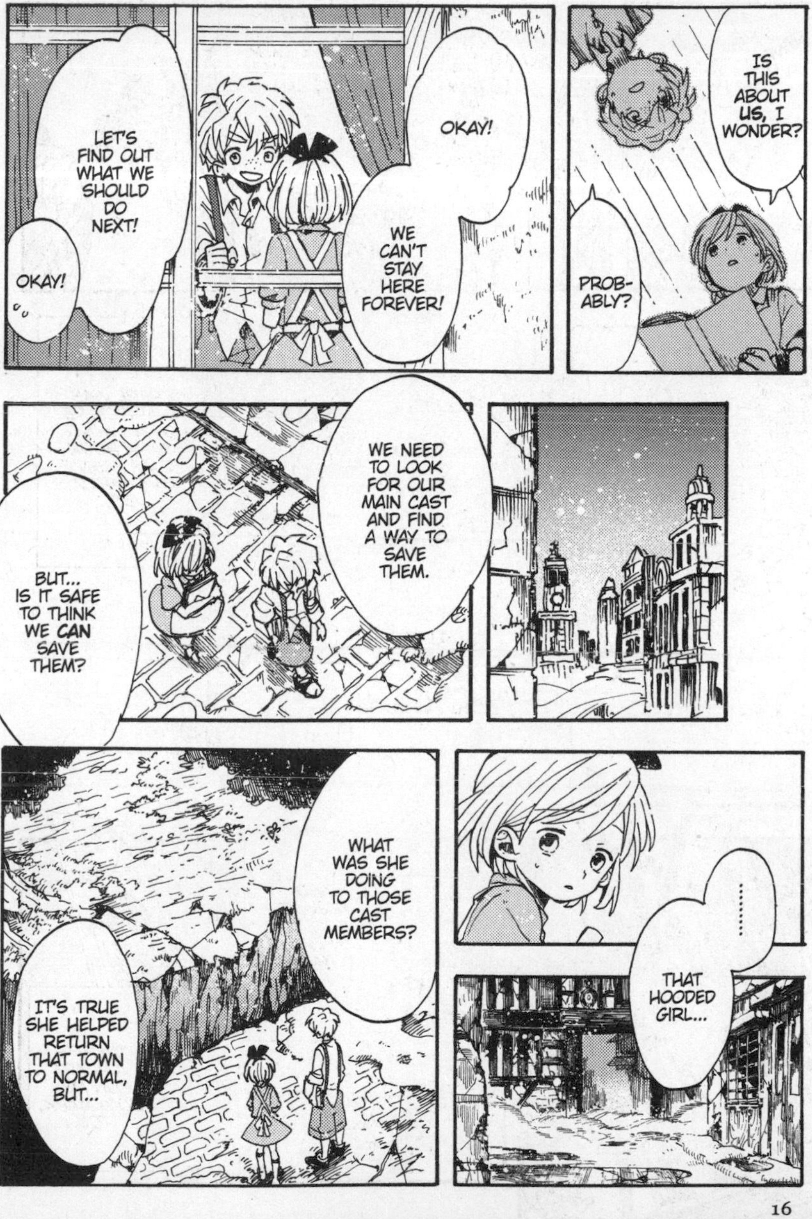
IS THIS ABOUT US, I WONDER?
PROBABLY?
OKAY!
WE CAN'T STAY HERE FOREVER!
LET'S FIND OUT WHAT WE SHOULD DO NEXT!
OKAY!
WE NEED TO LOOK FOR OUR MAIN CAST AND FIND A WAY TO SAVE THEM.
BUT... IS IT SAFE TO THINK WE **CAN** SAVE THEM?
......
THAT HOODED GIRL...
WHAT WAS SHE DOING TO THOSE CAST MEMBERS?
IT'S TRUE SHE HELPED RETURN THAT TOWN TO NORMAL, BUT...

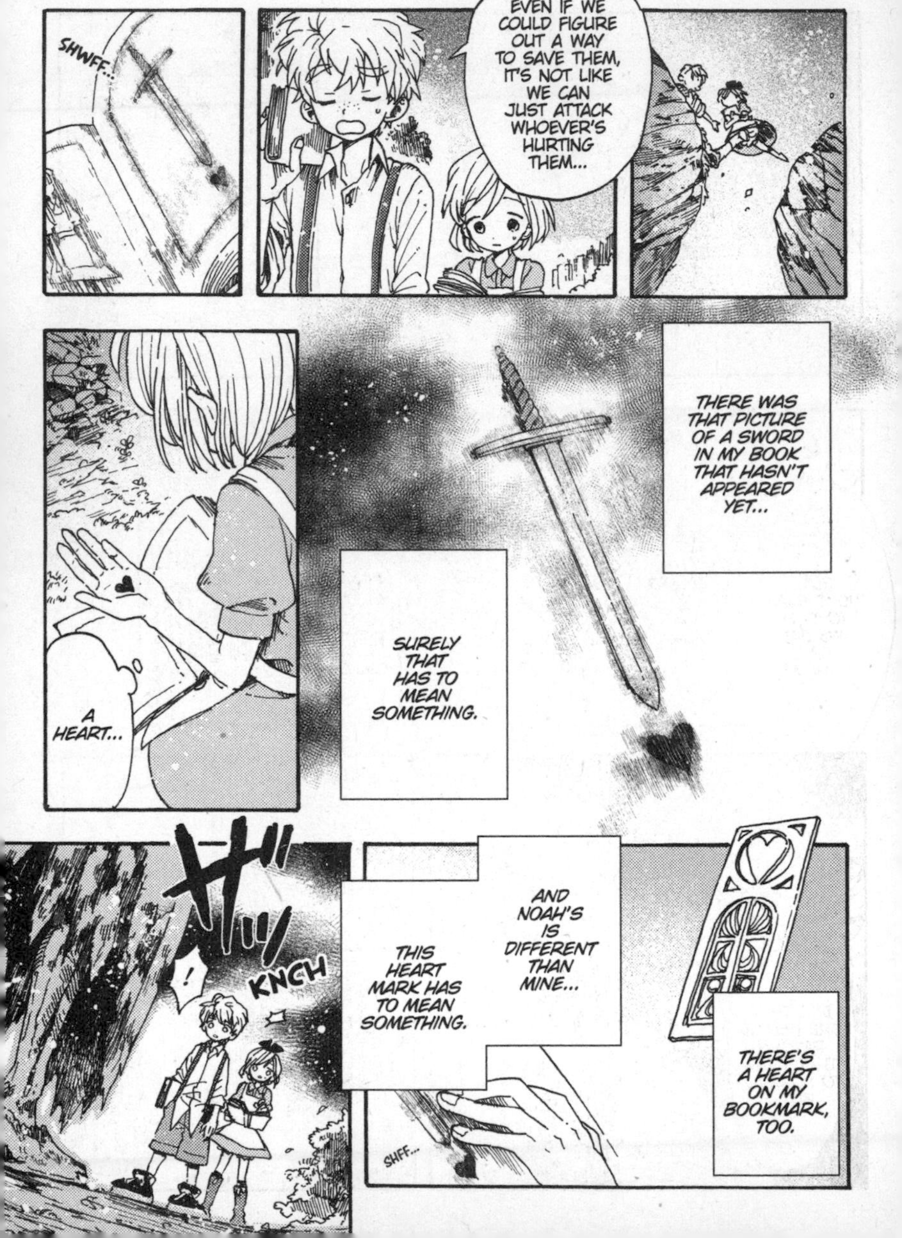
EVEN IF WE COULD FIGURE OUT A WAY TO SAVE THEM, IT'S NOT LIKE WE CAN JUST ATTACK WHOEVER'S HURTING THEM...
SHWFF...
THERE WAS THAT PICTURE OF A SWORD IN MY BOOK THAT HASN'T APPEARED YET...
SURELY THAT HAS TO MEAN SOMETHING.
A HEART...
THERE'S A HEART ON MY BOOKMARK, TOO.
AND NOAH'S IS DIFFERENT THAN MINE...
THIS HEART MARK HAS TO MEAN SOMETHING.
SHFF...
KNCH
!

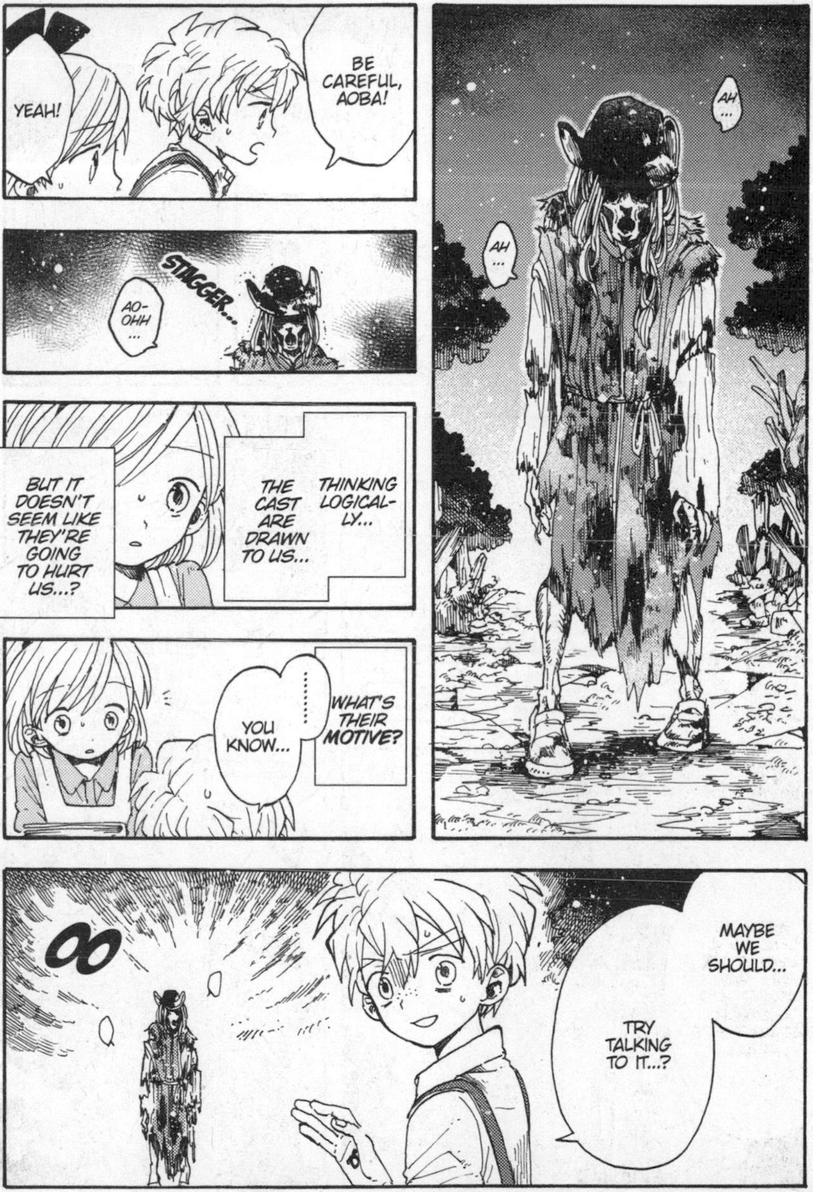
AH ...
AH ...
BE CAREFUL, AOBA!
YEAH!
STAGGER...
AO-OHH ...
THINKING LOGICAL-LY...
THE CAST ARE DRAWN TO US...
BUT IT DOESN'T SEEM LIKE THEY'RE GOING TO HURT US...?
WHAT'S THEIR MOTIVE?
......
YOU KNOW...
MAYBE WE SHOULD...
TRY TALKING TO IT...?
OO

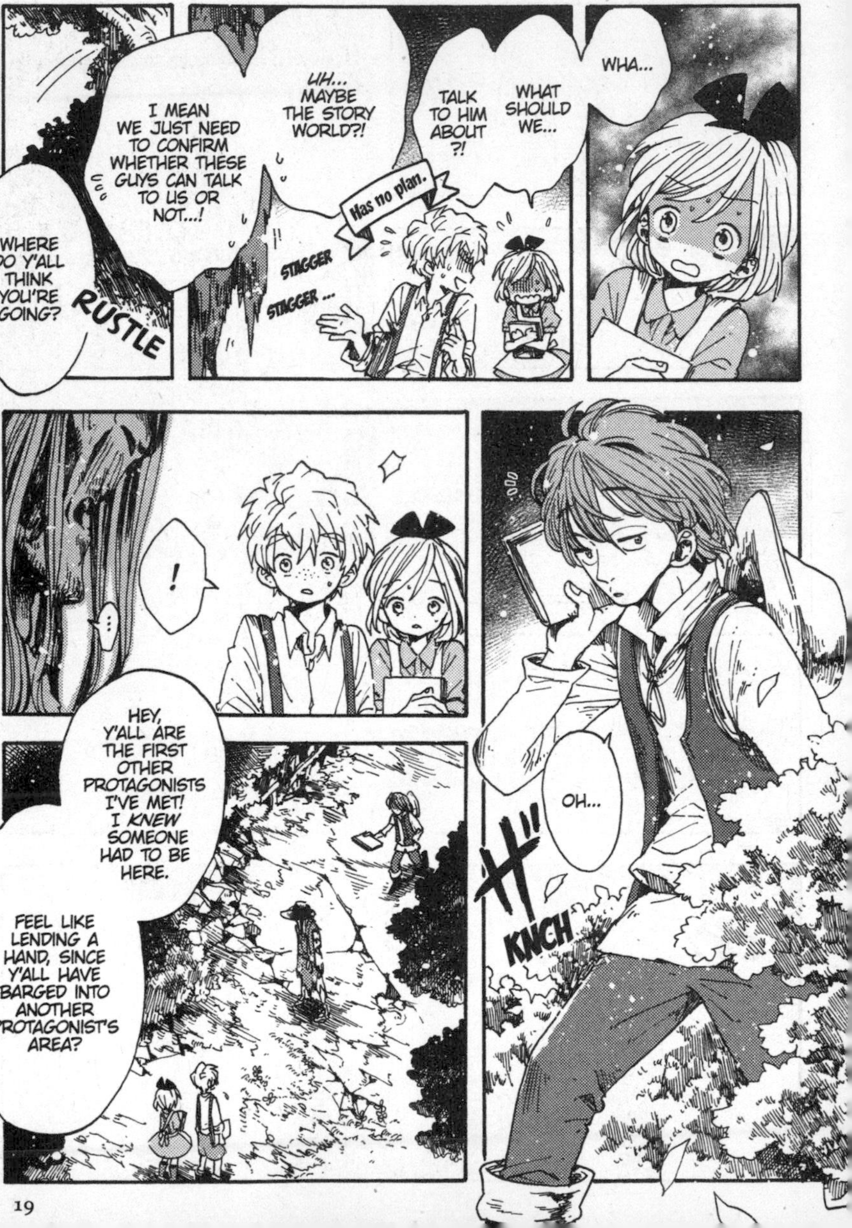
WHA...
WHAT SHOULD WE...
TALK TO HIM ABOUT ?!
UH... MAYBE THE STORY WORLD?!
Has no plan.
STAGGER
STAGGER ...
I MEAN WE JUST NEED TO CONFIRM WHETHER THESE GUYS CAN TALK TO US OR NOT...!
RUSTLE
WHERE DO Y'ALL THINK YOU'RE GOING?
OH...
KNCH
!
...
HEY, Y'ALL ARE THE FIRST OTHER PROTAGONISTS I'VE MET! I KNEW SOMEONE HAD TO BE HERE.
FEEL LIKE LENDING A HAND, SINCE Y'ALL HAVE BARGED INTO ANOTHER PROTAGONIST'S AREA?

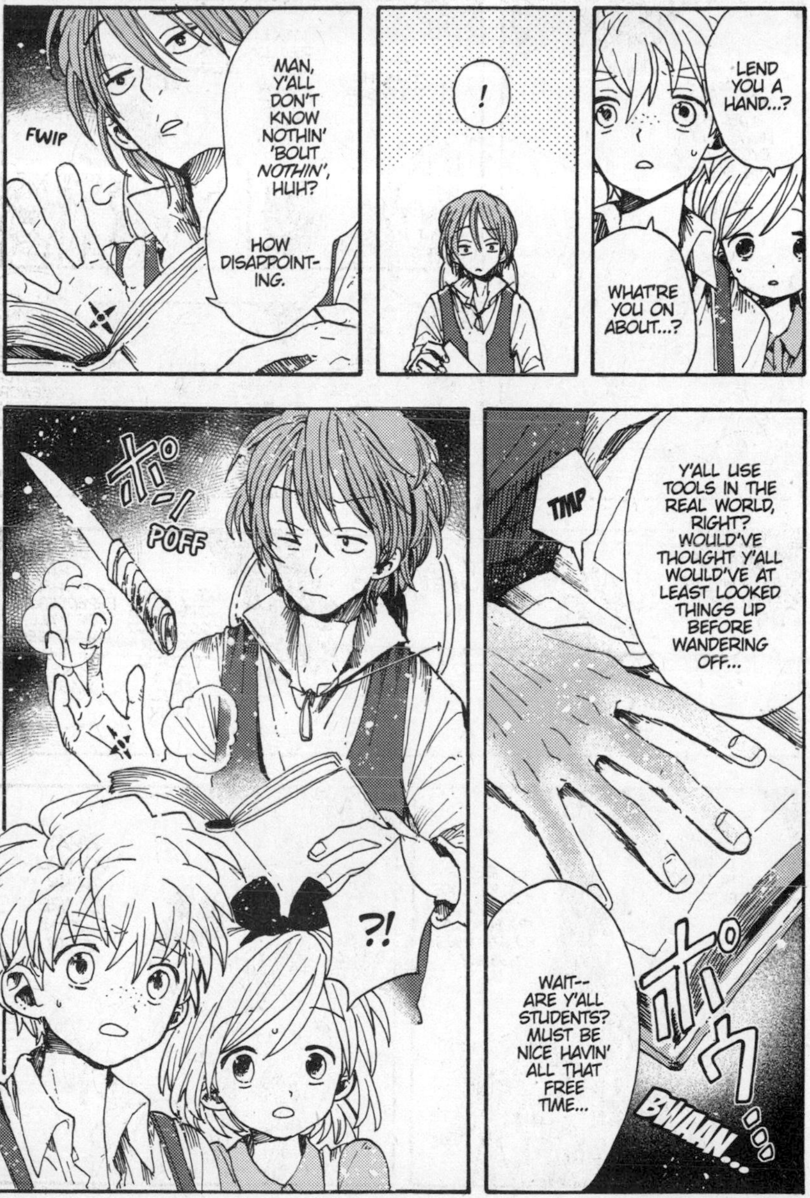
LEND YOU A HAND...?
WHAT'RE YOU ON ABOUT...?
!
MAN, Y'ALL DON'T KNOW NOTHIN' 'BOUT *NOTHIN'*, HUH?
HOW DISAPPOINT-ING.
FWIP
Y'ALL USE TOOLS IN THE REAL WORLD, RIGHT? WOULD'VE THOUGHT Y'ALL WOULD'VE AT LEAST LOOKED THINGS UP BEFORE WANDERING OFF...
TMP
WAIT-- ARE Y'ALL STUDENTS? MUST BE NICE HAVIN' ALL THAT FREE TIME...
BWAAAN...
POFF
?!

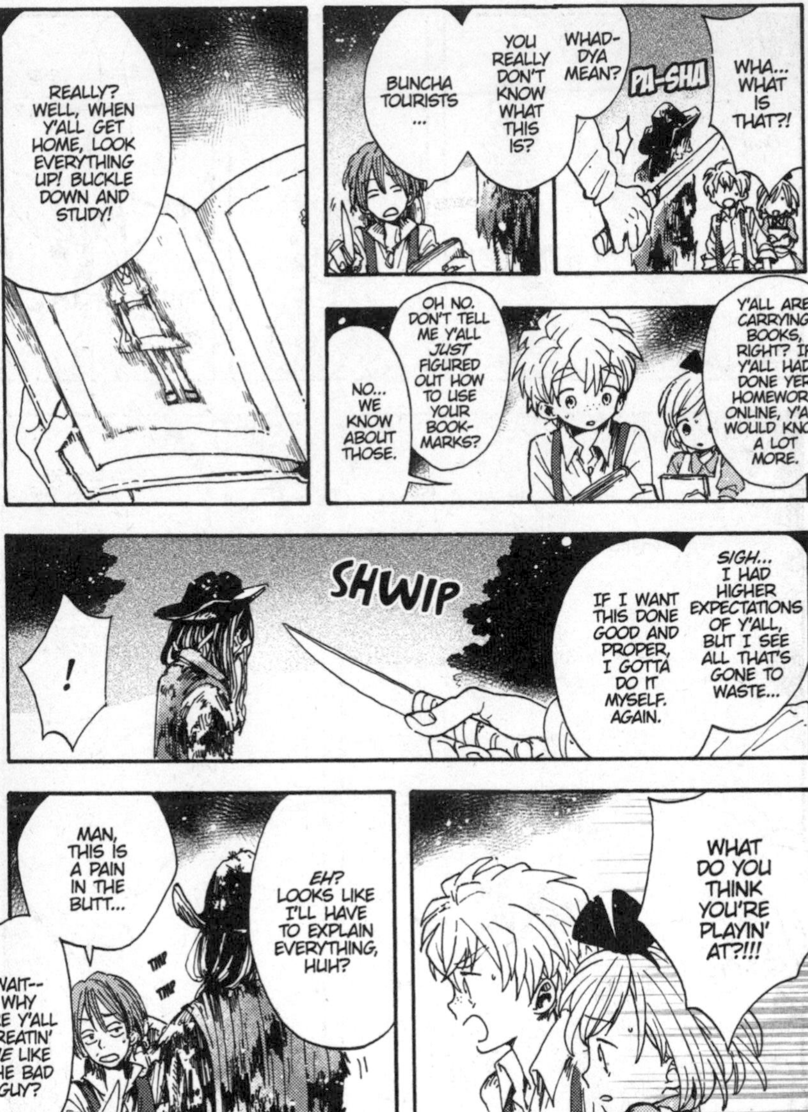

WHA... WHAT IS THAT?!
PA-SHA
WHAD-DYA MEAN?
YOU REALLY DON'T KNOW WHAT THIS IS?
BUNCHA TOURISTS ...
Y'ALL ARE CARRYING BOOKS, RIGHT? IF Y'ALL HAD DONE YER HOMEWORK ONLINE, Y'ALL WOULD KNOW A LOT MORE.
OH NO. DON'T TELL ME Y'ALL *JUST* FIGURED OUT HOW TO USE YOUR BOOK-MARKS?
NO... WE KNOW ABOUT THOSE.
REALLY? WELL, WHEN Y'ALL GET HOME, LOOK EVERYTHING UP! BUCKLE DOWN AND STUDY!
SIGH... I HAD HIGHER EXPECTATIONS OF Y'ALL, BUT I SEE ALL THAT'S GONE TO WASTE...
IF I WANT THIS DONE GOOD AND PROPER, I GOTTA DO IT MYSELF. AGAIN.
SHWIP
!
WHAT DO YOU THINK YOU'RE PLAYIN' AT?!!!
EH? LOOKS LIKE I'LL HAVE TO EXPLAIN EVERYTHING, HUH?
MAN, THIS IS A PAIN IN THE BUTT...
TMP
TMP
WAIT-- WHY ARE Y'ALL TREATIN' *ME* LIKE THE BAD GUY?
STAGGER

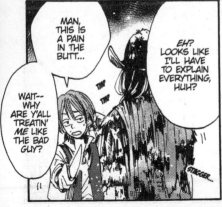

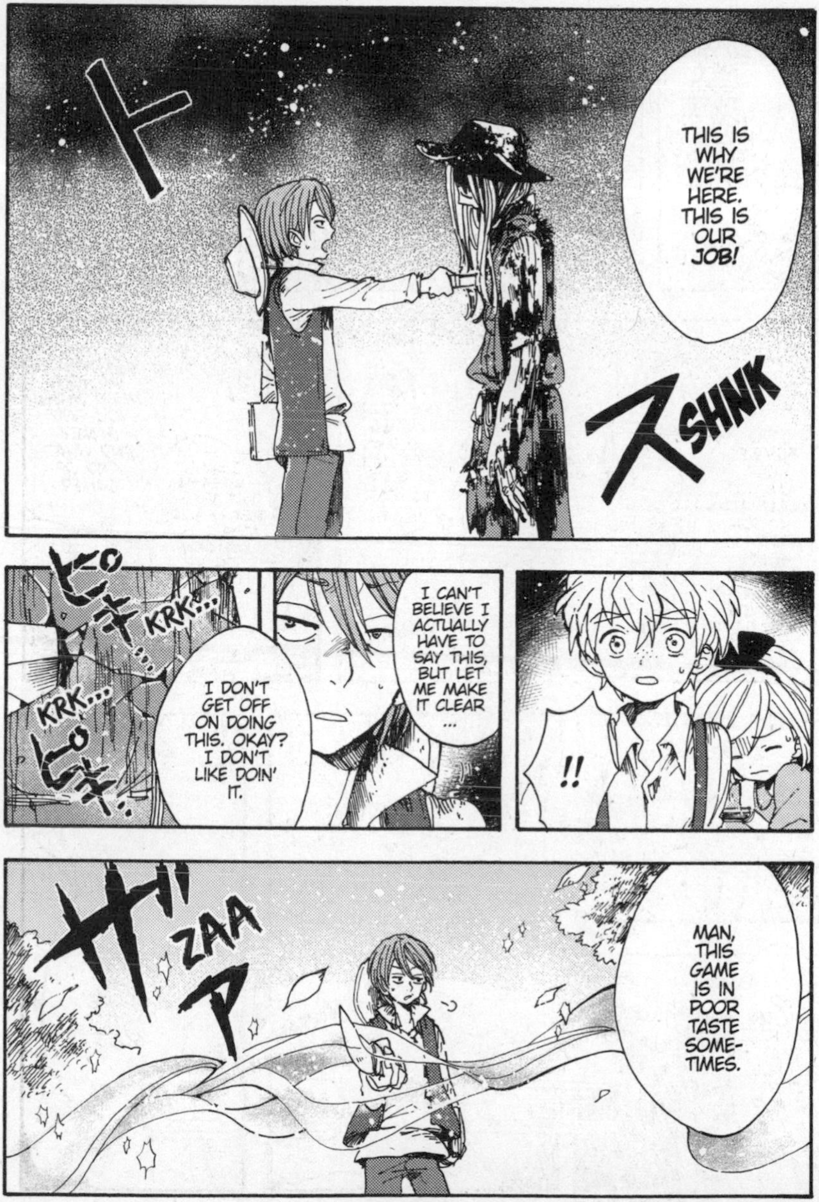
THIS IS WHY WE'RE HERE. THIS IS OUR JOB!
ト
ス SHNK
!!
I CAN'T BELIEVE I ACTUALLY HAVE TO SAY THIS, BUT LET ME MAKE IT CLEAR ...
I DON'T GET OFF ON DOING THIS. OKAY? I DON'T LIKE DOIN' IT.
KRK...
KRK...
MAN, THIS GAME IS IN POOR TASTE SOME-TIMES.
ZAA

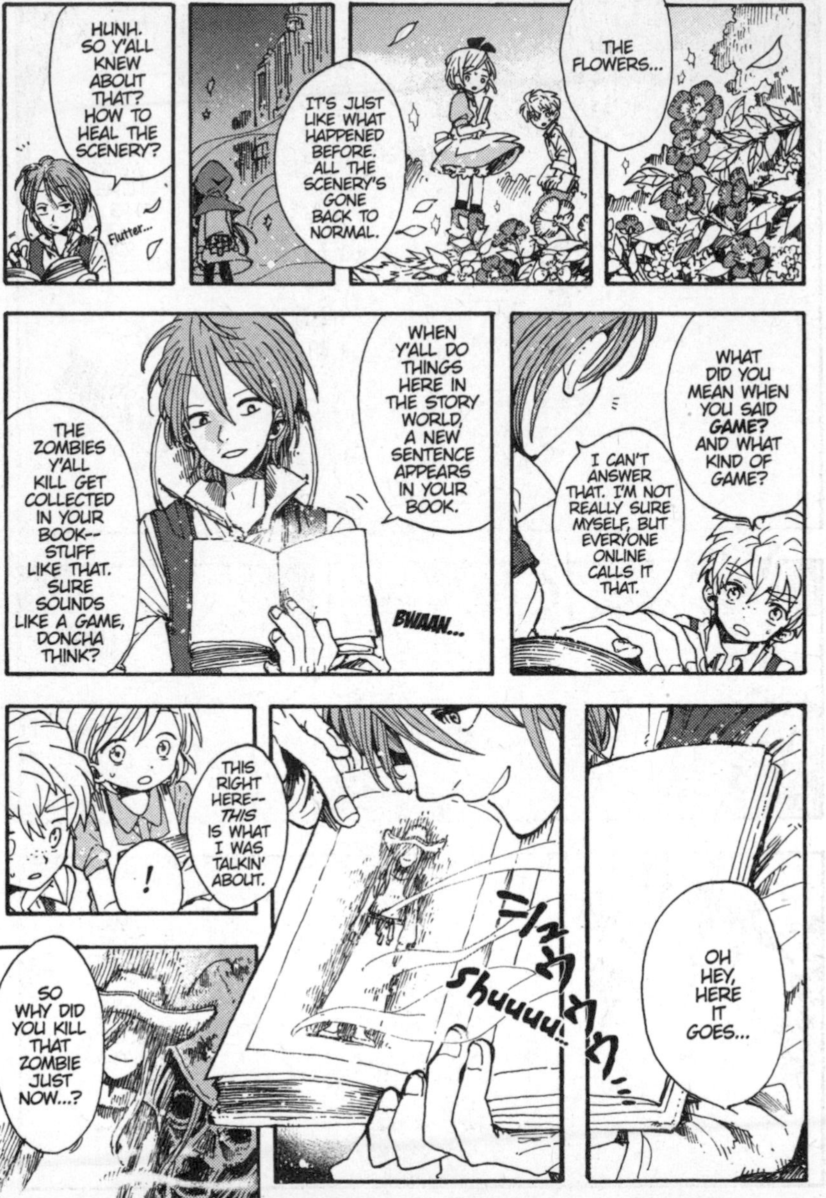
THE FLOWERS...
IT'S JUST LIKE WHAT HAPPENED BEFORE. ALL THE SCENERY'S GONE BACK TO NORMAL.
HUNH. SO Y'ALL KNEW ABOUT THAT? HOW TO HEAL THE SCENERY?
Flutter...
WHAT DID YOU MEAN WHEN YOU SAID GAME? AND WHAT KIND OF GAME?
I CAN'T ANSWER THAT. I'M NOT REALLY SURE MYSELF, BUT EVERYONE ONLINE CALLS IT THAT.
WHEN Y'ALL DO THINGS HERE IN THE STORY WORLD, A NEW SENTENCE APPEARS IN YOUR BOOK.
THE ZOMBIES Y'ALL KILL GET COLLECTED IN YOUR BOOK--STUFF LIKE THAT. SURE SOUNDS LIKE A GAME, DONCHA THINK?
BWAAN...
OH HEY, HERE IT GOES...
Shuuuu...
THIS RIGHT HERE--*THIS* IS WHAT I WAS TALKIN' ABOUT.
!
SO WHY DID YOU KILL THAT ZOMBIE JUST NOW...?

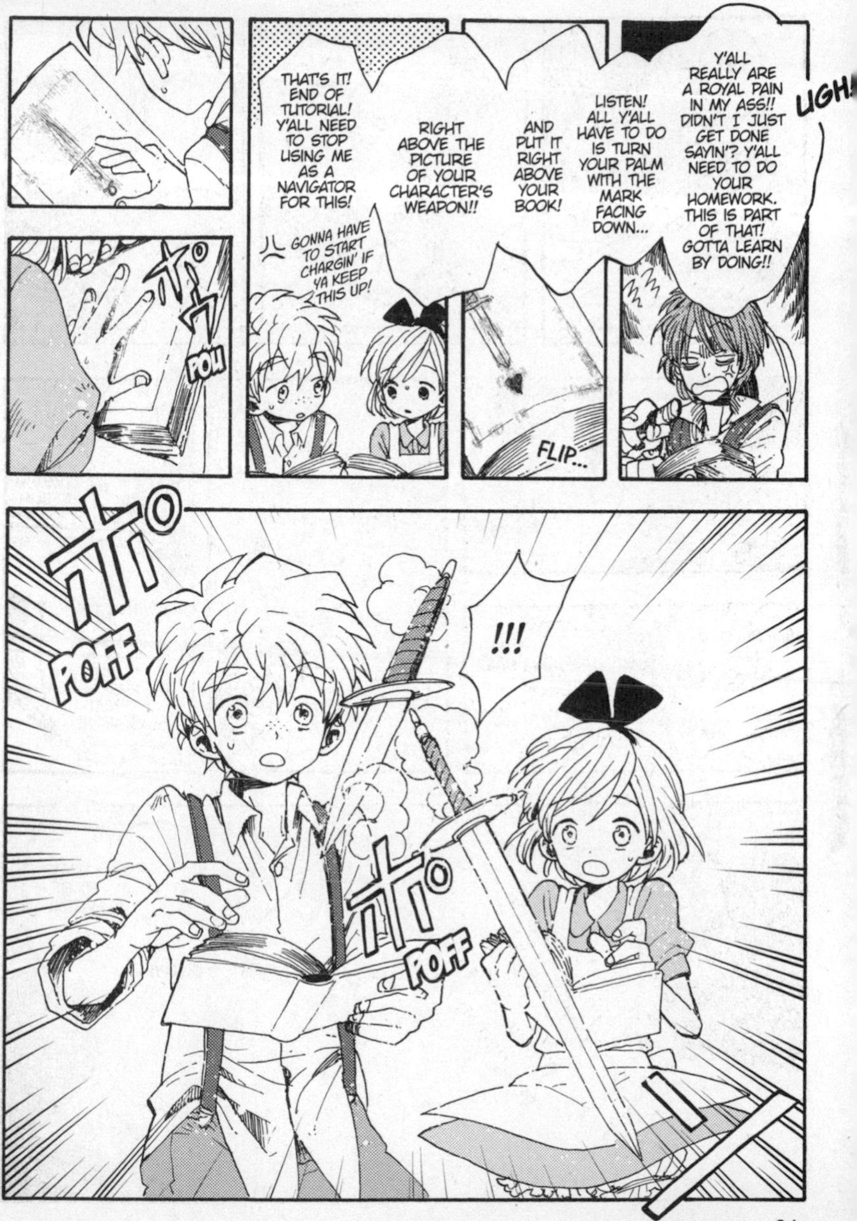
UGH!
Y'ALL REALLY ARE A ROYAL PAIN IN MY ASS!! DIDN'T I JUST GET DONE SAYIN'? Y'ALL NEED TO DO YOUR HOMEWORK. THIS IS PART OF THAT! GOTTA LEARN BY DOING!!
LISTEN! ALL Y'ALL HAVE TO DO IS TURN YOUR PALM WITH THE MARK FACING DOWN...
AND PUT IT RIGHT ABOVE YOUR BOOK!
FLIP...
RIGHT ABOVE THE PICTURE OF YOUR CHARACTER'S WEAPON!!
THAT'S IT! END OF TUTORIAL! Y'ALL NEED TO STOP USING ME AS A NAVIGATOR FOR THIS!
GONNA HAVE TO START CHARGIN' IF YA KEEP THIS UP!
POW
POFF
!!!
POFF

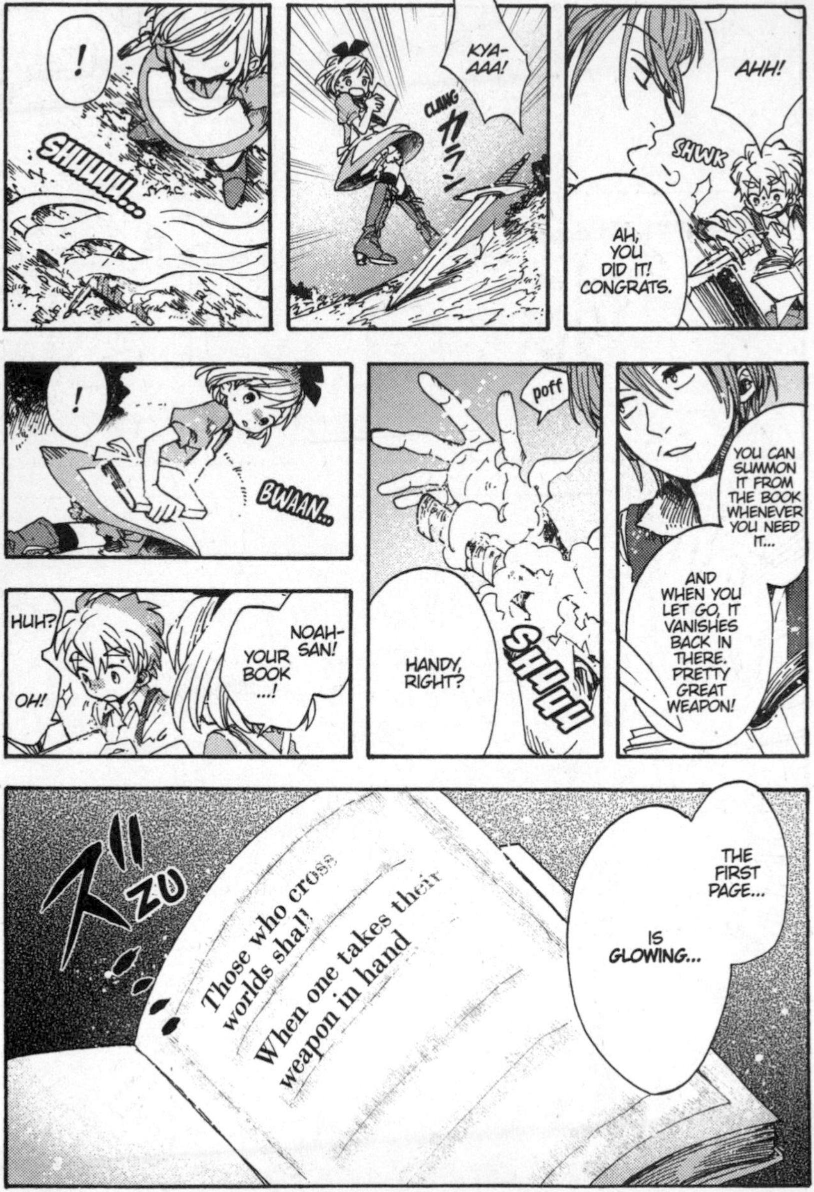
AHH!
SHWK
AH, YOU DID IT! CONGRATS.
KYA-AAA!
CLANG カラン
!
SHUUUN...
YOU CAN SUMMON IT FROM THE BOOK WHENEVER YOU NEED IT...
AND WHEN YOU LET GO, IT VANISHES BACK IN THERE. PRETTY GREAT WEAPON!
poff
HANDY, RIGHT?
SHUUU
!
BWAAN...
NOAH-SAN!
YOUR BOOK ...!
HUH?
OH!
THE FIRST PAGE...
IS GLOWING...
Those who cross worlds shall
When one takes their weapon in hand
ZU

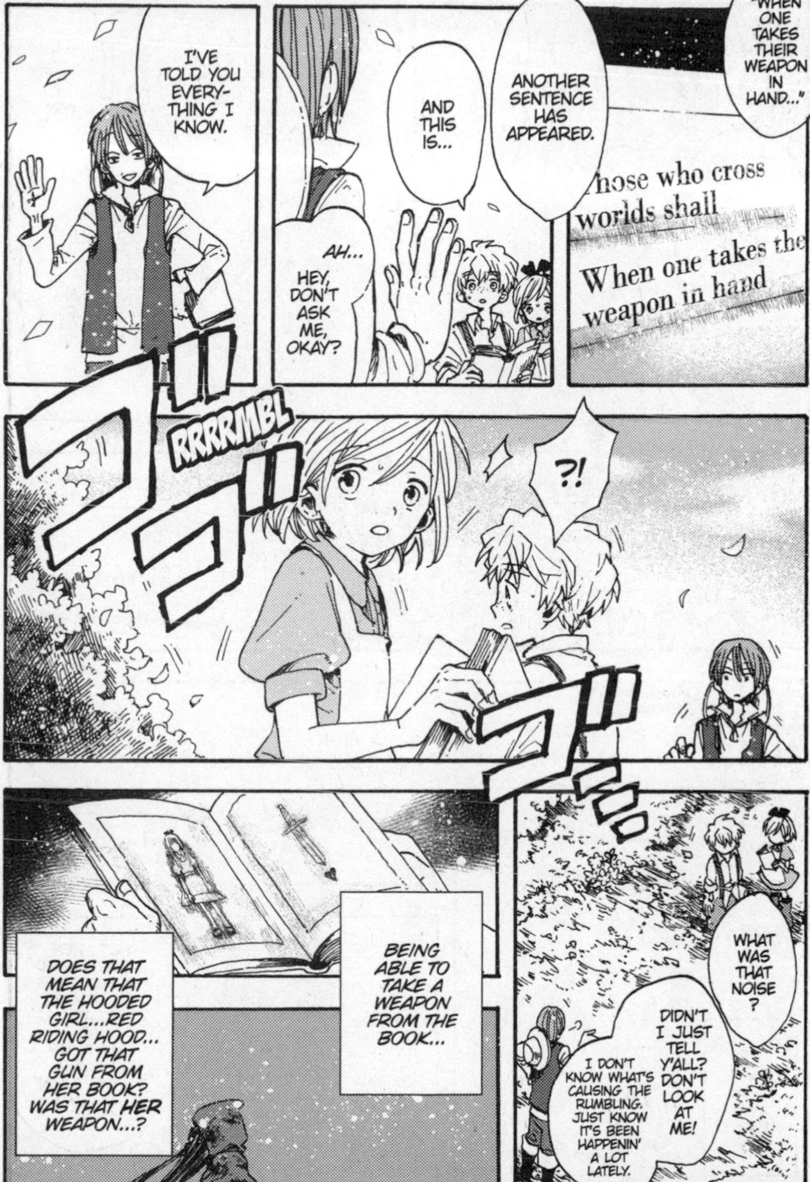
"WHEN ONE TAKES THEIR WEAPON IN HAND..."
ANOTHER SENTENCE HAS APPEARED.
hose who cross worlds shall
When one takes the weapon in hand
AND THIS IS...
AH... HEY, DON'T ASK ME, OKAY?
I'VE TOLD YOU EVERY-THING I KNOW.
?!
RRRRMBL
WHAT WAS THAT NOISE?
DIDN'T I JUST TELL Y'ALL? DON'T LOOK AT ME!
I DON'T KNOW WHAT'S CAUSING THE RUMBLING. JUST KNOW IT'S BEEN HAPPENIN' A LOT LATELY.
BEING ABLE TO TAKE A WEAPON FROM THE BOOK...
DOES THAT MEAN THAT THE HOODED GIRL...RED RIDING HOOD... GOT THAT GUN FROM HER BOOK? WAS THAT HER WEAPON...?

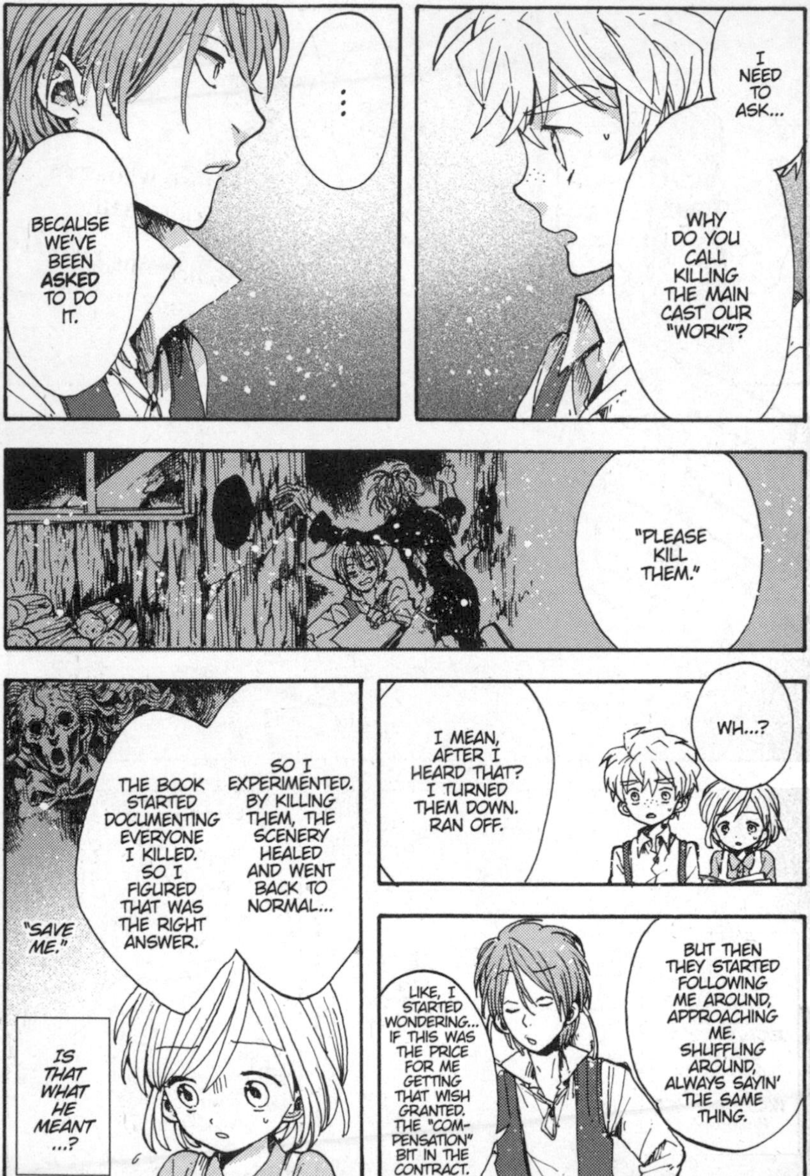
I NEED TO ASK...
WHY DO YOU CALL KILLING THE MAIN CAST OUR "WORK"?
...
BECAUSE WE'VE BEEN ASKED TO DO IT.
"PLEASE KILL THEM."
WH...?
I MEAN, AFTER I HEARD THAT? I TURNED THEM DOWN. RAN OFF.
BUT THEN THEY STARTED FOLLOWING ME AROUND, APPROACHING ME. SHUFFLING AROUND, ALWAYS SAYIN' THE SAME THING.
LIKE, I STARTED WONDERING... IF THIS WAS THE PRICE FOR ME GETTING THAT WISH GRANTED. THE "COMPENSATION" BIT IN THE CONTRACT.
SO I EXPERIMENTED. BY KILLING THEM, THE SCENERY HEALED AND WENT BACK TO NORMAL...
THE BOOK STARTED DOCUMENTING EVERYONE I KILLED. SO I FIGURED THAT WAS THE RIGHT ANSWER.
"SAVE ME."
IS THAT WHAT HE MEANT ...?

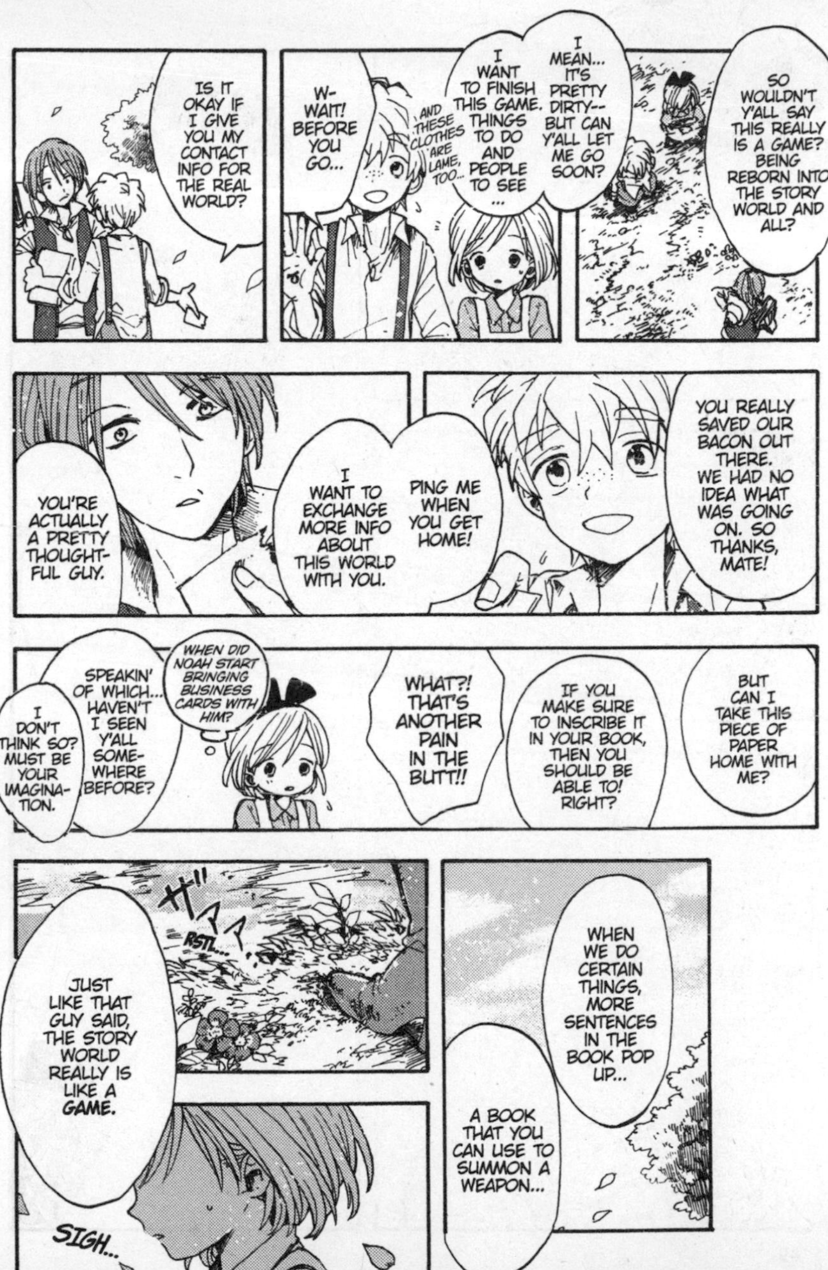
SO WOULDN'T Y'ALL SAY THIS REALLY IS A GAME? BEING REBORN INTO THE STORY WORLD AND ALL?
I MEAN... IT'S PRETTY DIRTY-- BUT CAN Y'ALL LET ME GO SOON?
I WANT TO FINISH THIS GAME. THINGS TO DO AND PEOPLE TO SEE...
AND THESE CLOTHES ARE LAME, TOO...
W-WAIT! BEFORE YOU GO...
IS IT OKAY IF I GIVE YOU MY CONTACT INFO FOR THE REAL WORLD?
YOU REALLY SAVED OUR BACON OUT THERE. WE HAD NO IDEA WHAT WAS GOING ON. SO THANKS, MATE!
PING ME WHEN YOU GET HOME!
I WANT TO EXCHANGE MORE INFO ABOUT THIS WORLD WITH YOU.
YOU'RE ACTUALLY A PRETTY THOUGHTFUL GUY.
BUT CAN I TAKE THIS PIECE OF PAPER HOME WITH ME?
IF YOU MAKE SURE TO INSCRIBE IT IN YOUR BOOK, THEN YOU SHOULD BE ABLE TO! RIGHT?
WHAT?! THAT'S ANOTHER PAIN IN THE BUTT!!
WHEN DID NOAH START BRINGING BUSINESS CARDS WITH HIM?
SPEAKIN' OF WHICH... HAVEN'T I SEEN Y'ALL SOMEWHERE BEFORE?
I DON'T THINK SO? MUST BE YOUR IMAGINATION.
WHEN WE DO CERTAIN THINGS, MORE SENTENCES IN THE BOOK POP UP...
A BOOK THAT YOU CAN USE TO SUMMON A WEAPON...
ザァァ
RSTL...
JUST LIKE THAT GUY SAID, THE STORY WORLD REALLY IS LIKE A GAME.
SIGH...

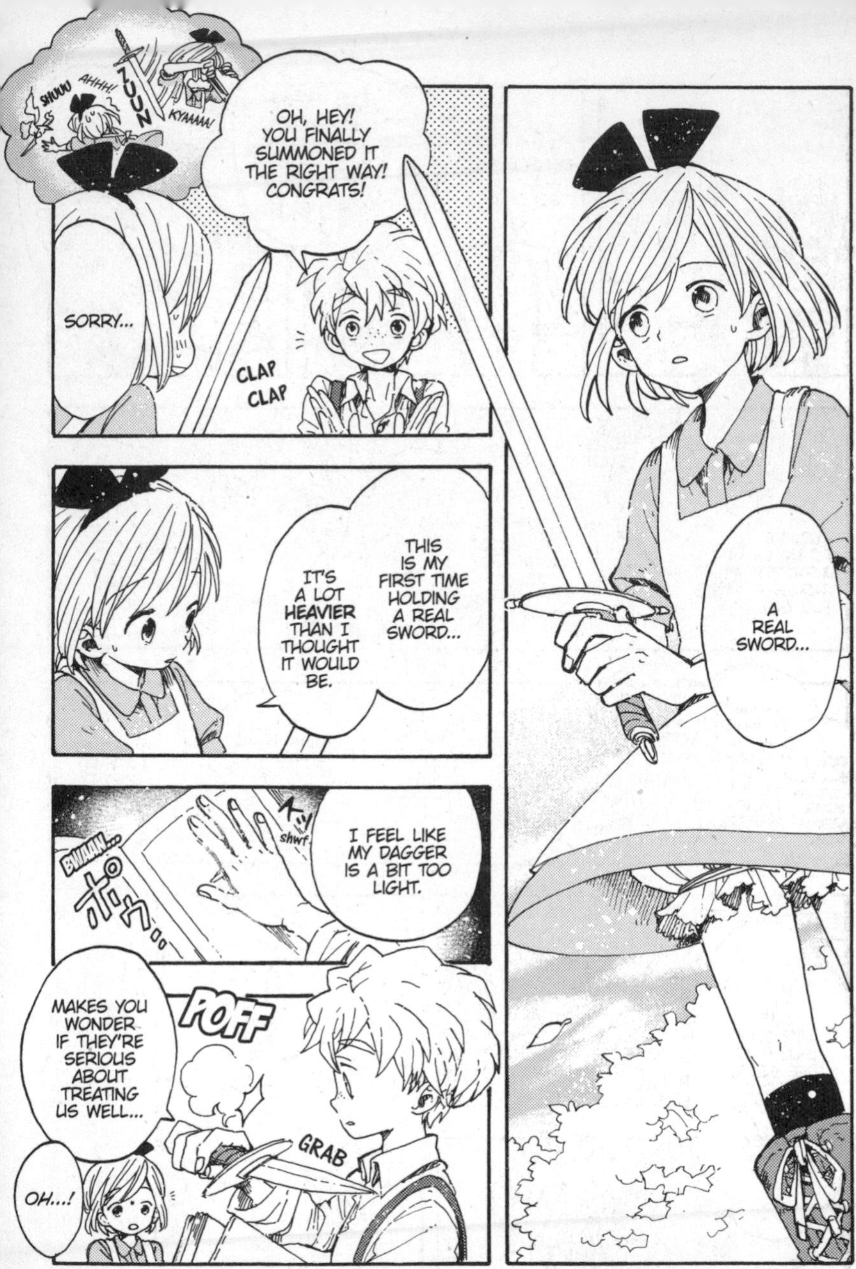
A REAL SWORD...
SHUUU
AHHH!
ZUUN
KYAAAA!
OH, HEY! YOU FINALLY SUMMONED IT THE RIGHT WAY! CONGRATS!
CLAP CLAP
SORRY...
THIS IS MY FIRST TIME HOLDING A REAL SWORD...
IT'S A LOT HEAVIER THAN I THOUGHT IT WOULD BE.
shwf
I FEEL LIKE MY DAGGER IS A BIT TOO LIGHT.
BWAAN...
POFF
MAKES YOU WONDER IF THEY'RE SERIOUS ABOUT TREATING US WELL...
GRAB
OH...!

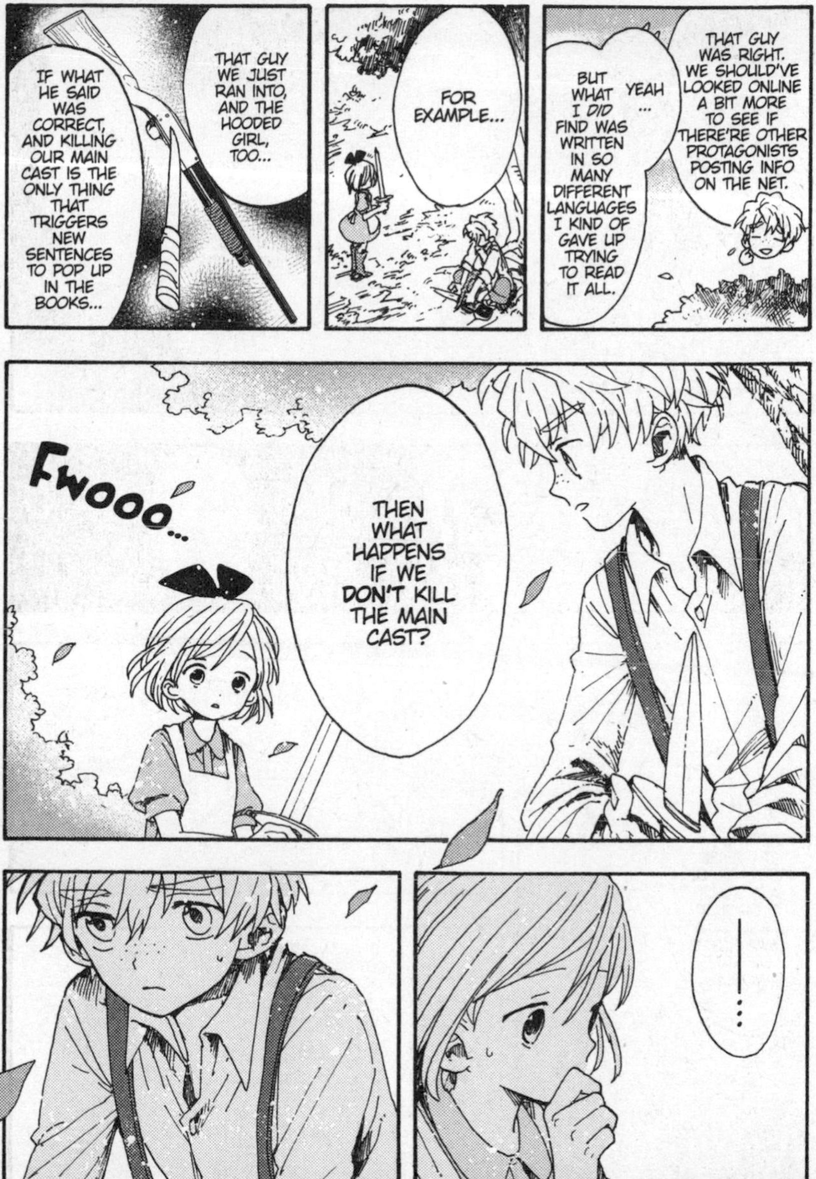
THAT GUY WAS RIGHT. WE SHOULD'VE LOOKED ONLINE A BIT MORE TO SEE IF THERE'RE OTHER PROTAGONISTS POSTING INFO ON THE NET.
YEAH ...
BUT WHAT I *DID* FIND WAS WRITTEN IN SO MANY DIFFERENT LANGUAGES I KIND OF GAVE UP TRYING TO READ IT ALL.
FOR EXAMPLE...
THAT GUY WE JUST RAN INTO, AND THE HOODED GIRL, TOO...
IF WHAT HE SAID WAS CORRECT, AND KILLING OUR MAIN CAST IS THE ONLY THING THAT TRIGGERS NEW SENTENCES TO POP UP IN THE BOOKS...
THEN WHAT HAPPENS IF WE DON'T KILL THE MAIN CAST?
Fwooo...
!...

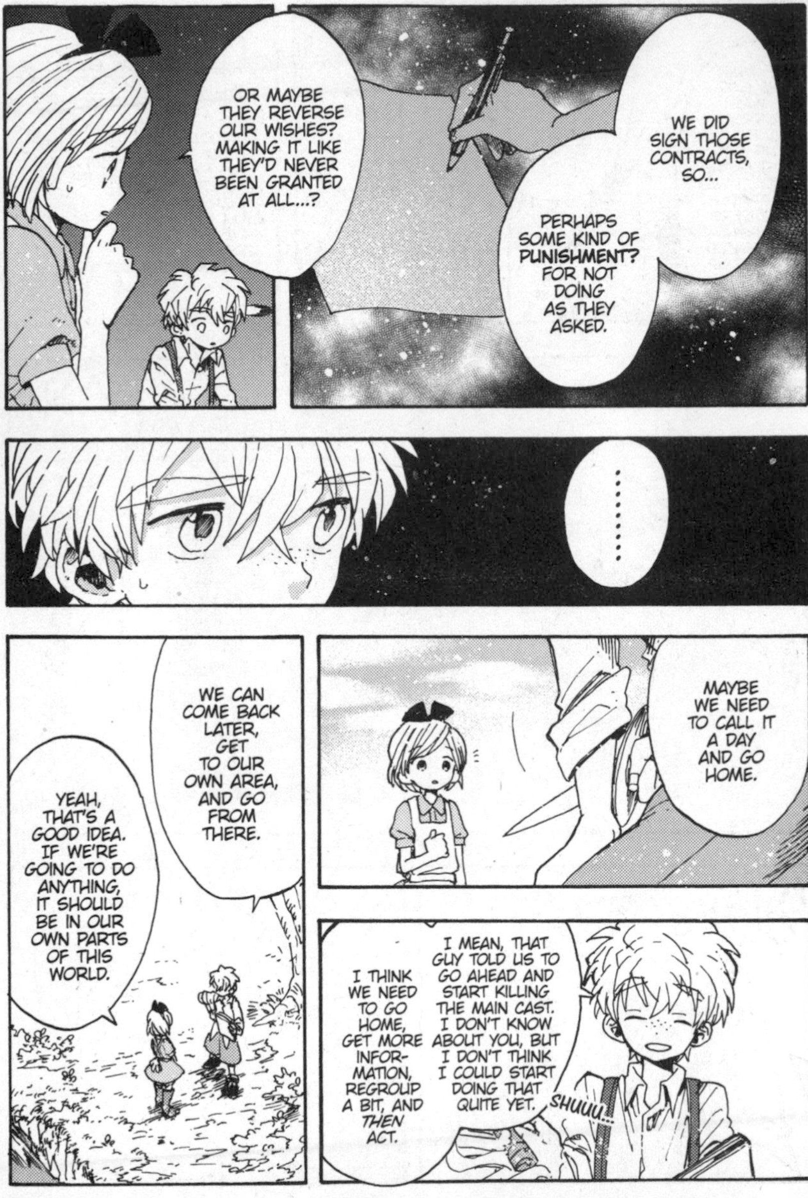
WE DID SIGN THOSE CONTRACTS, SO...
PERHAPS SOME KIND OF PUNISHMENT? FOR NOT DOING AS THEY ASKED.
OR MAYBE THEY REVERSE OUR WISHES? MAKING IT LIKE THEY'D NEVER BEEN GRANTED AT ALL...?
....
MAYBE WE NEED TO CALL IT A DAY AND GO HOME.
I MEAN, THAT GUY TOLD US TO GO AHEAD AND START KILLING THE MAIN CAST. I DON'T KNOW ABOUT YOU, BUT I DON'T THINK I COULD START DOING THAT QUITE YET.
I THINK WE NEED TO GO HOME, GET MORE INFORMATION, REGROUP A BIT, AND THEN ACT.
SHUUU...
WE CAN COME BACK LATER, GET TO OUR OWN AREA, AND GO FROM THERE.
YEAH, THAT'S A GOOD IDEA. IF WE'RE GOING TO DO ANYTHING, IT SHOULD BE IN OUR OWN PARTS OF THIS WORLD.

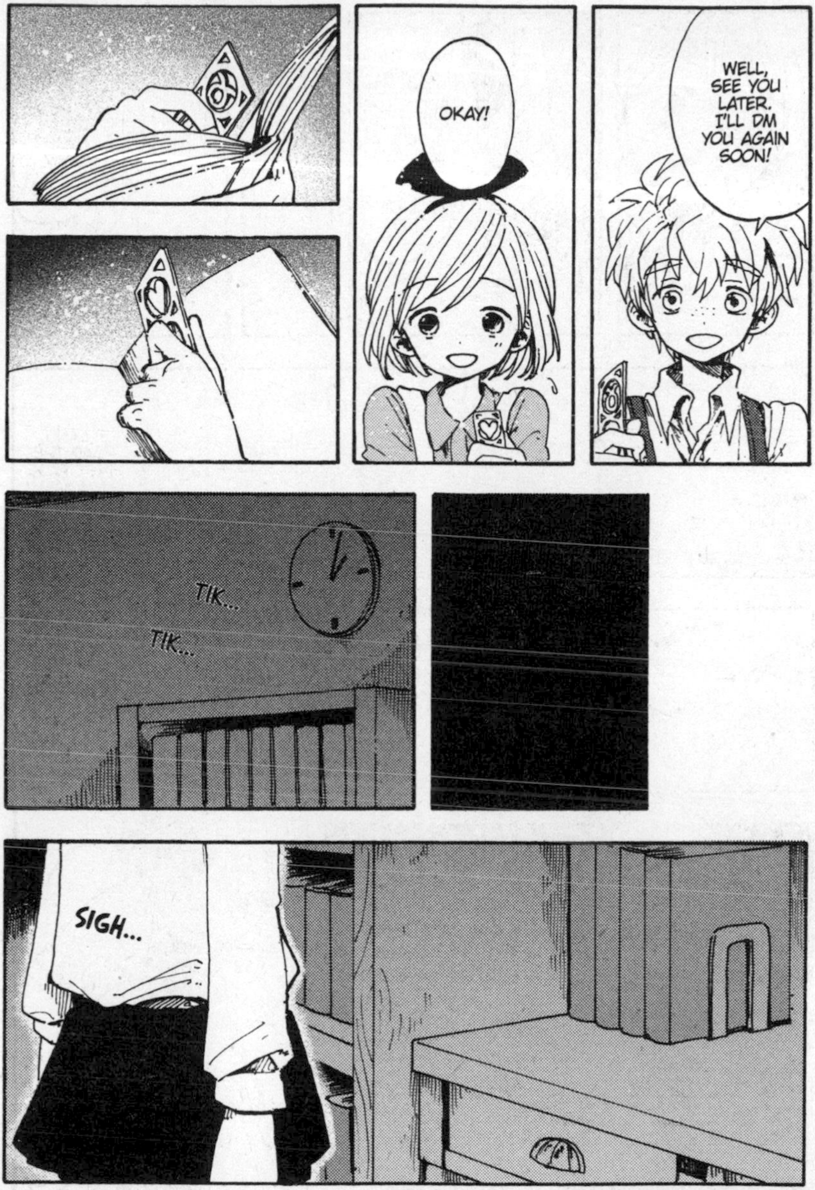
WELL, SEE YOU LATER. I'LL DM YOU AGAIN SOON!
OKAY!
TIK...
TIK...
SIGH...

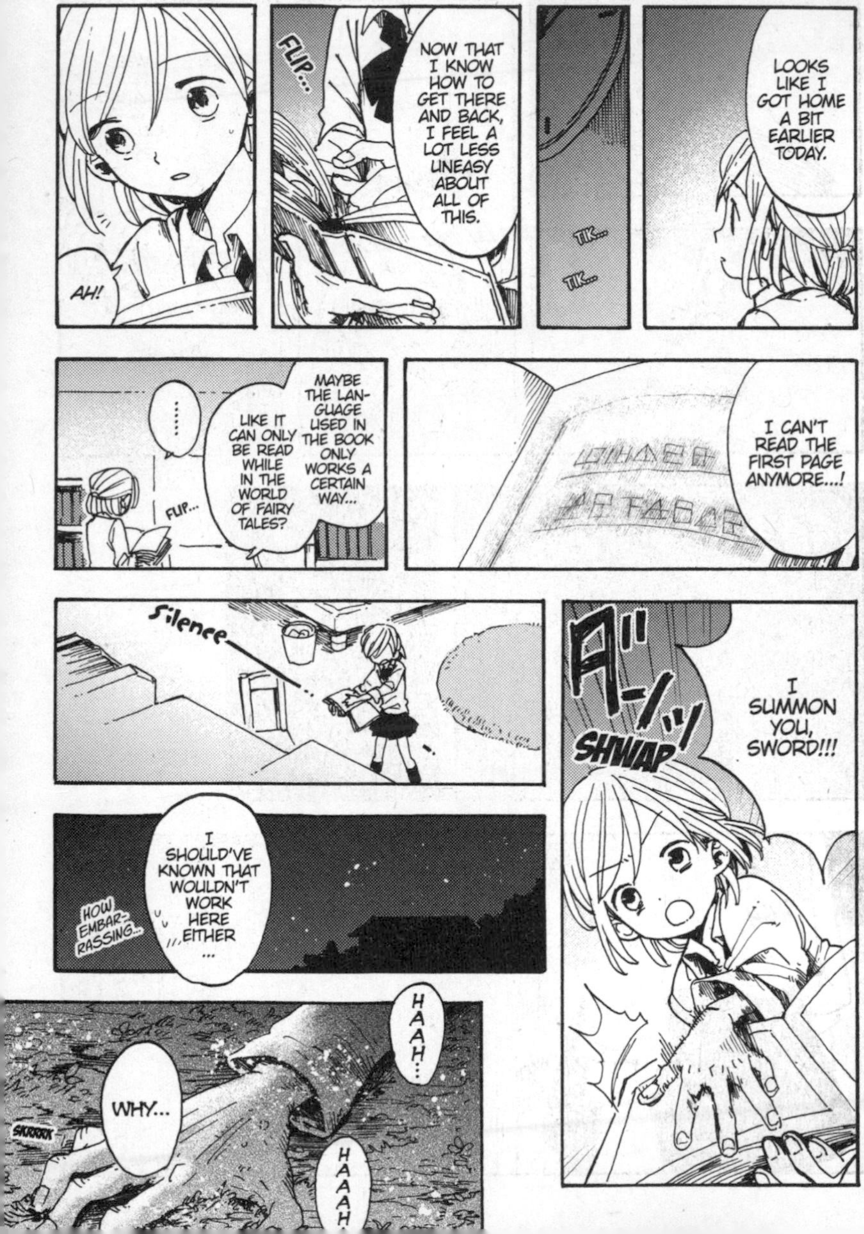
LOOKS LIKE I GOT HOME A BIT EARLIER TODAY.
TIK...
TIK...
FLIP...
NOW THAT I KNOW HOW TO GET THERE AND BACK, I FEEL A LOT LESS UNEASY ABOUT ALL OF THIS.
AH!
I CAN'T READ THE FIRST PAGE ANYMORE...!
MAYBE THE LANGUAGE USED IN THE BOOK ONLY WORKS A CERTAIN WAY...
LIKE IT CAN ONLY BE READ WHILE IN THE WORLD OF FAIRY TALES?
......
FLIP...
I SUMMON YOU, SWORD!!!
SHWAP
Silence...
I SHOULD'VE KNOWN THAT WOULDN'T WORK HERE EITHER ...
HOW EMBARRASSING...
HAAAH...
WHY...
HAAAH
SKRRRK

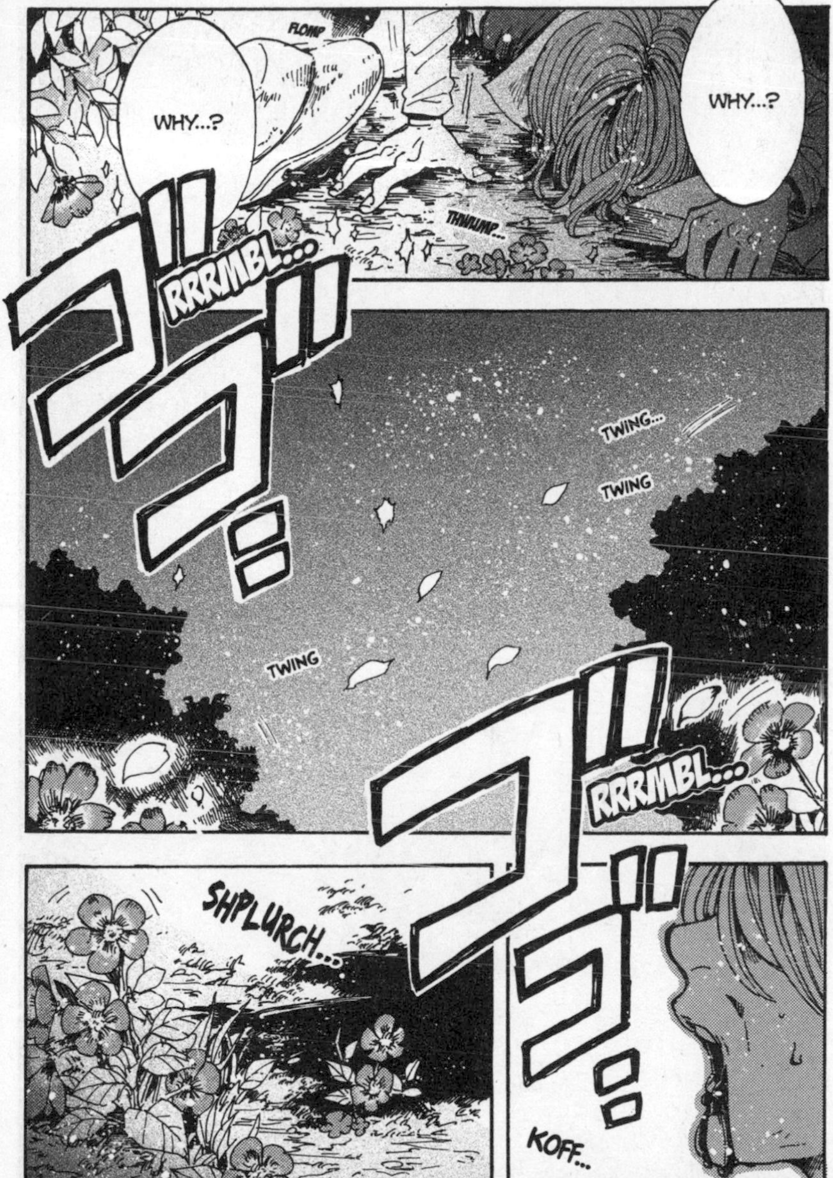
WHY...?
FLOMP
WHY...?
THWUMP...
RRRMBL...
TWING...
TWING
TWING
RRRMBL...
KOFF...
SHPLURCH...

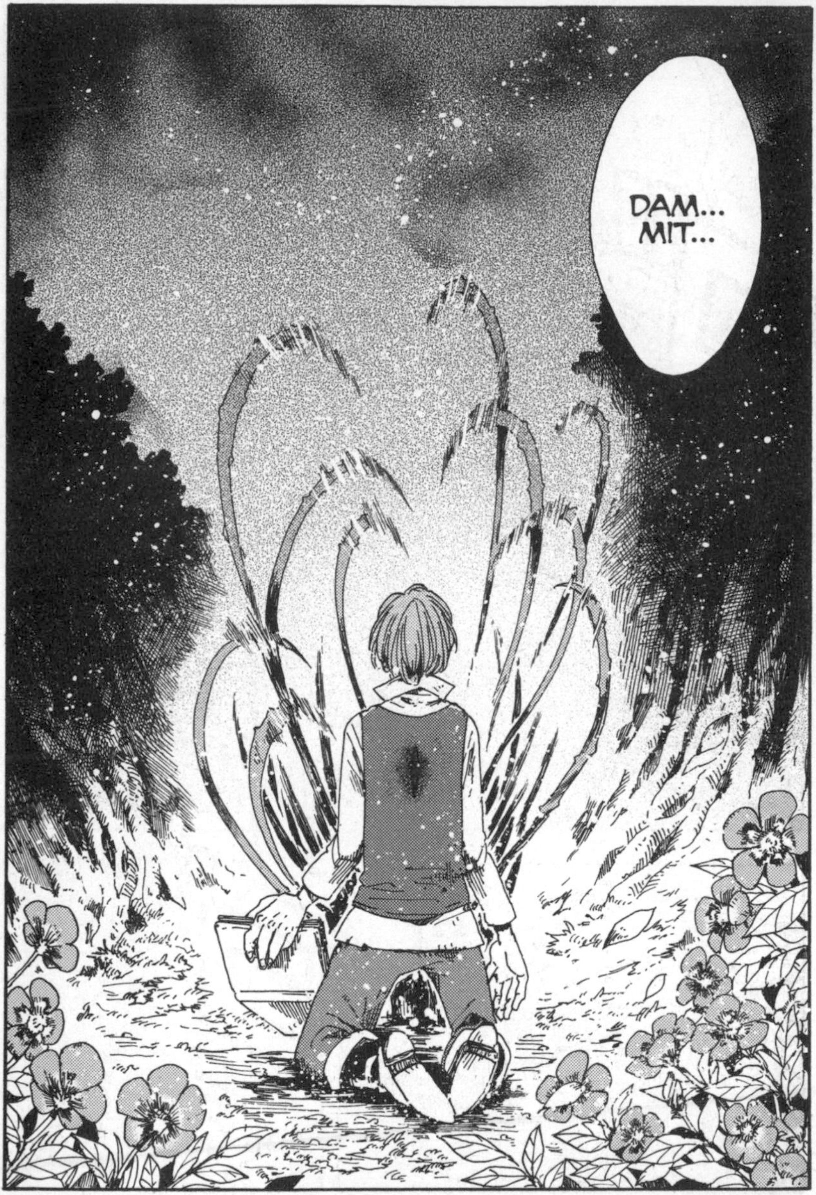
DAM...
MIT...

FAIRY
TALE
BATTLE
ROYALE

Chapter 6: Wishes

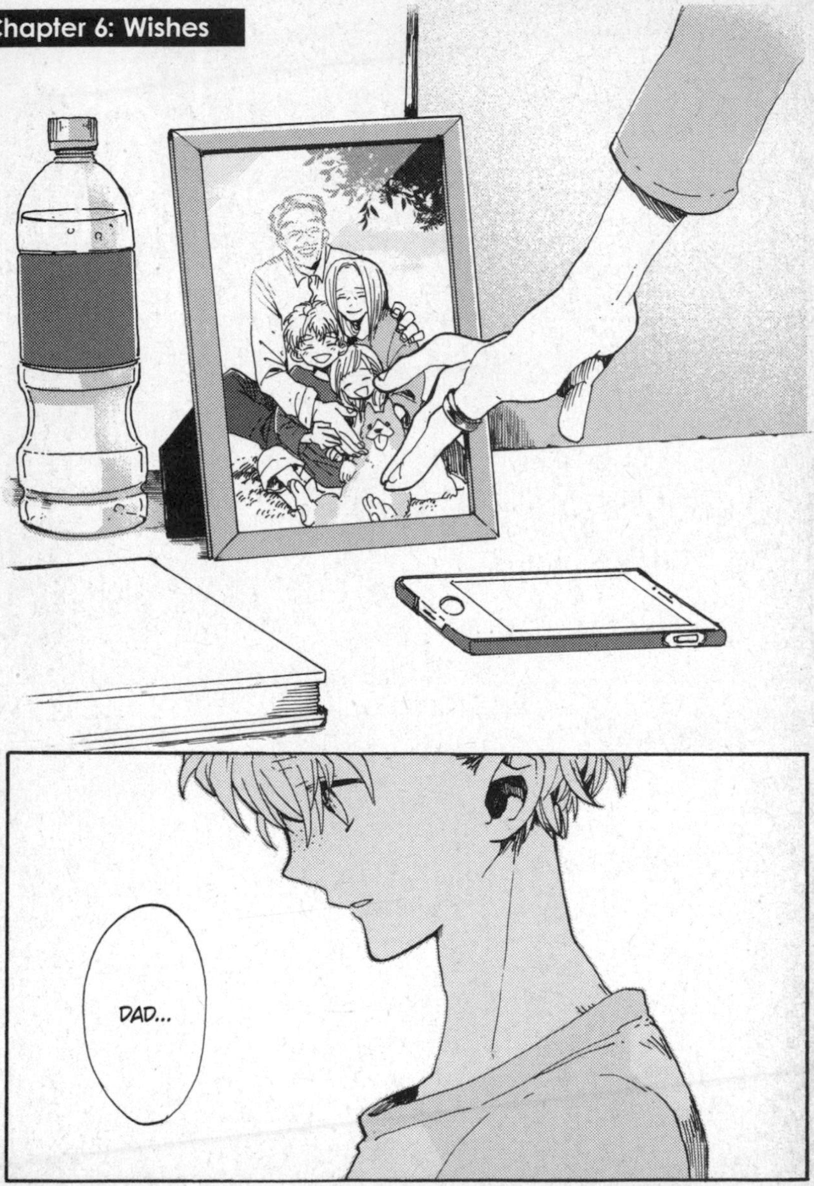

DAD...

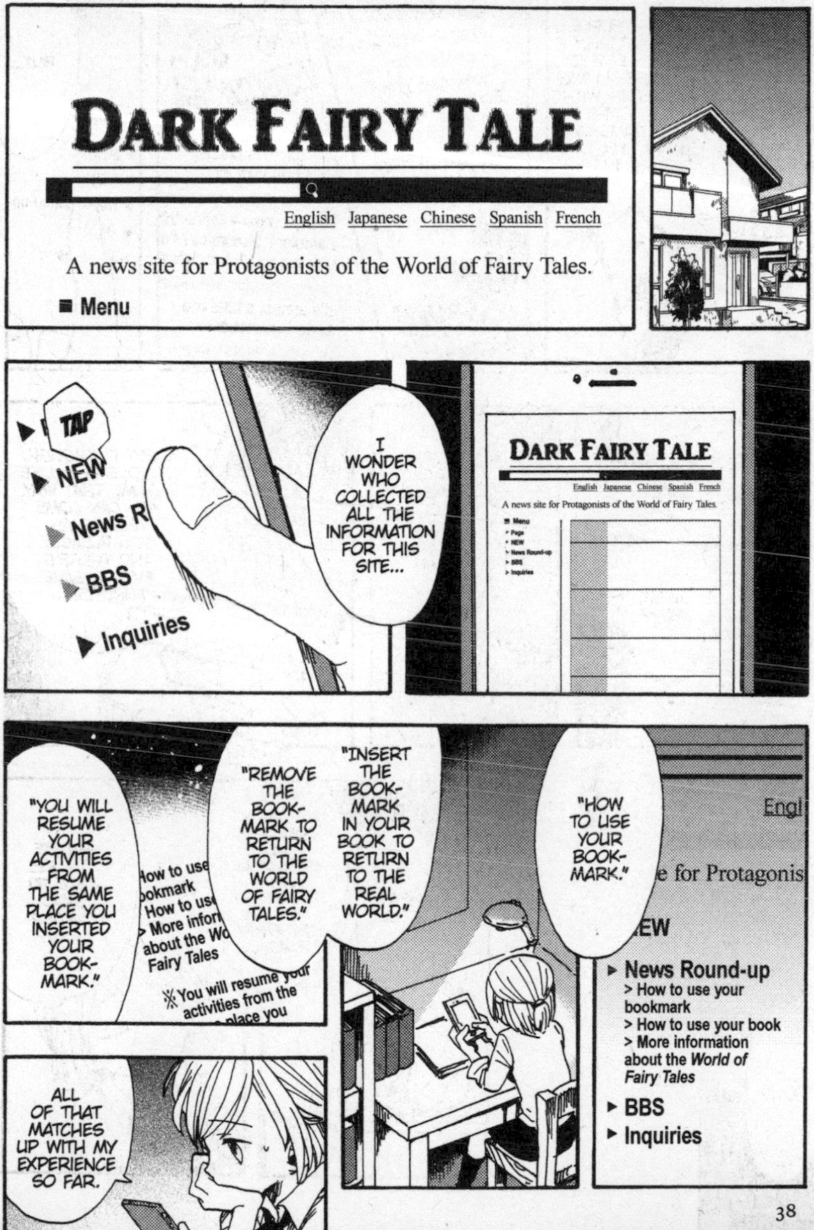
DARK FAIRY TALE
English Japanese Chinese Spanish French
A news site for Protagonists of the World of Fairy Tales.
Menu
DARK FAIRY TALE
English Japanese Chinese Spanish French
A news site for Protagonists of the World of Fairy Tales.
TAP
NEW
News R
BBS
Inquiries
I WONDER WHO COLLECTED ALL THE INFORMATION FOR THIS SITE...
Engl
e for Protagonis
EW
News Round-up
> How to use your bookmark
> How to use your book
> More information about the World of Fairy Tales
BBS
Inquiries
"HOW TO USE YOUR BOOK-MARK."
"INSERT THE BOOK-MARK IN YOUR BOOK TO RETURN TO THE REAL WORLD."
"REMOVE THE BOOK-MARK TO RETURN TO THE WORLD OF FAIRY TALES."
"YOU WILL RESUME YOUR ACTIVITIES FROM THE SAME PLACE YOU INSERTED YOUR BOOK-MARK."
How to use
ookmark
How to us
> More infor
about the Wo
Fairy Tales
※You will resume your
activities from the
ALL OF THAT MATCHES UP WITH MY EXPERIENCE SO FAR.

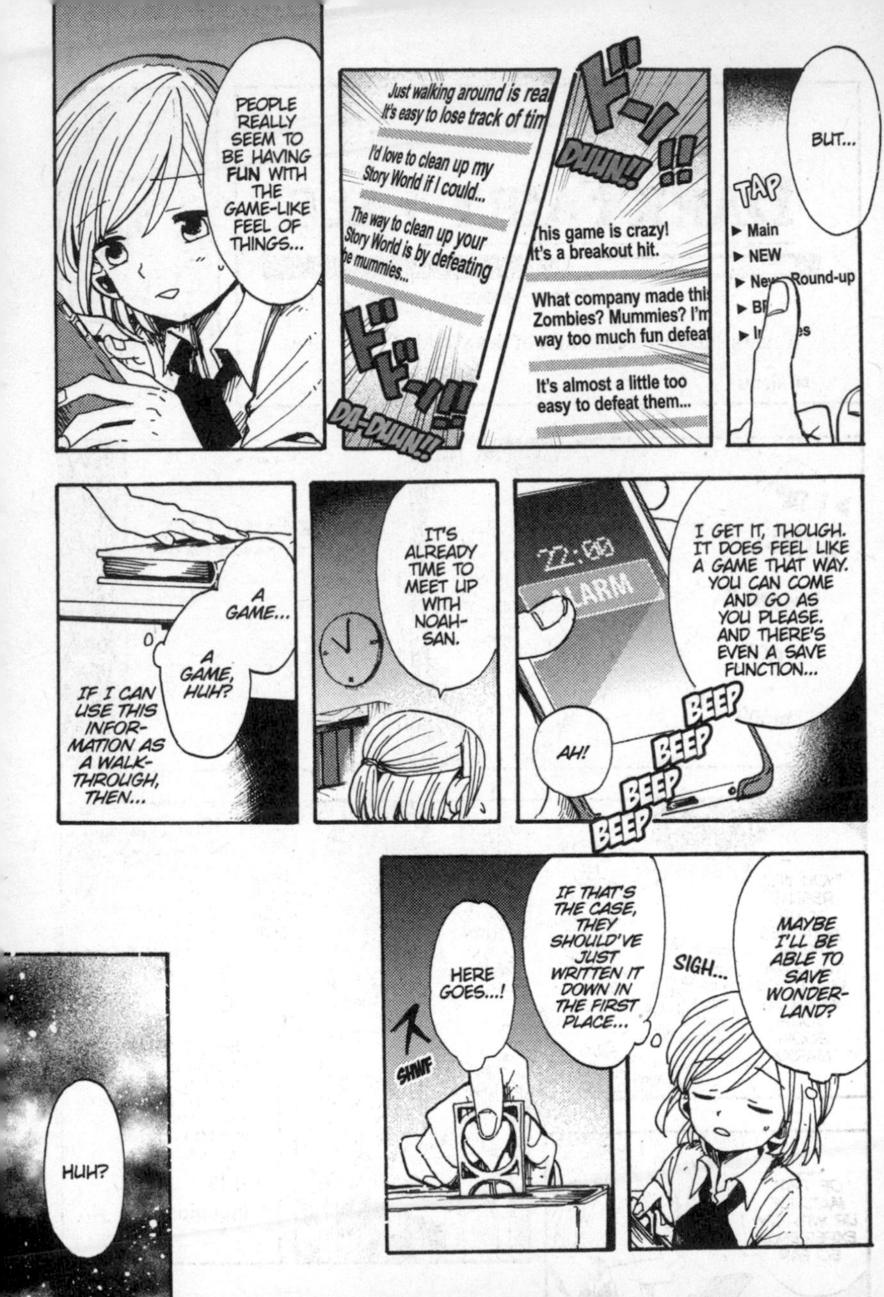
BUT...
TAP
Main
NEW
DUUN!!
This game is crazy! It's a breakout hit.
What company made this
It's almost a little too easy to defeat them...
I'd love to clean up my Story World if I could...
The way to clean up your Story World is by defeating the mummies...
DA-DUUN!!
PEOPLE REALLY SEEM TO BE HAVING FUN WITH THE GAME-LIKE FEEL OF THINGS...
I GET IT, THOUGH. IT DOES FEEL LIKE A GAME THAT WAY. YOU CAN COME AND GO AS YOU PLEASE. AND THERE'S EVEN A SAVE FUNCTION...
22:00
ALARM
AH!
BEEP BEEP BEEP BEEP
IT'S ALREADY TIME TO MEET UP WITH NOAH-SAN.
A GAME...
A GAME, HUH?
IF I CAN USE THIS INFORMATION AS A WALKTHROUGH, THEN...
MAYBE I'LL BE ABLE TO SAVE WONDERLAND?
SIGH...
IF THAT'S THE CASE, THEY SHOULD'VE JUST WRITTEN IT DOWN IN THE FIRST PLACE...
HERE GOES...!
SHUF
HUH?

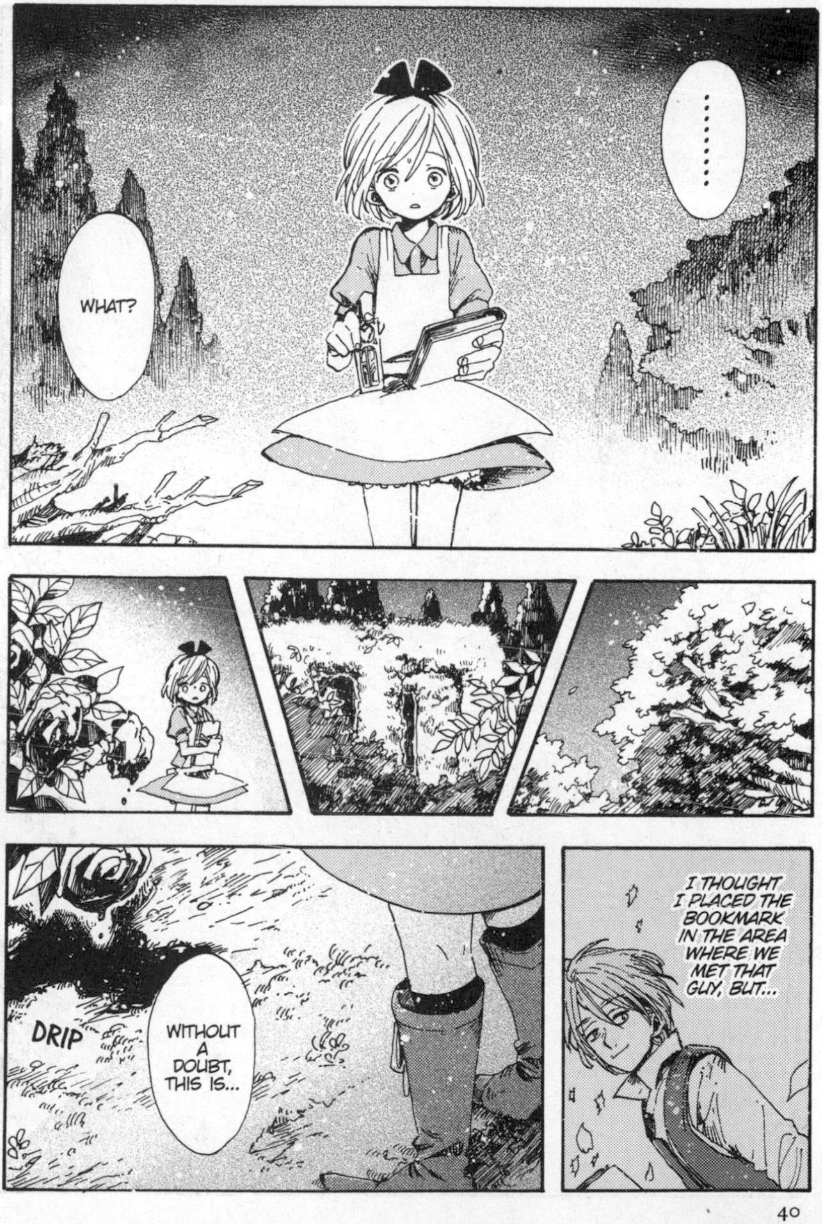
......
WHAT?
I THOUGHT I PLACED THE BOOKMARK IN THE AREA WHERE WE MET THAT GUY, BUT...
WITHOUT A DOUBT, THIS IS...
DRIP

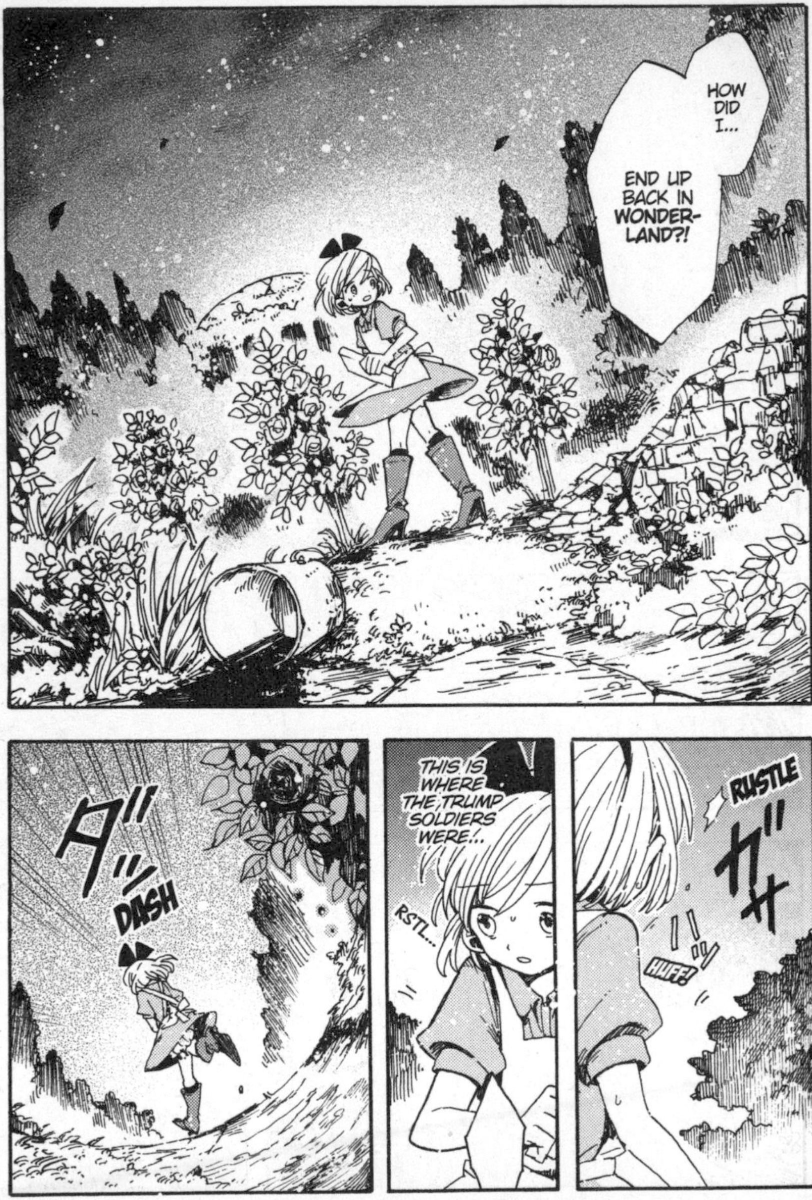
HOW DID I...
END UP BACK IN WONDERLAND?!
RUSTLE
ガサ
HUFF!
THIS IS WHERE THE TRUMP SOLDIERS WERE...
RSTL...
ダッ
DASH

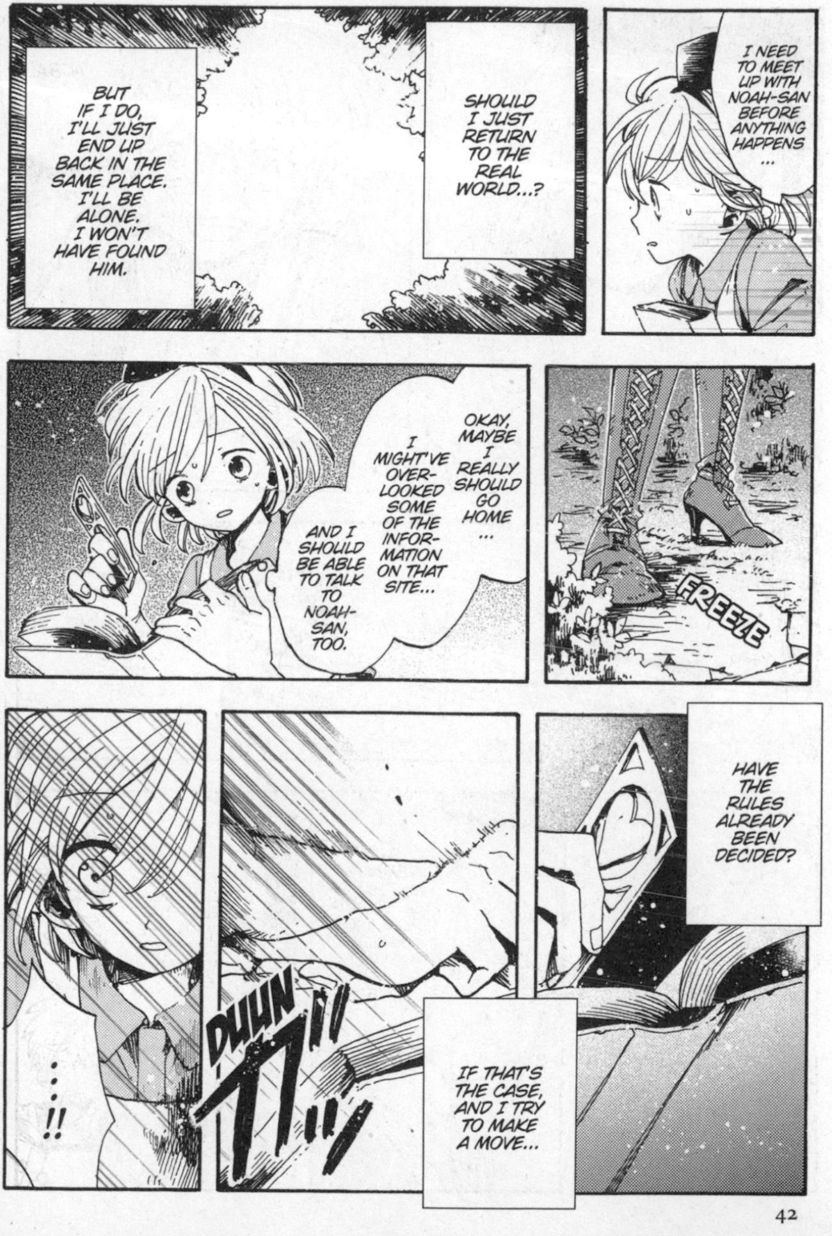
I NEED TO MEET UP WITH NOAH-SAN BEFORE ANYTHING HAPPENS ...
SHOULD I JUST RETURN TO THE REAL WORLD...?
BUT IF I DO, I'LL JUST END UP BACK IN THE SAME PLACE. I'LL BE ALONE. I WON'T HAVE FOUND HIM.
FREEZE
OKAY, MAYBE I REALLY SHOULD GO HOME ...
I MIGHT'VE OVERLOOKED SOME OF THE INFORMATION ON THAT SITE...
AND I SHOULD BE ABLE TO TALK TO NOAH-SAN, TOO.
HAVE THE RULES ALREADY BEEN DECIDED?
IF THAT'S THE CASE, AND I TRY TO MAKE A MOVE...
DUUN!!
...!!

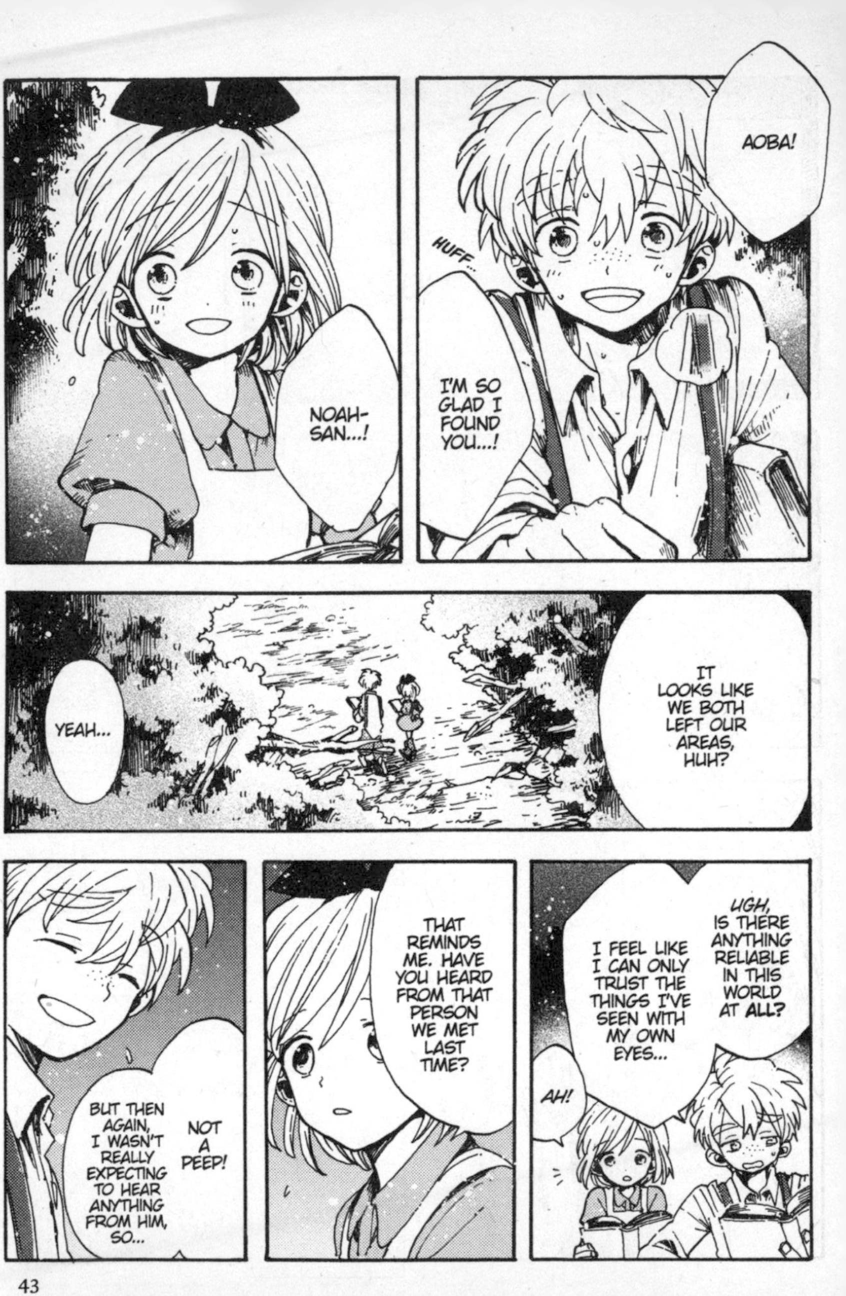
AOBA!
HUFF...
I'M SO GLAD I FOUND YOU...!
NOAH-SAN...!
IT LOOKS LIKE WE BOTH LEFT OUR AREAS, HUH?
YEAH...
UGH, IS THERE ANYTHING RELIABLE IN THIS WORLD AT ALL?
I FEEL LIKE I CAN ONLY TRUST THE THINGS I'VE SEEN WITH MY OWN EYES...
AH!
THAT REMINDS ME. HAVE YOU HEARD FROM THAT PERSON WE MET LAST TIME?
NOT A PEEP!
BUT THEN AGAIN, I WASN'T REALLY EXPECTING TO HEAR ANYTHING FROM HIM, SO...

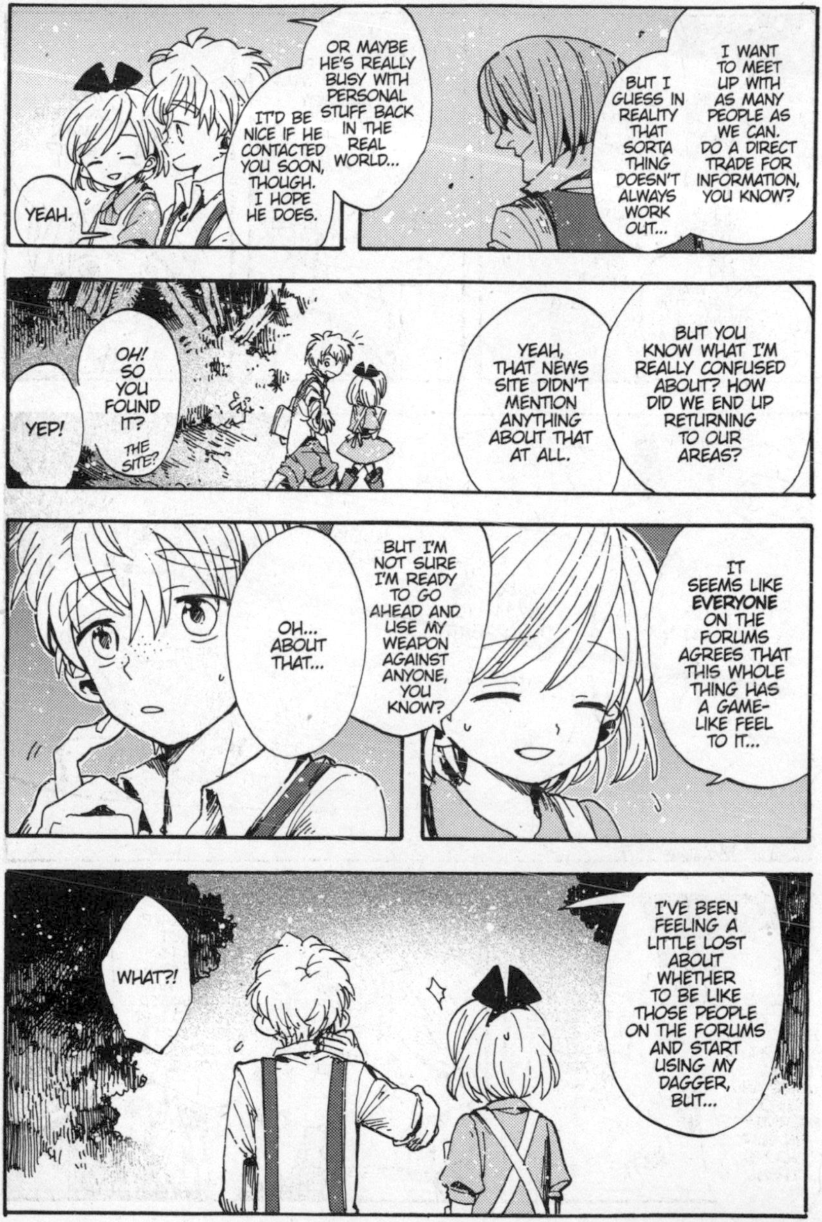
I WANT TO MEET UP WITH AS MANY PEOPLE AS WE CAN. DO A DIRECT TRADE FOR INFORMATION, YOU KNOW?
BUT I GUESS IN REALITY THAT SORTA THING DOESN'T ALWAYS WORK OUT...
OR MAYBE HE'S REALLY BUSY WITH PERSONAL STUFF BACK IN THE REAL WORLD...
IT'D BE NICE IF HE CONTACTED YOU SOON, THOUGH. I HOPE HE DOES.
YEAH.
BUT YOU KNOW WHAT I'M REALLY CONFUSED ABOUT? HOW DID WE END UP RETURNING TO OUR AREAS?
YEAH, THAT NEWS SITE DIDN'T MENTION ANYTHING ABOUT THAT AT ALL.
OH! SO YOU FOUND IT?
THE SITE?
YEP!
IT SEEMS LIKE **EVERYONE** ON THE FORUMS AGREES THAT THIS WHOLE THING HAS A GAME-LIKE FEEL TO IT...
BUT I'M NOT SURE I'M READY TO GO AHEAD AND USE MY WEAPON AGAINST ANYONE, YOU KNOW?
OH... ABOUT THAT...
I'VE BEEN FEELING A LITTLE LOST ABOUT WHETHER TO BE LIKE THOSE PEOPLE ON THE FORUMS AND START USING MY DAGGER, BUT...
WHAT?!

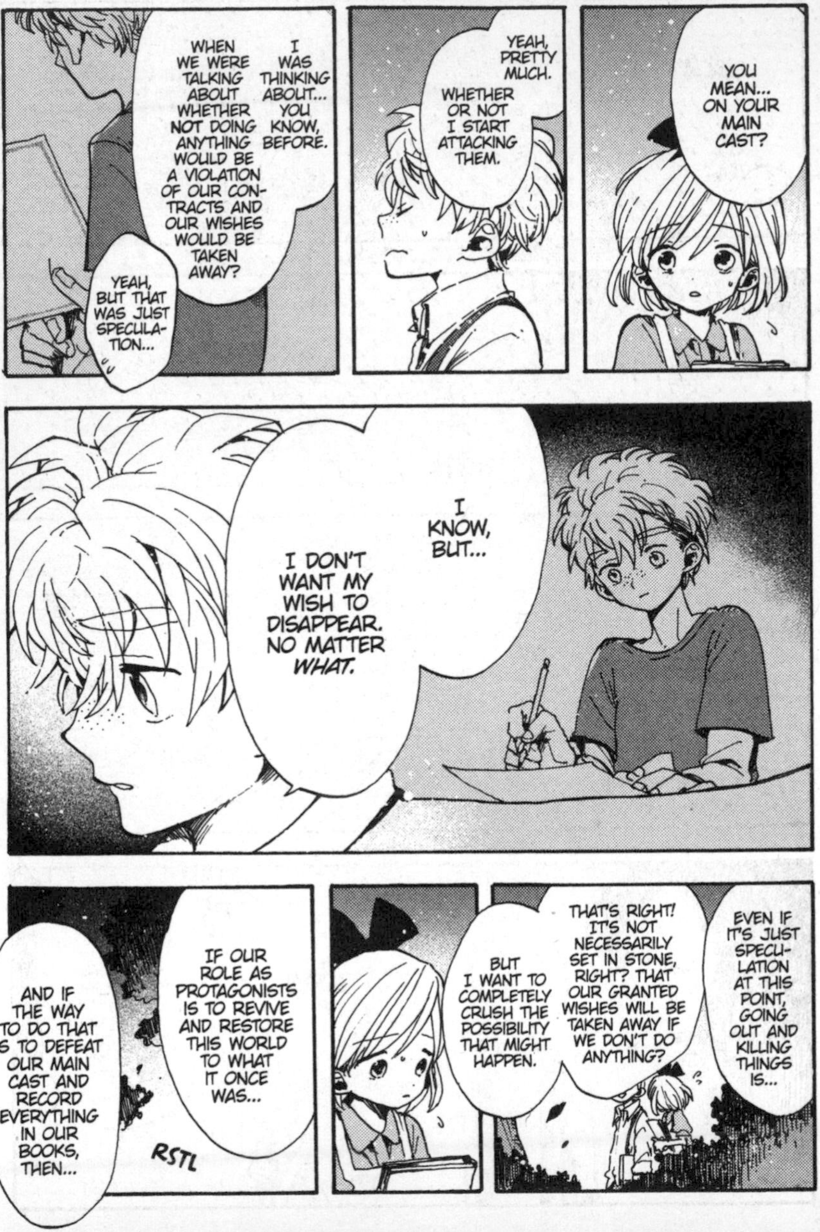
YOU MEAN... ON YOUR MAIN CAST?
YEAH, PRETTY MUCH.
WHETHER OR NOT I START ATTACKING THEM.
I WAS THINKING ABOUT... YOU KNOW, BEFORE.
WHEN WE WERE TALKING ABOUT WHETHER NOT DOING ANYTHING WOULD BE A VIOLATION OF OUR CONTRACTS AND OUR WISHES WOULD BE TAKEN AWAY?
YEAH, BUT THAT WAS JUST SPECULATION...
I KNOW, BUT...
I DON'T WANT MY WISH TO DISAPPEAR. NO MATTER *WHAT.*
EVEN IF IT'S JUST SPECULATION AT THIS POINT, GOING OUT AND KILLING THINGS IS...
THAT'S RIGHT! IT'S NOT NECESSARILY SET IN STONE, RIGHT? THAT OUR GRANTED WISHES WILL BE TAKEN AWAY IF WE DON'T DO ANYTHING?
BUT I WANT TO COMPLETELY CRUSH THE POSSIBILITY THAT MIGHT HAPPEN.
IF OUR ROLE AS PROTAGONISTS IS TO REVIVE AND RESTORE THIS WORLD TO WHAT IT ONCE WAS...
AND IF THE WAY TO DO THAT IS TO DEFEAT OUR MAIN CAST AND RECORD EVERYTHING IN OUR BOOKS, THEN...
RSTL

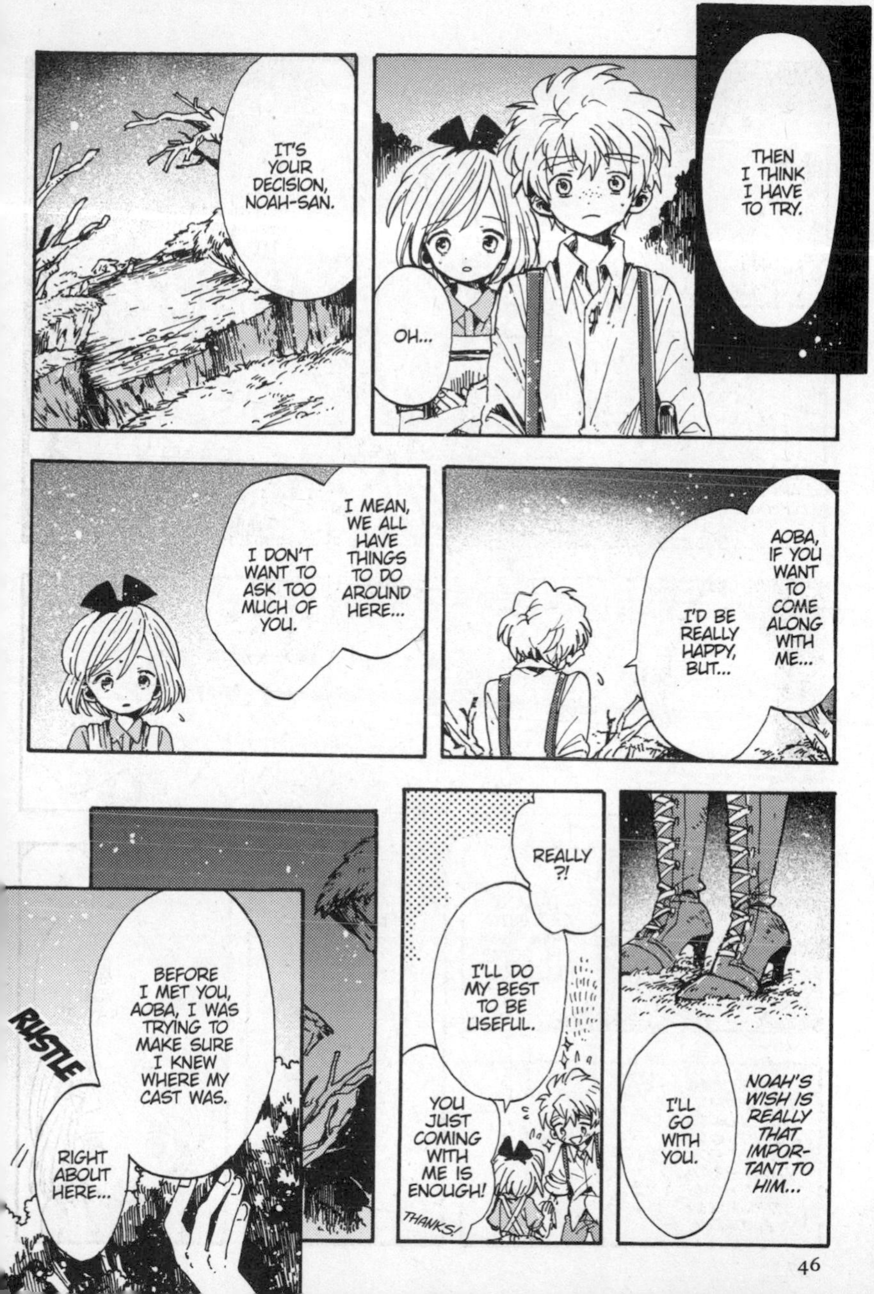
THEN I THINK I HAVE TO TRY.
OH...
IT'S YOUR DECISION, NOAH-SAN.
AOBA, IF YOU WANT TO COME ALONG WITH ME...
I'D BE REALLY HAPPY, BUT...
I MEAN, WE ALL HAVE THINGS TO DO AROUND HERE...
I DON'T WANT TO ASK TOO MUCH OF YOU.
NOAH'S WISH IS REALLY THAT IMPOR-TANT TO HIM...
I'LL GO WITH YOU.
REALLY?!
I'LL DO MY BEST TO BE USEFUL.
YOU JUST COMING WITH ME IS ENOUGH!
THANKS!
RUSTLE
BEFORE I MET YOU, AOBA, I WAS TRYING TO MAKE SURE I KNEW WHERE MY CAST WAS.
RIGHT ABOUT HERE...

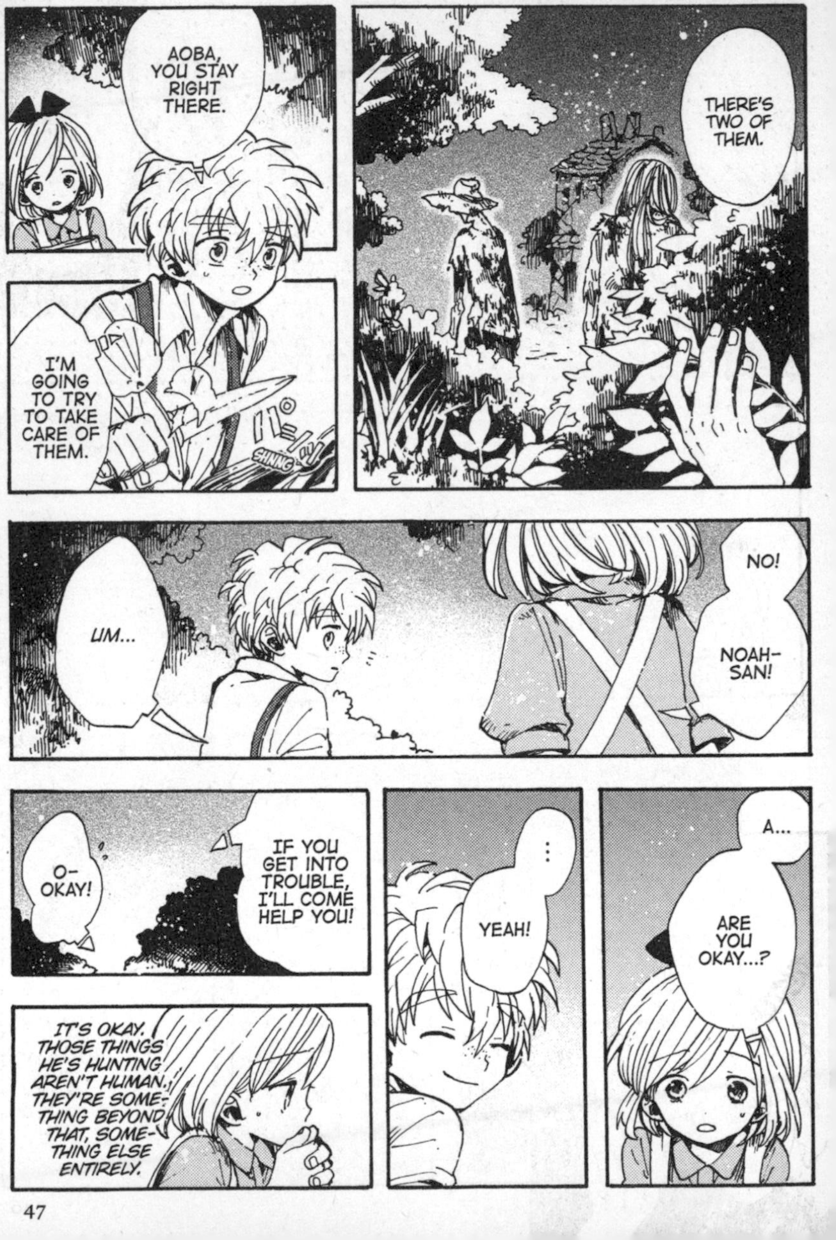
THERE'S TWO OF THEM.
AOBA, YOU STAY RIGHT THERE.
I'M GOING TO TRY TO TAKE CARE OF THEM.
SHING
NO!
NOAH-SAN!
UM...
A...
ARE YOU OKAY...?
...
YEAH!
IF YOU GET INTO TROUBLE, I'LL COME HELP YOU!
O-OKAY!
IT'S OKAY. THOSE THINGS HE'S HUNTING AREN'T HUMAN. THEY'RE SOMETHING BEYOND THAT, SOMETHING ELSE ENTIRELY.

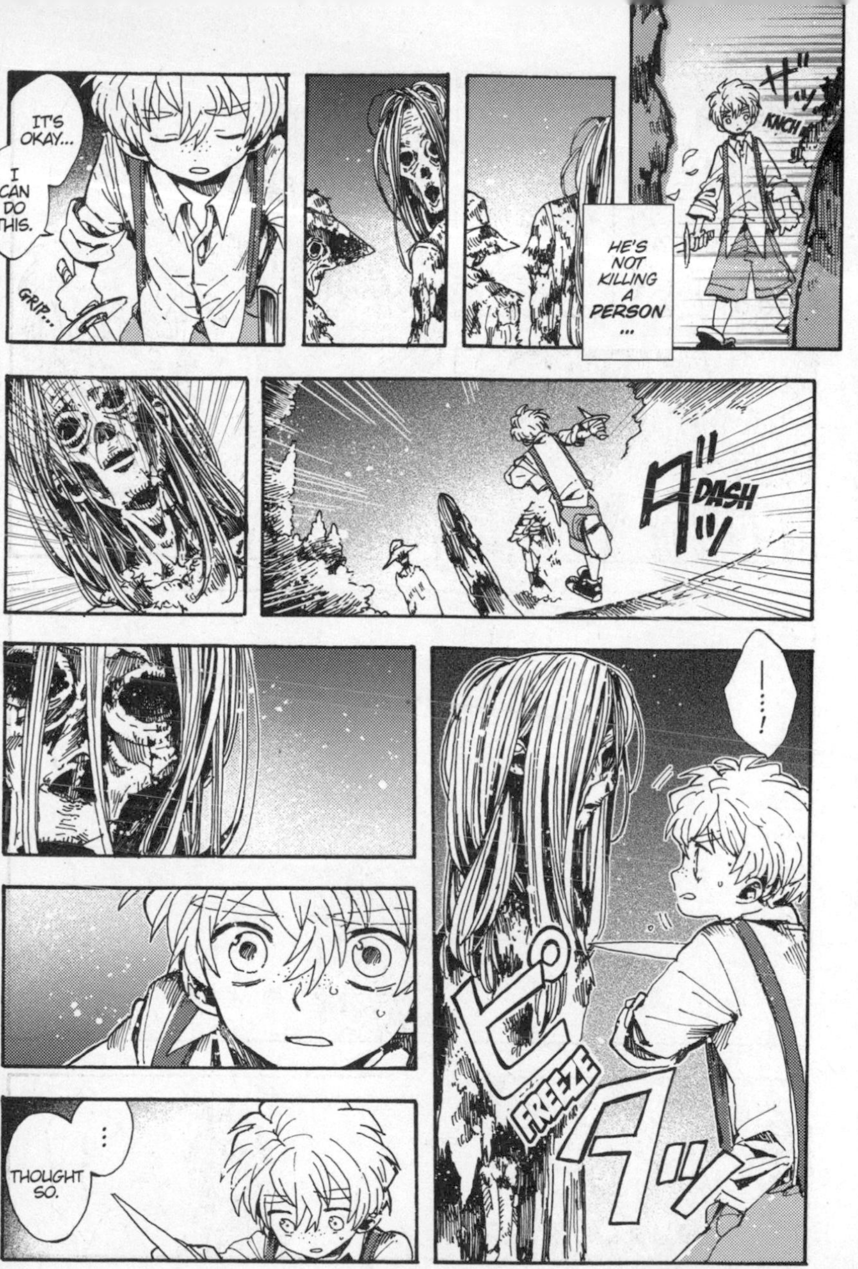
KNCH
HE'S NOT KILLING A PERSON ...
IT'S OKAY... I CAN DO THIS.
GRIP...
DASH
—...!
FREEZE
... THOUGHT SO.

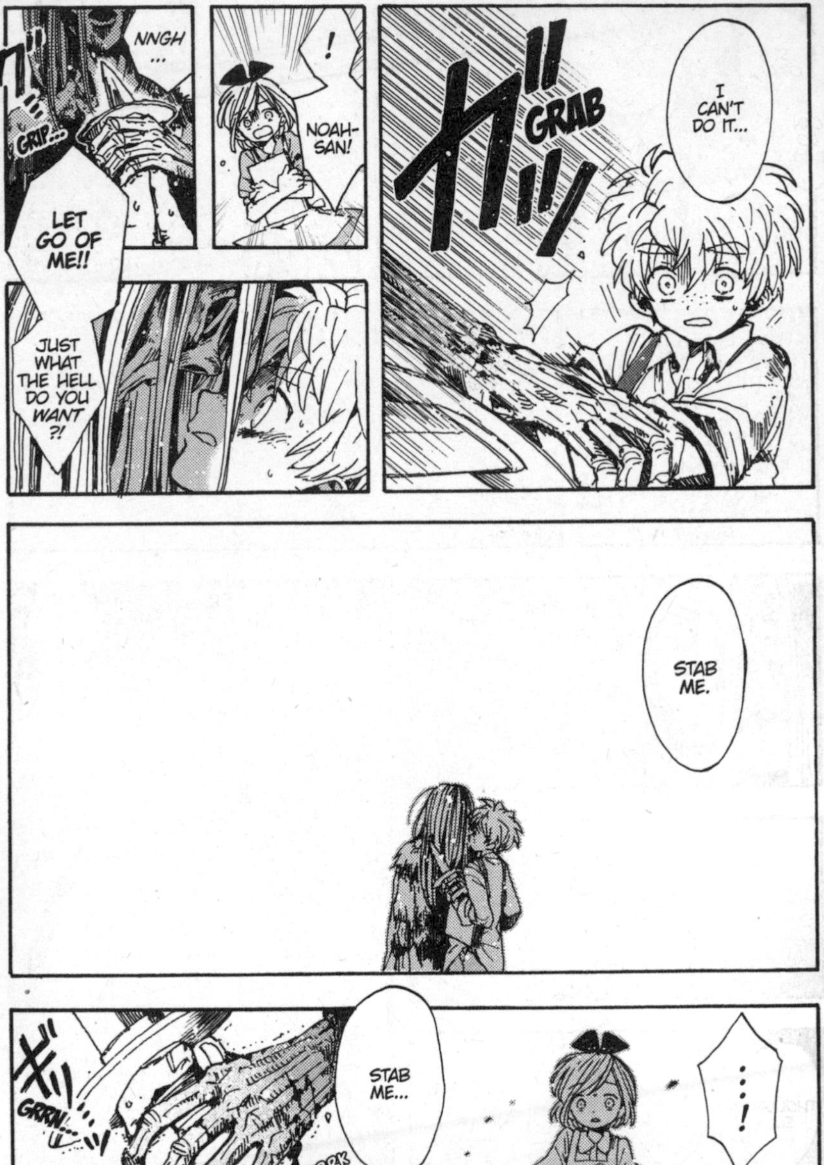
I CAN'T DO IT...
GRAB
!
NOAH-SAN!
NNGH ...
GRIP...
LET GO OF ME!!
JUST WHAT THE HELL DO YOU WANT ?!
STAB ME.
...!
STAB ME...
GRRN...
KRRK

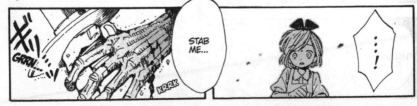

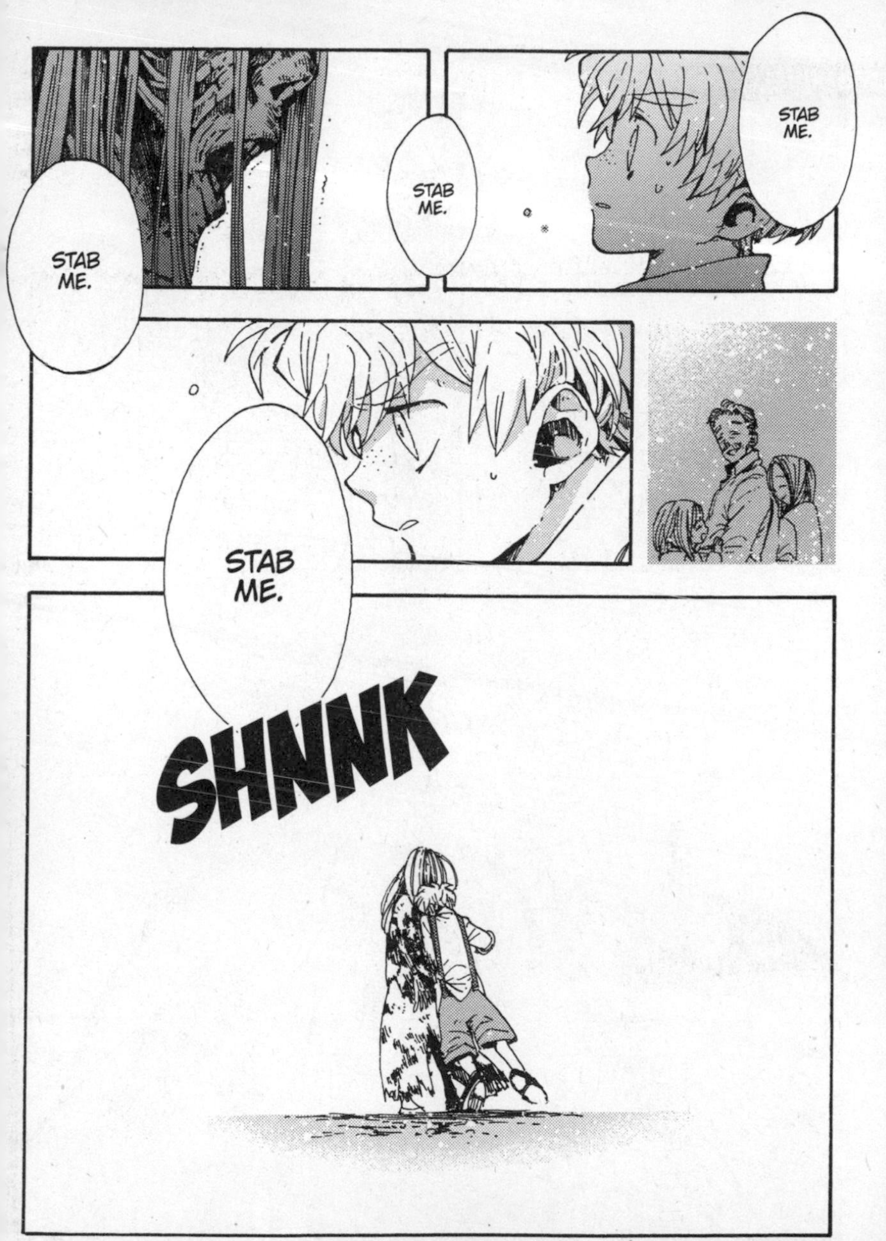
STAB ME.
STAB ME.
STAB ME.
STAB ME.
SHNNK

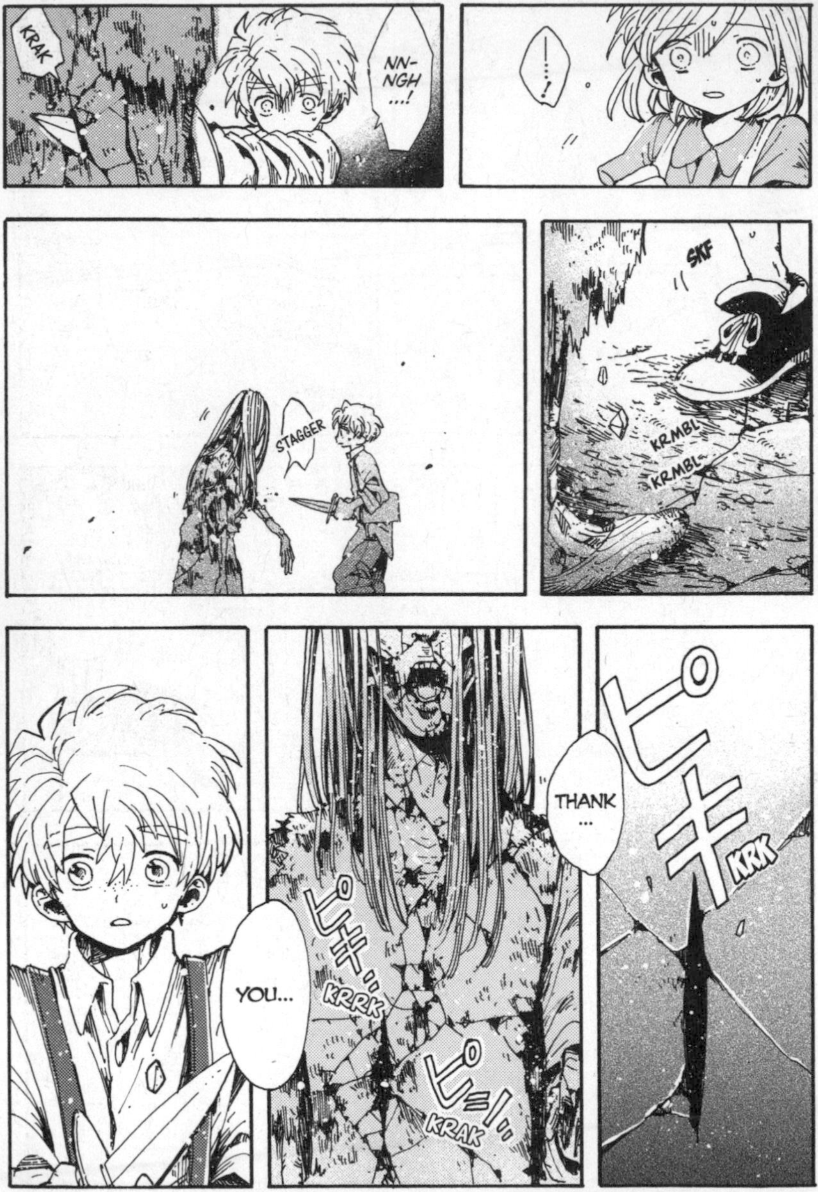
!...!
NN-NGH...!
KRAK
SKF
KRMBL
KRMBL
STAGGER
THANK...
ピキ
KRK
KRRK
KRAK
YOU...

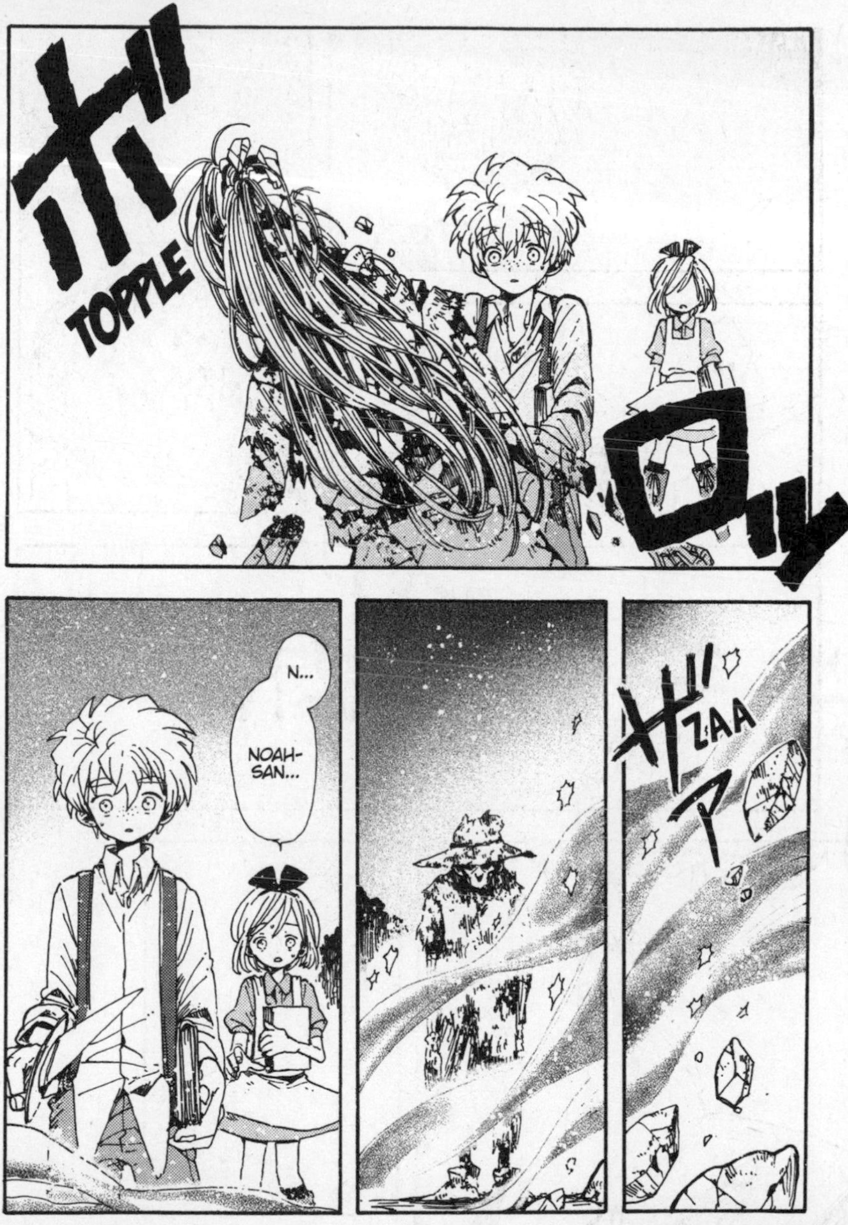
TOPPLE
ZAA
N... NOAH-SAN...

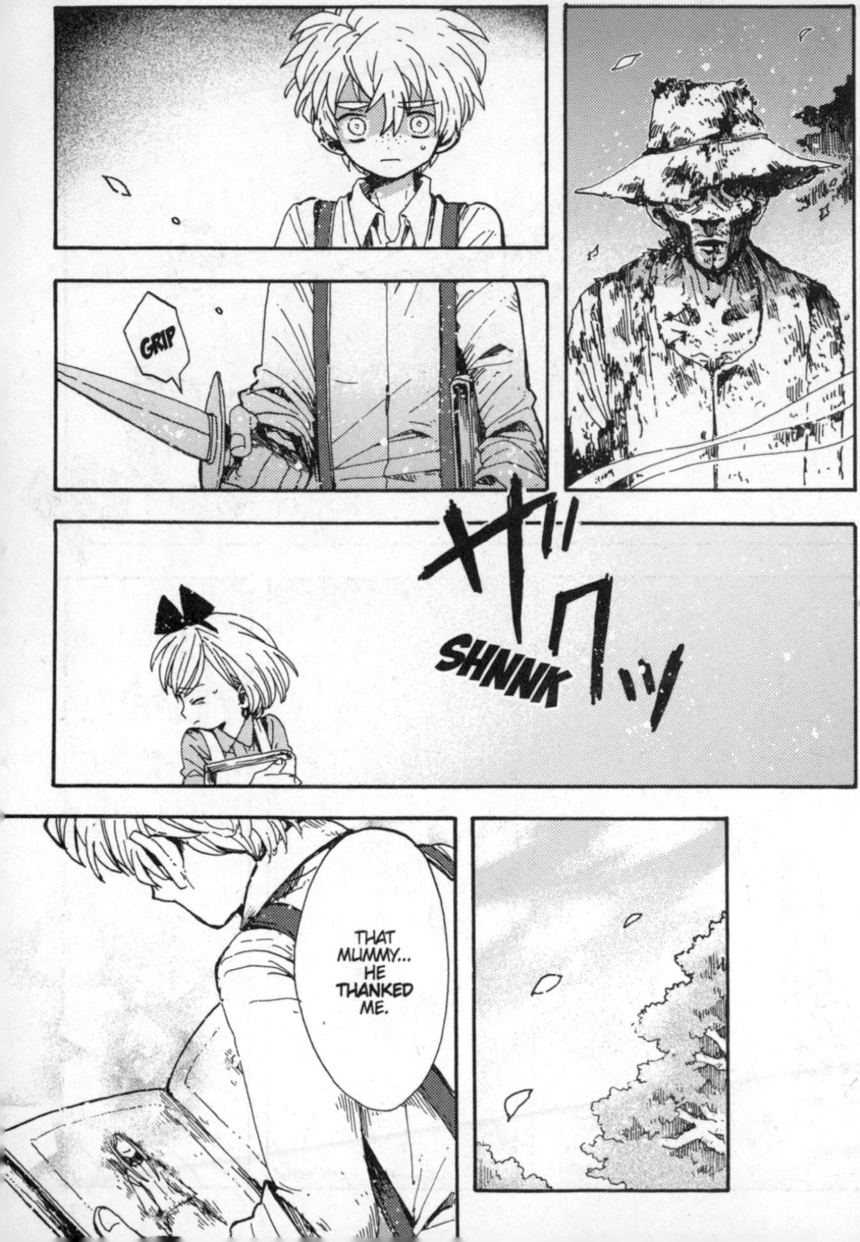
GRIP
ザクッ
SHNNK
THAT MUMMY... HE THANKED ME.

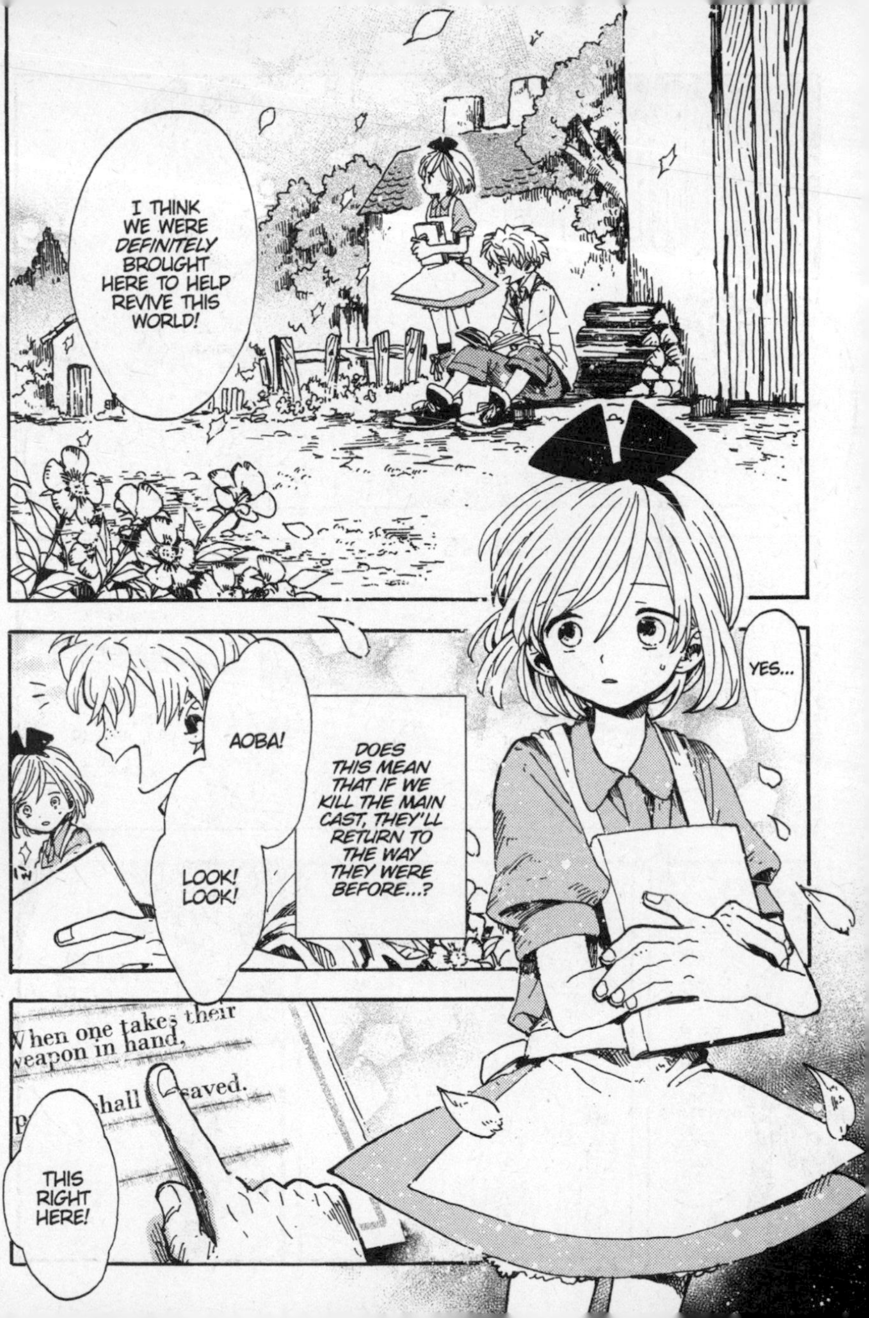
I THINK WE WERE DEFINITELY BROUGHT HERE TO HELP REVIVE THIS WORLD!
YES...
DOES THIS MEAN THAT IF WE KILL THE MAIN CAST, THEY'LL RETURN TO THE WAY THEY WERE BEFORE...?
AOBA!
LOOK! LOOK!
When one takes their
weapon in hand,
saved.
THIS RIGHT HERE!

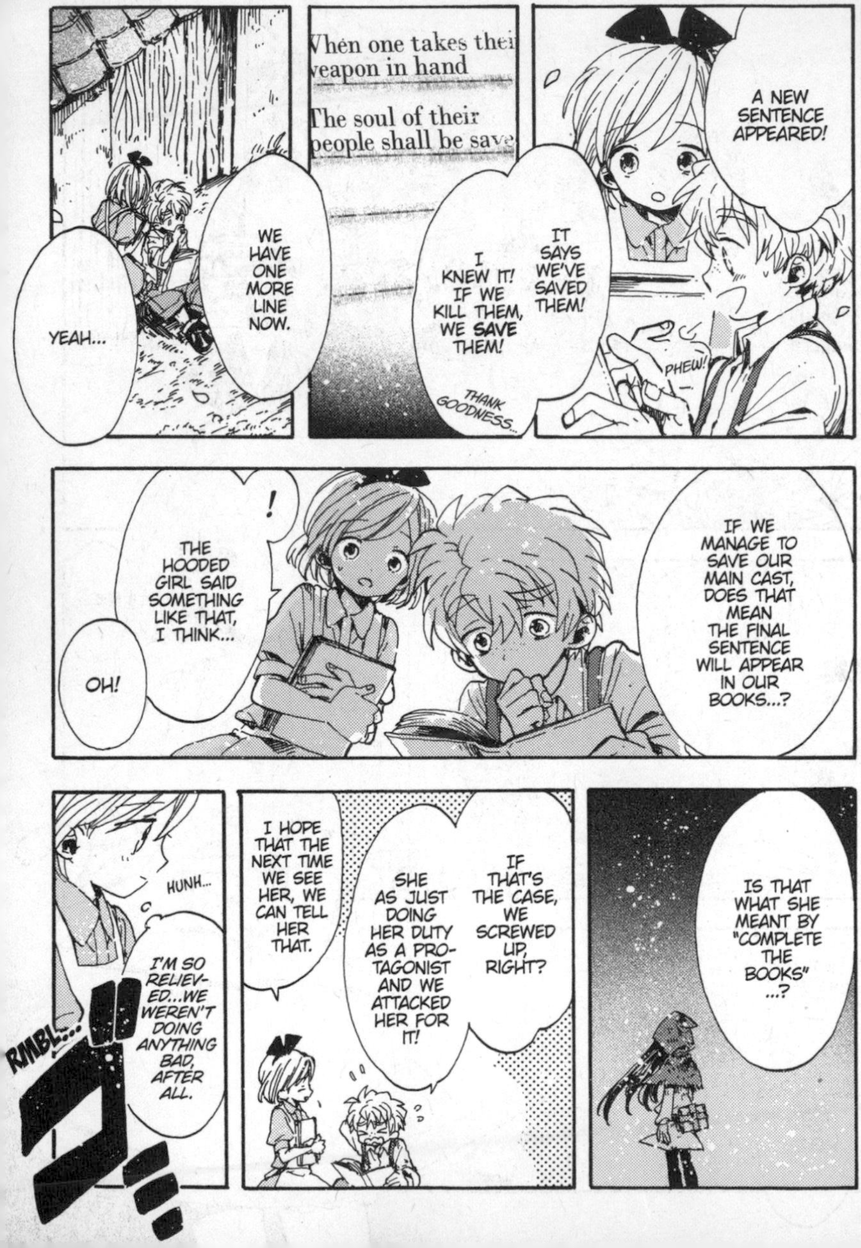
A NEW SENTENCE APPEARED!
IT SAYS WE'VE SAVED THEM!
I KNEW IT! IF WE KILL THEM, WE SAVE THEM!
PHEW!
THANK GOODNESS...
Vhen one takes thei
veapon in hand
The soul of their
people shall be save
WE HAVE ONE MORE LINE NOW.
YEAH...
IF WE MANAGE TO SAVE OUR MAIN CAST, DOES THAT MEAN THE FINAL SENTENCE WILL APPEAR IN OUR BOOKS...?
!
THE HOODED GIRL SAID SOMETHING LIKE THAT, I THINK...
OH!
IS THAT WHAT SHE MEANT BY "COMPLETE THE BOOKS"...?
IF THAT'S THE CASE, WE SCREWED UP, RIGHT?
SHE AS JUST DOING HER DUTY AS A PROTAGONIST AND WE ATTACKED HER FOR IT!
I HOPE THAT THE NEXT TIME WE SEE HER, WE CAN TELL HER THAT.
HUNH...
I'M SO RELIEVED...WE WEREN'T DOING ANYTHING BAD, AFTER ALL.
RMBL...

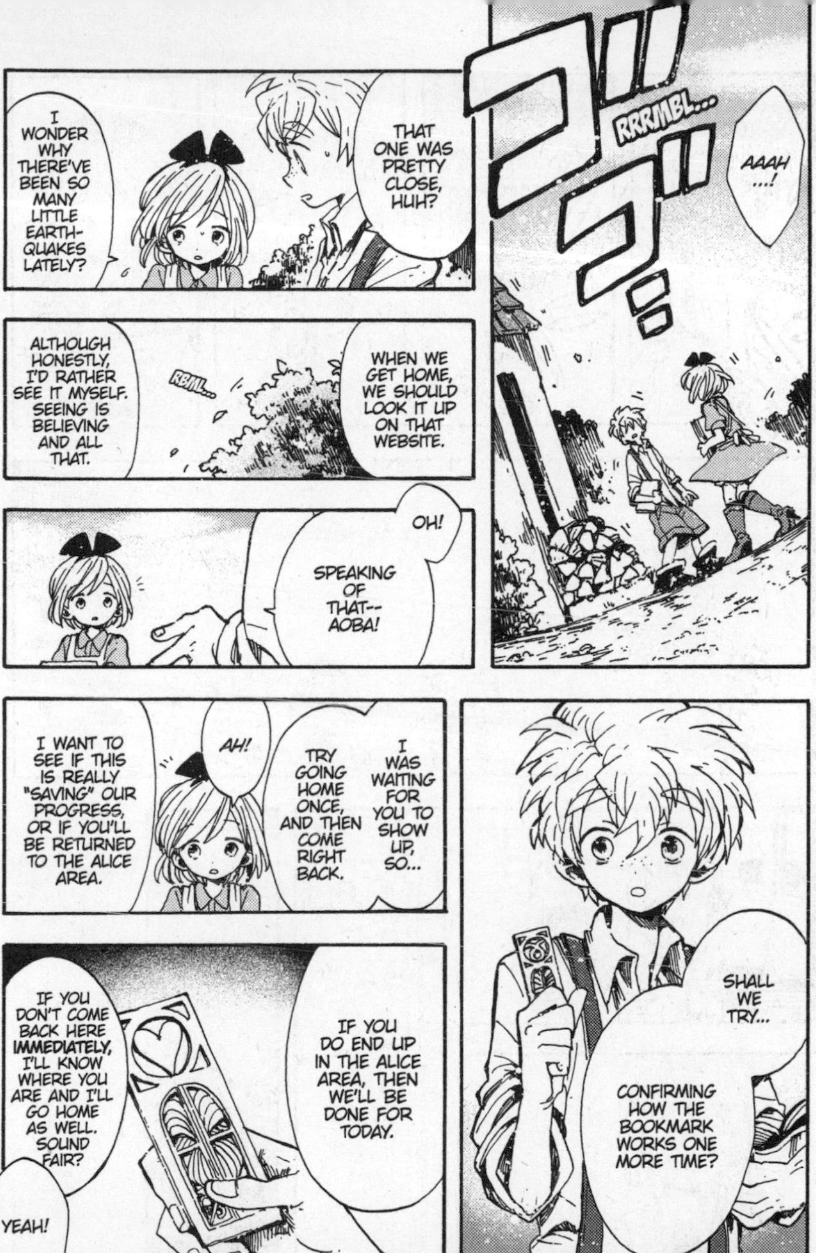
RRRMBL...
AAAH ...!
THAT ONE WAS PRETTY CLOSE, HUH?
I WONDER WHY THERE'VE BEEN SO MANY LITTLE EARTH-QUAKES LATELY?
WHEN WE GET HOME, WE SHOULD LOOK IT UP ON THAT WEBSITE.
RBML...
ALTHOUGH HONESTLY, I'D RATHER SEE IT MYSELF. SEEING IS BELIEVING AND ALL THAT.
OH!
SPEAKING OF THAT-- AOBA!
SHALL WE TRY...
CONFIRMING HOW THE BOOKMARK WORKS ONE MORE TIME?
I WAS WAITING FOR YOU TO SHOW UP, SO...
TRY GOING HOME ONCE, AND THEN COME RIGHT BACK.
AH!
I WANT TO SEE IF THIS IS REALLY "SAVING" OUR PROGRESS, OR IF YOU'LL BE RETURNED TO THE ALICE AREA.
IF YOU DO END UP IN THE ALICE AREA, THEN WE'LL BE DONE FOR TODAY.
IF YOU DON'T COME BACK HERE IMMEDIATELY, I'LL KNOW WHERE YOU ARE AND I'LL GO HOME AS WELL. SOUND FAIR?
YEAH!

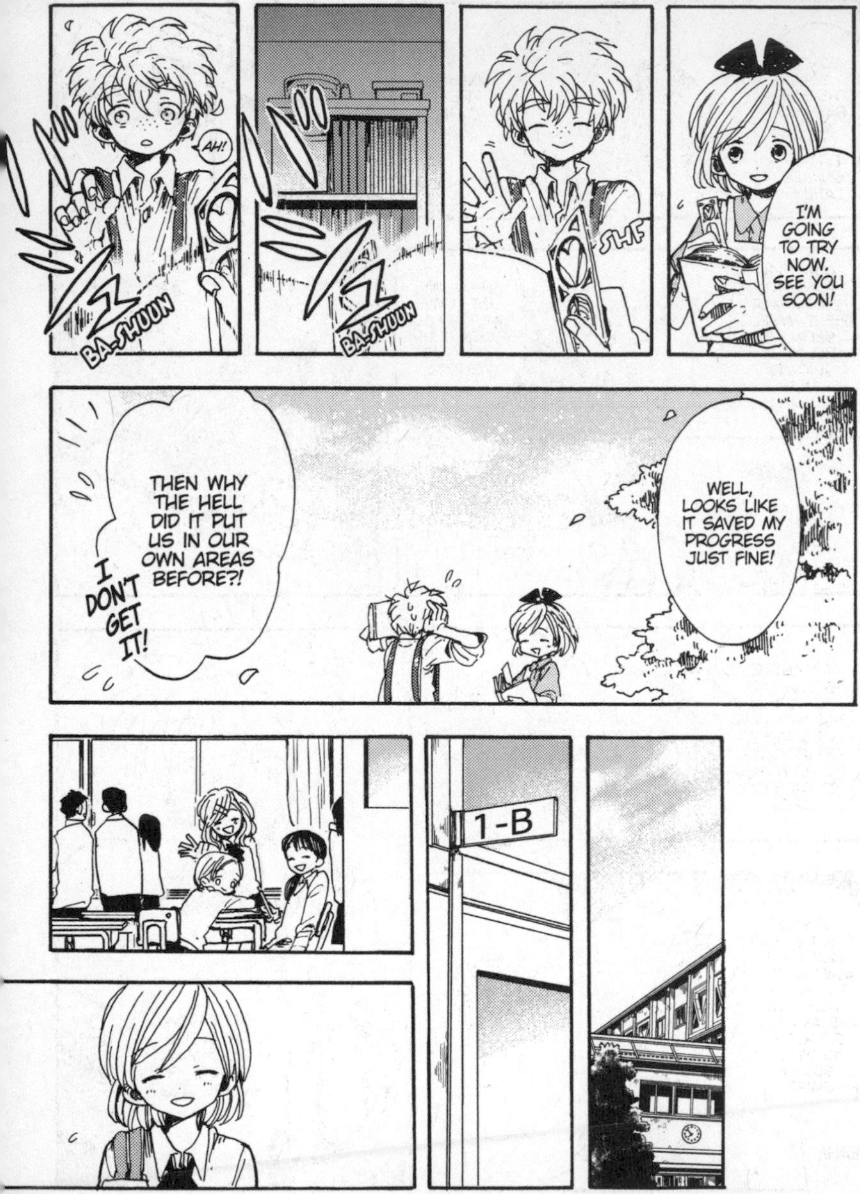
I'M GOING TO TRY NOW. SEE YOU SOON!
SHF
BA-SHUUN
AH!
BA-SHUUN
WELL, LOOKS LIKE IT SAVED MY PROGRESS JUST FINE!
THEN WHY THE HELL DID IT PUT US IN OUR OWN AREAS BEFORE?!
I DON'T GET IT!
1-B

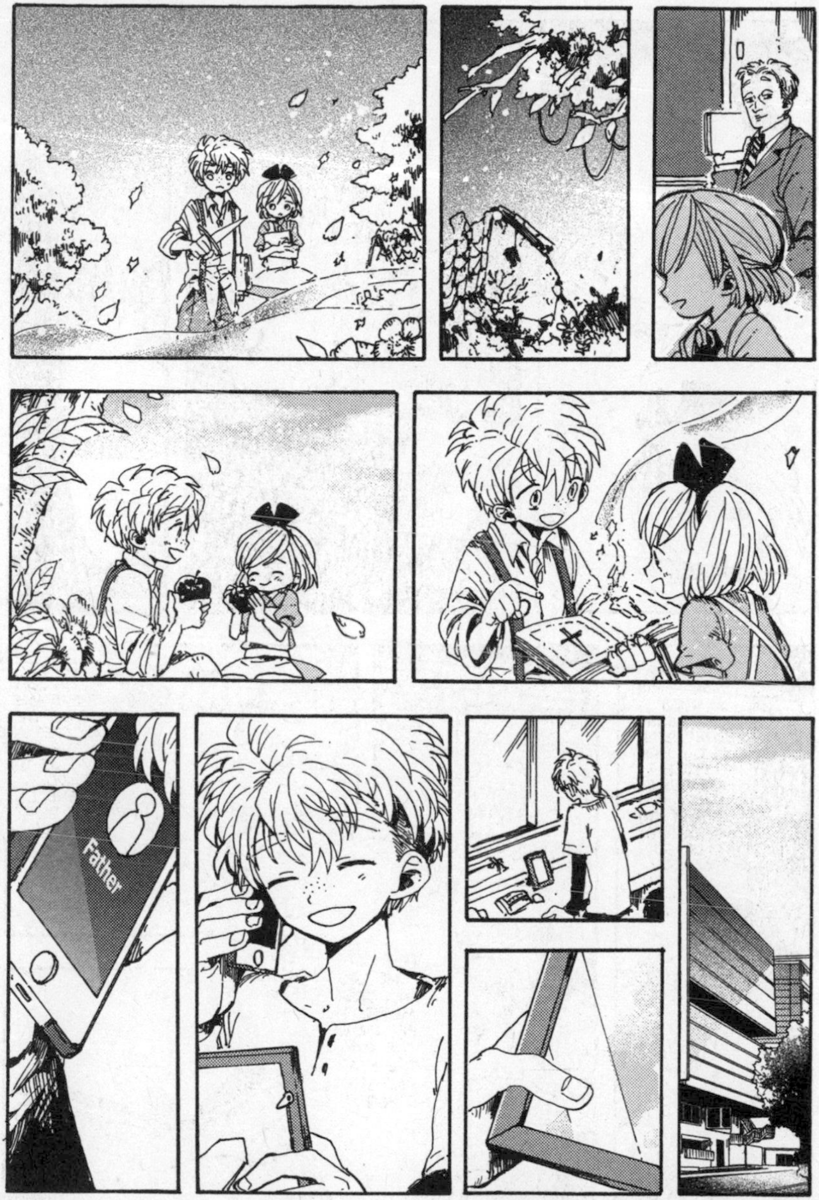
Father

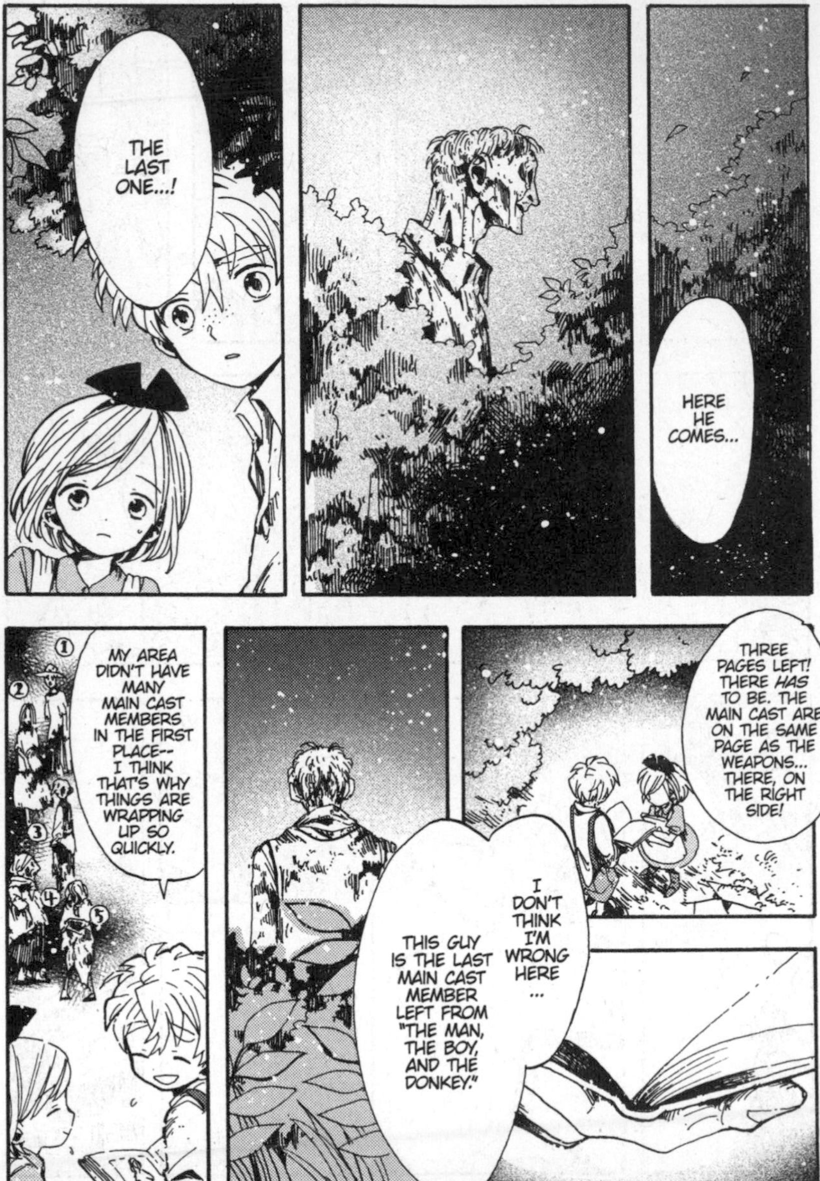
HERE HE COMES...
THE LAST ONE...!
THREE PAGES LEFT! THERE *HAS* TO BE. THE MAIN CAST ARE ON THE SAME PAGE AS THE WEAPONS... THERE, ON THE RIGHT SIDE!
I DON'T THINK I'M WRONG HERE...
THIS GUY IS THE LAST MAIN CAST MEMBER LEFT FROM "THE MAN, THE BOY, AND THE DONKEY."
MY AREA DIDN'T HAVE MANY MAIN CAST MEMBERS IN THE FIRST PLACE-- I THINK THAT'S WHY THINGS ARE WRAPPING UP SO QUICKLY.

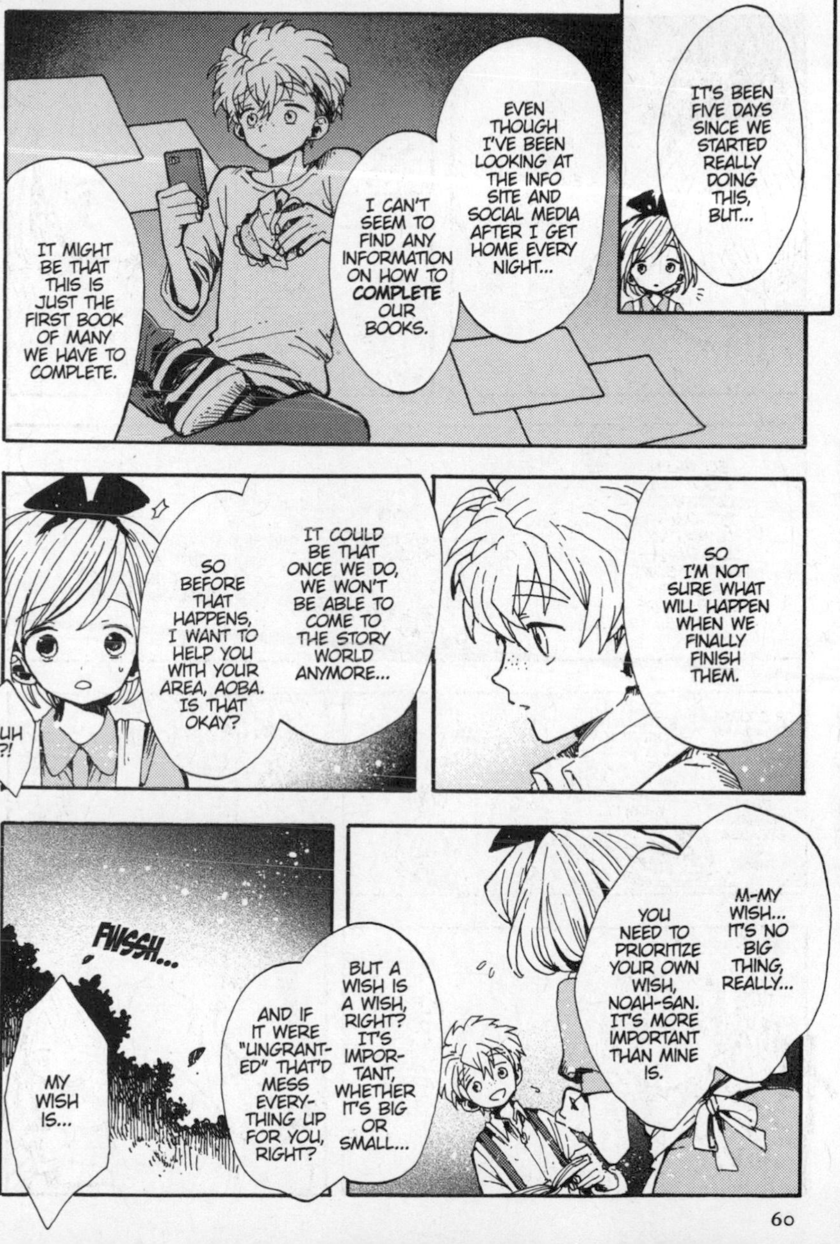
IT'S BEEN FIVE DAYS SINCE WE STARTED REALLY DOING THIS, BUT...
EVEN THOUGH I'VE BEEN LOOKING AT THE INFO SITE AND SOCIAL MEDIA AFTER I GET HOME EVERY NIGHT...
I CAN'T SEEM TO FIND ANY INFORMATION ON HOW TO **COMPLETE** OUR BOOKS.
IT MIGHT BE THAT THIS IS JUST THE FIRST BOOK OF MANY WE HAVE TO COMPLETE.
SO I'M NOT SURE WHAT WILL HAPPEN WHEN WE FINALLY FINISH THEM.
IT COULD BE THAT ONCE WE DO, WE WON'T BE ABLE TO COME TO THE STORY WORLD ANYMORE...
SO BEFORE THAT HAPPENS, I WANT TO HELP YOU WITH YOUR AREA, AOBA. IS THAT OKAY?
HUH?!
M-MY WISH... IT'S NO BIG THING, REALLY...
YOU NEED TO PRIORITIZE YOUR OWN WISH, NOAH-SAN. IT'S MORE IMPORTANT THAN MINE IS.
BUT A WISH IS A WISH, RIGHT? IT'S IMPOR-TANT, WHETHER IT'S BIG OR SMALL...
AND IF IT WERE "UNGRANT-ED" THAT'D MESS EVERY-THING UP FOR YOU, RIGHT?
FWSSH...
MY WISH IS...

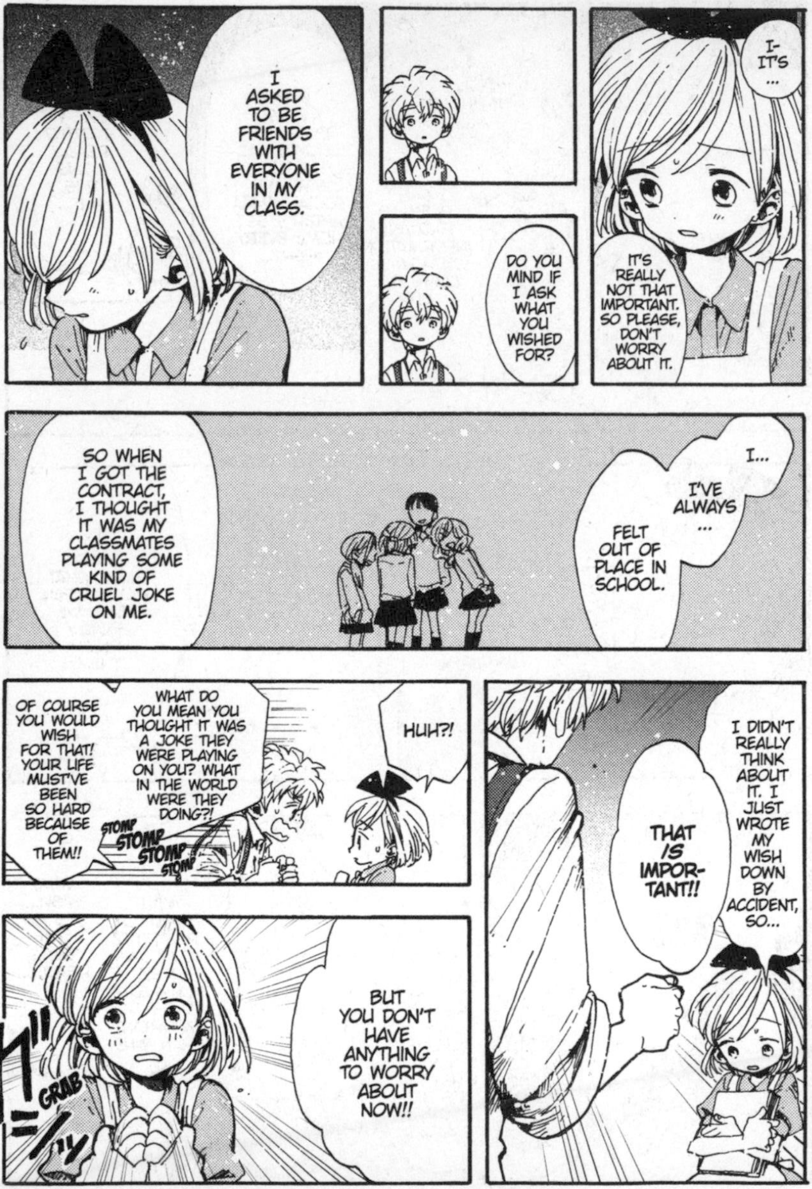
I- IT'S ...
IT'S REALLY NOT THAT IMPORTANT. SO PLEASE, DON'T WORRY ABOUT IT.
DO YOU MIND IF I ASK WHAT YOU WISHED FOR?
I ASKED TO BE FRIENDS WITH EVERYONE IN MY CLASS.
I...
I'VE ALWAYS ...
FELT OUT OF PLACE IN SCHOOL.
SO WHEN I GOT THE CONTRACT, I THOUGHT IT WAS MY CLASSMATES PLAYING SOME KIND OF CRUEL JOKE ON ME.
I DIDN'T REALLY THINK ABOUT IT. I JUST WROTE MY WISH DOWN BY ACCIDENT, SO...
THAT IS IMPORTANT!!
HUH?!
WHAT DO YOU MEAN YOU THOUGHT IT WAS A JOKE THEY WERE PLAYING ON YOU? WHAT IN THE WORLD WERE THEY DOING?!
OF COURSE YOU WOULD WISH FOR THAT! YOUR LIFE MUST'VE BEEN SO HARD BECAUSE OF THEM!!
STOMP STOMP STOMP STOMP
BUT YOU DON'T HAVE ANYTHING TO WORRY ABOUT NOW!!
GRAB

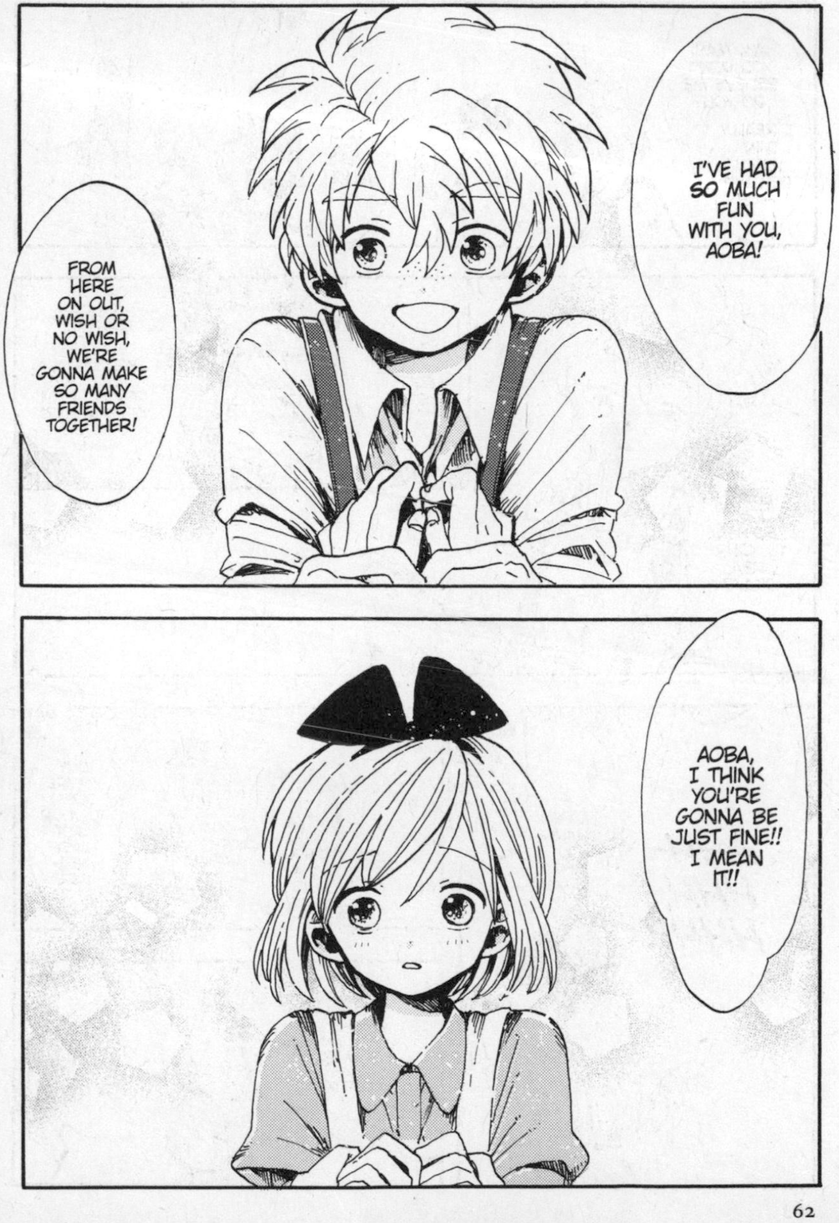
I'VE HAD SO MUCH FUN WITH YOU, AOBA!
FROM HERE ON OUT, WISH OR NO WISH, WE'RE GONNA MAKE SO MANY FRIENDS TOGETHER!
AOBA, I THINK YOU'RE GONNA BE JUST FINE!! I MEAN IT!!

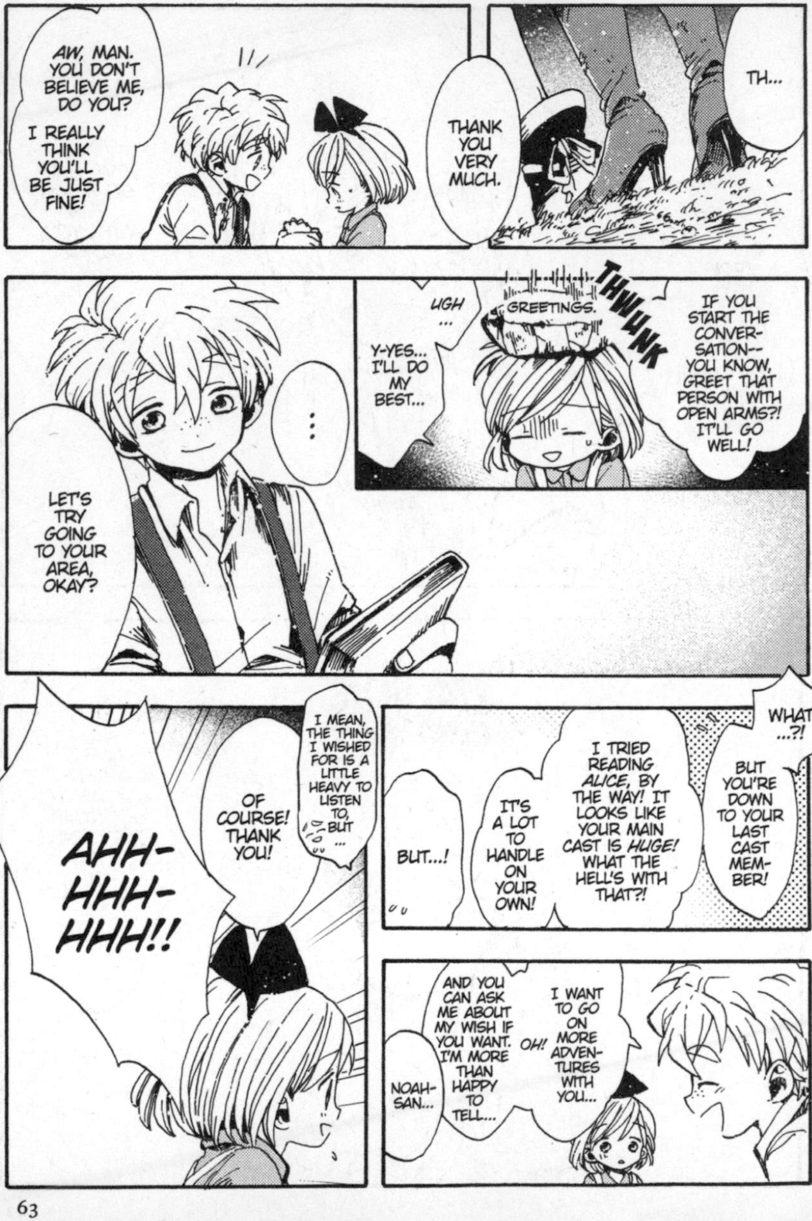
TH...
THANK YOU VERY MUCH.
AW, MAN. YOU DON'T BELIEVE ME, DO YOU?
I REALLY THINK YOU'LL BE JUST FINE!
IF YOU START THE CONVERSATION--YOU KNOW, GREET THAT PERSON WITH OPEN ARMS?! IT'LL GO WELL!
THWUNK
GREETINGS.
UGH ...
Y-YES... I'LL DO MY BEST...
...
LET'S TRY GOING TO YOUR AREA, OKAY?
WHAT ...?!
BUT YOU'RE DOWN TO YOUR LAST CAST MEMBER!
I TRIED READING *ALICE*, BY THE WAY! IT LOOKS LIKE YOUR MAIN CAST IS *HUGE!* WHAT THE HELL'S WITH THAT?!
IT'S A LOT TO HANDLE ON YOUR OWN!
BUT...!
I WANT TO GO ON MORE ADVENTURES WITH YOU...
OH!
AND YOU CAN ASK ME ABOUT MY WISH IF YOU WANT. I'M MORE THAN HAPPY TO TELL...
NOAH-SAN...
I MEAN, THE THING I WISHED FOR IS A LITTLE HEAVY TO LISTEN TO, BUT ...
OF COURSE! THANK YOU!
AHHHHHHHHH!!

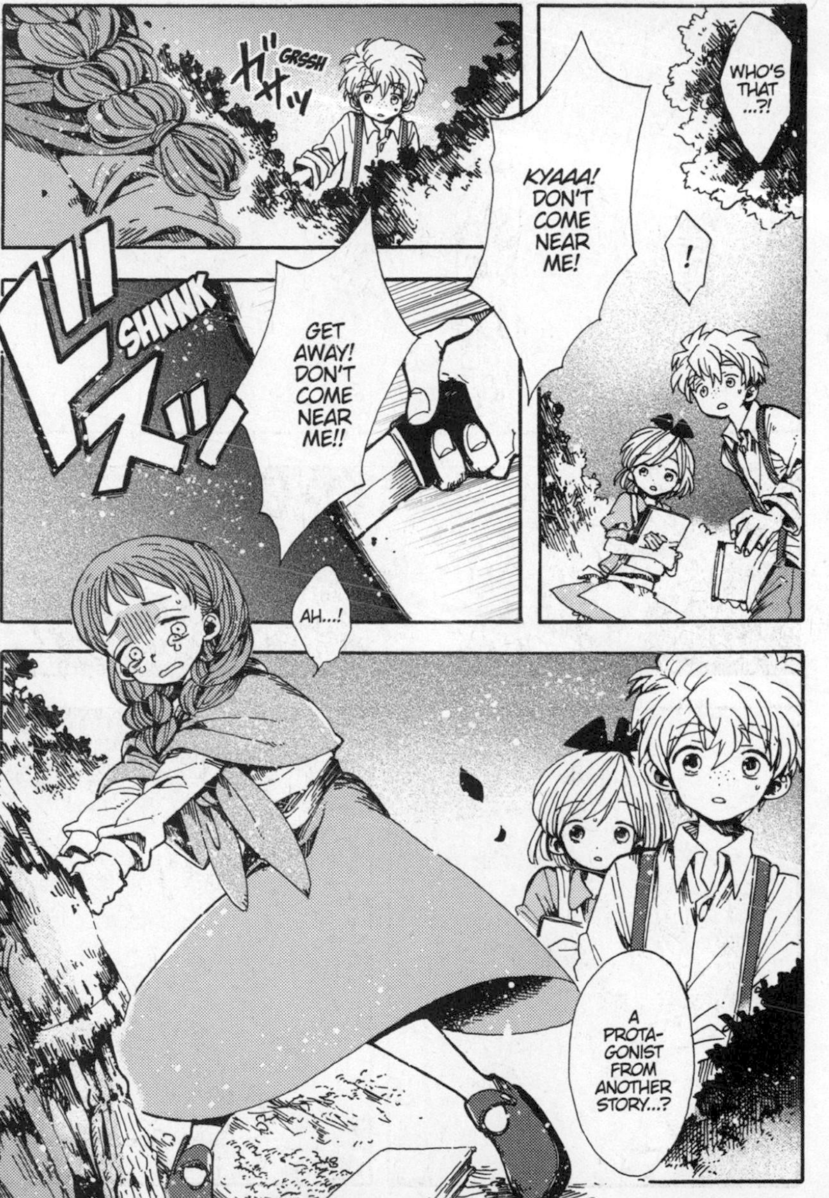
WHO'S THAT ...?!
KYAAA! DON'T COME NEAR ME!
!
GRSSH
SHNNK
GET AWAY! DON'T COME NEAR ME!!
AH...!
A PROTAGONIST FROM ANOTHER STORY...?

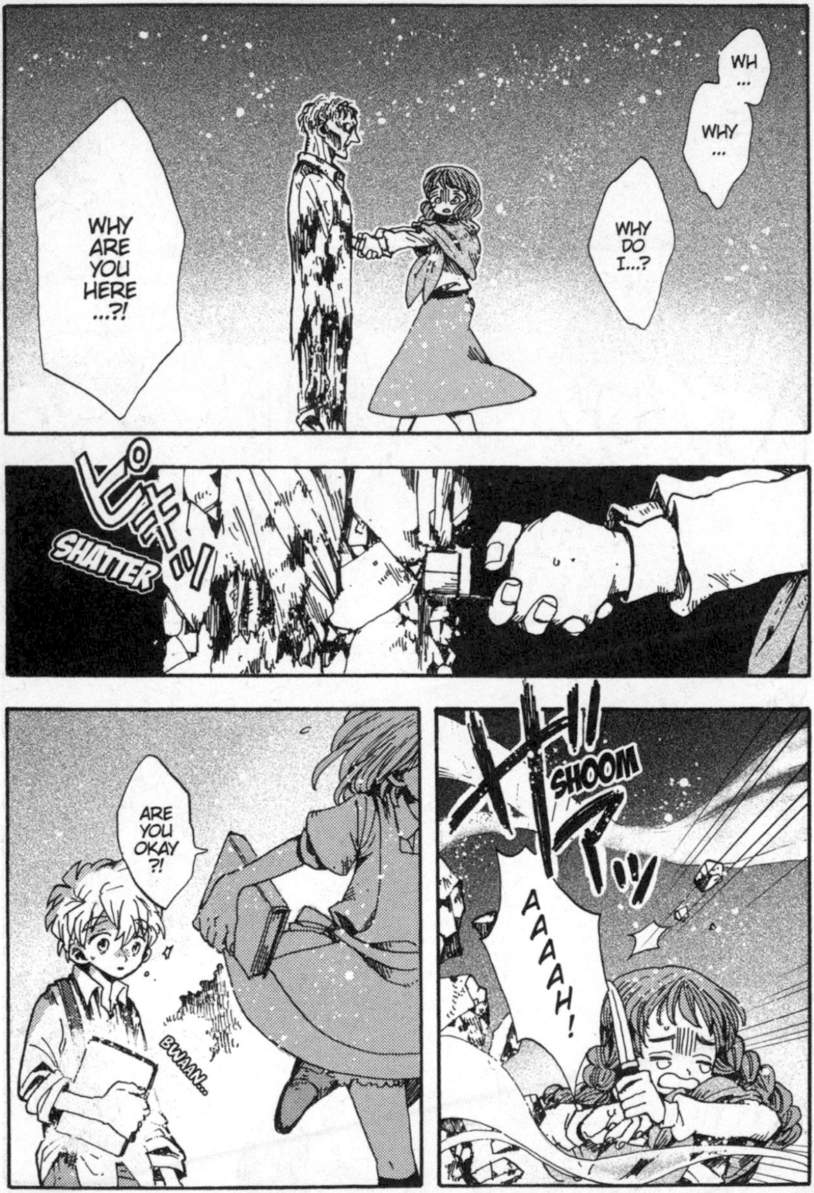
WH... WHY...
WHY DO I...?
WHY ARE YOU HERE...?!
SHATTER
SHOOM
AAAAAH!
ARE YOU OKAY?!
BWAAN...

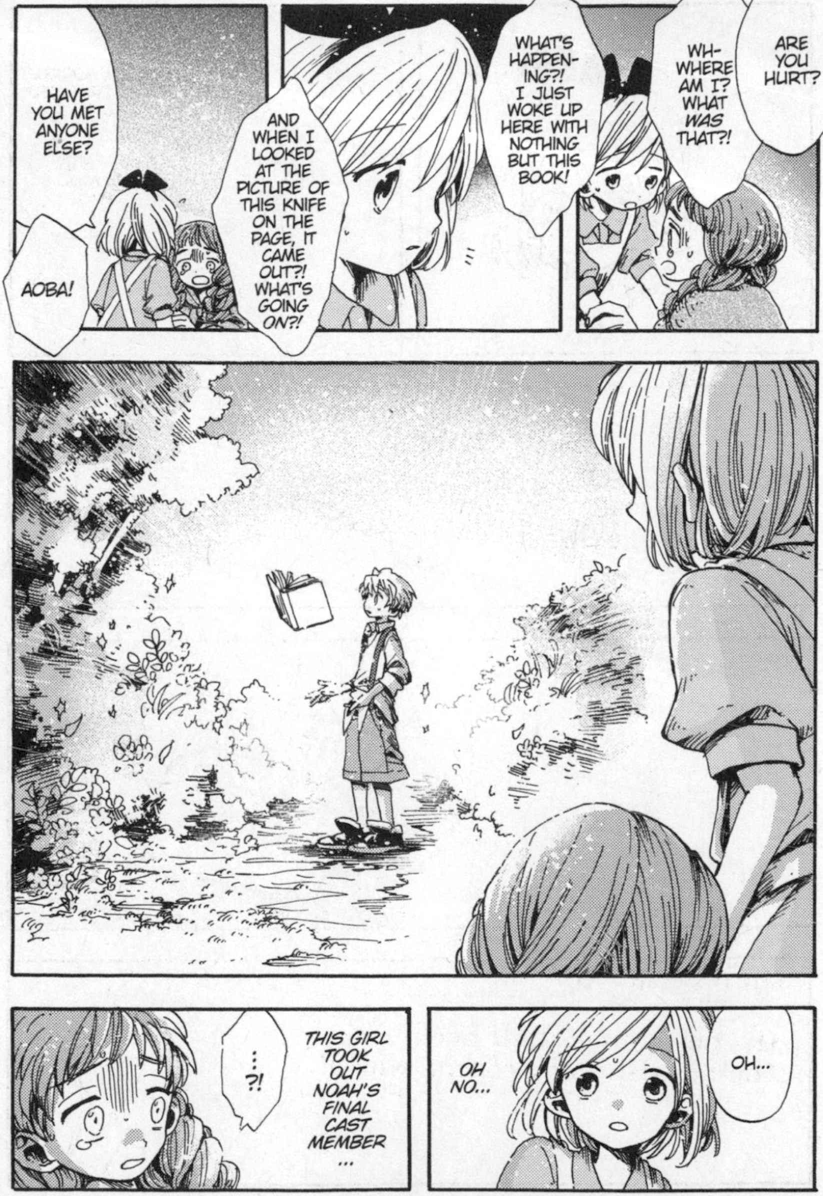
ARE YOU HURT?
WH-WHERE AM I? WHAT WAS THAT?!
WHAT'S HAPPENING?! I JUST WOKE UP HERE WITH NOTHING BUT THIS BOOK!
AND WHEN I LOOKED AT THE PICTURE OF THIS KNIFE ON THE PAGE, IT CAME OUT?! WHAT'S GOING ON?!
HAVE YOU MET ANYONE ELSE?
AOBA!
OH...
OH NO...
THIS GIRL TOOK OUT NOAH'S FINAL CAST MEMBER ...
...?!

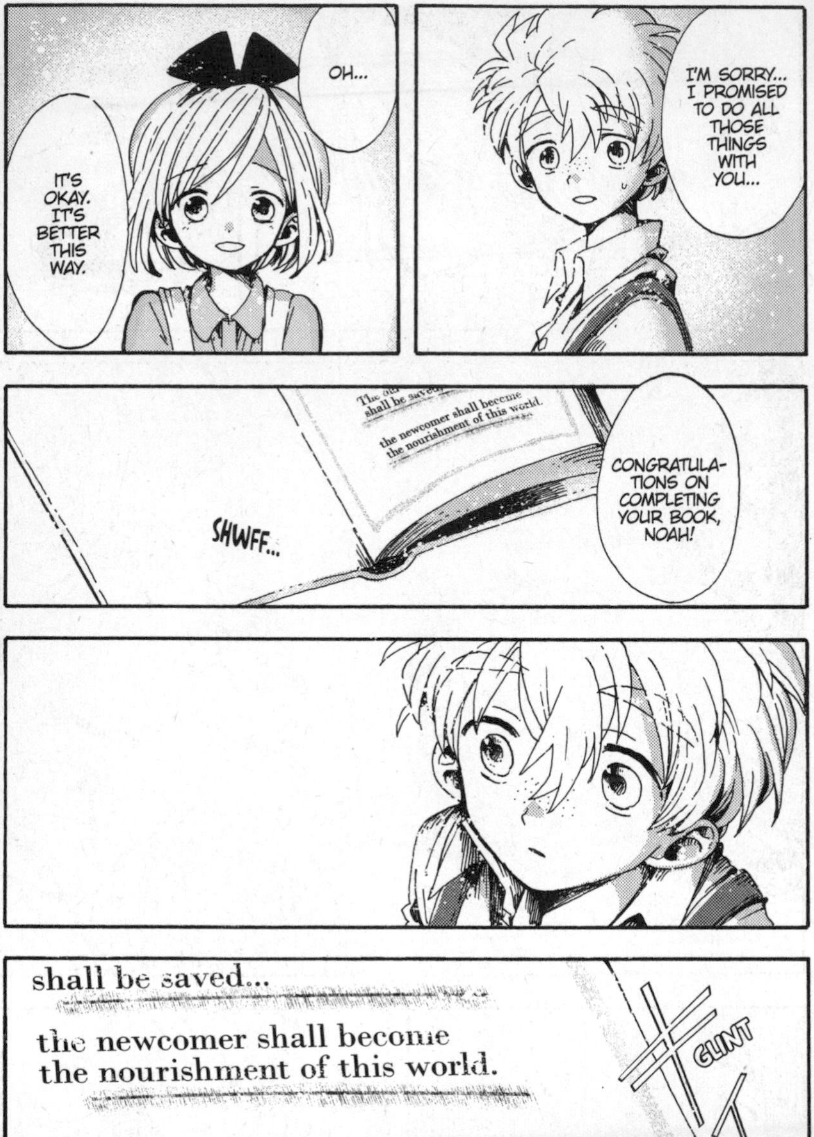
I'M SORRY... I PROMISED TO DO ALL THOSE THINGS WITH YOU...
OH...
IT'S OKAY. IT'S BETTER THIS WAY.
CONGRATULATIONS ON COMPLETING YOUR BOOK, NOAH!
shall be saved
the newcomer shall become the nourishment of this world.
SHWFF...
shall be saved...
the newcomer shall become the nourishment of this world.
GLINT

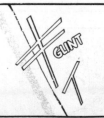

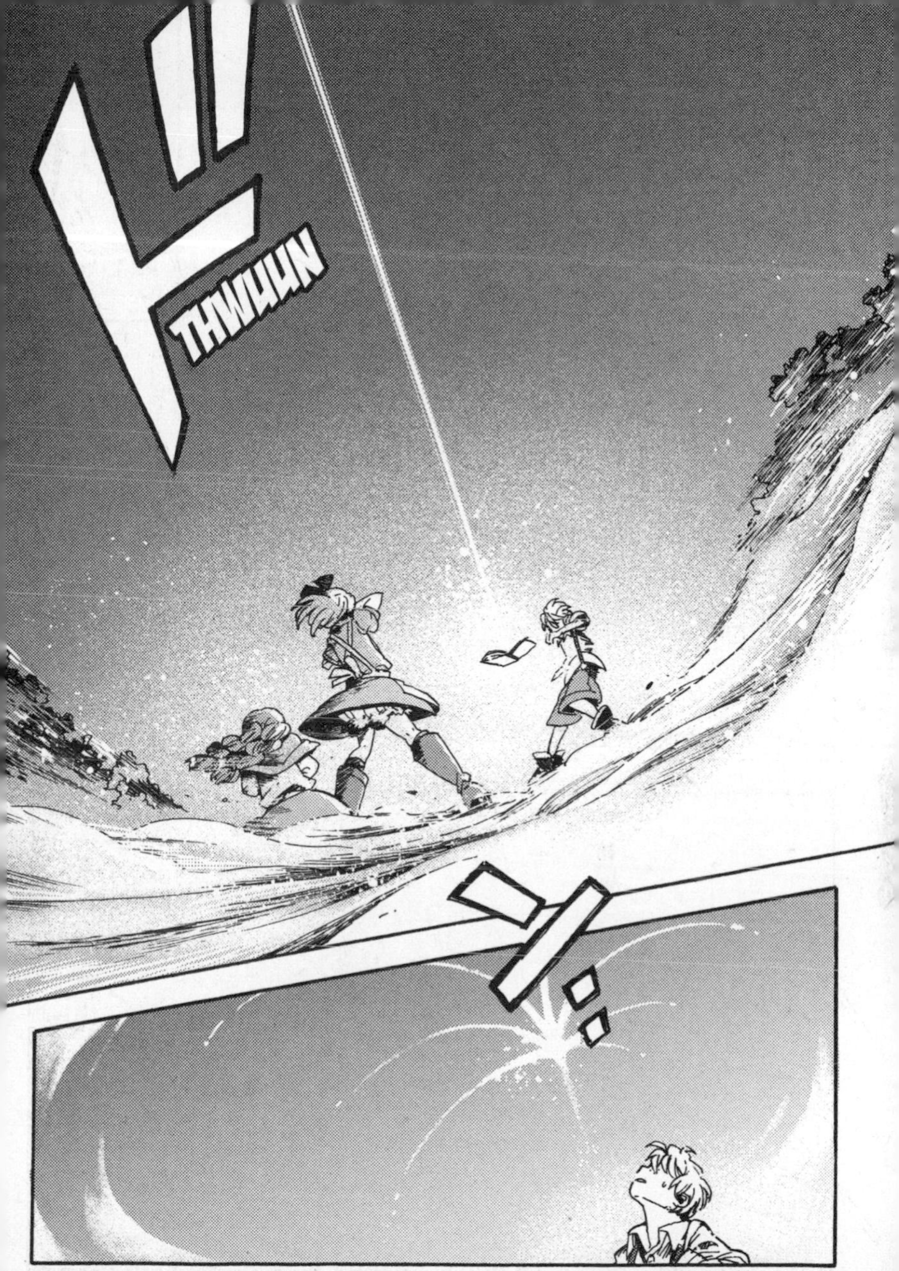
THWUUN

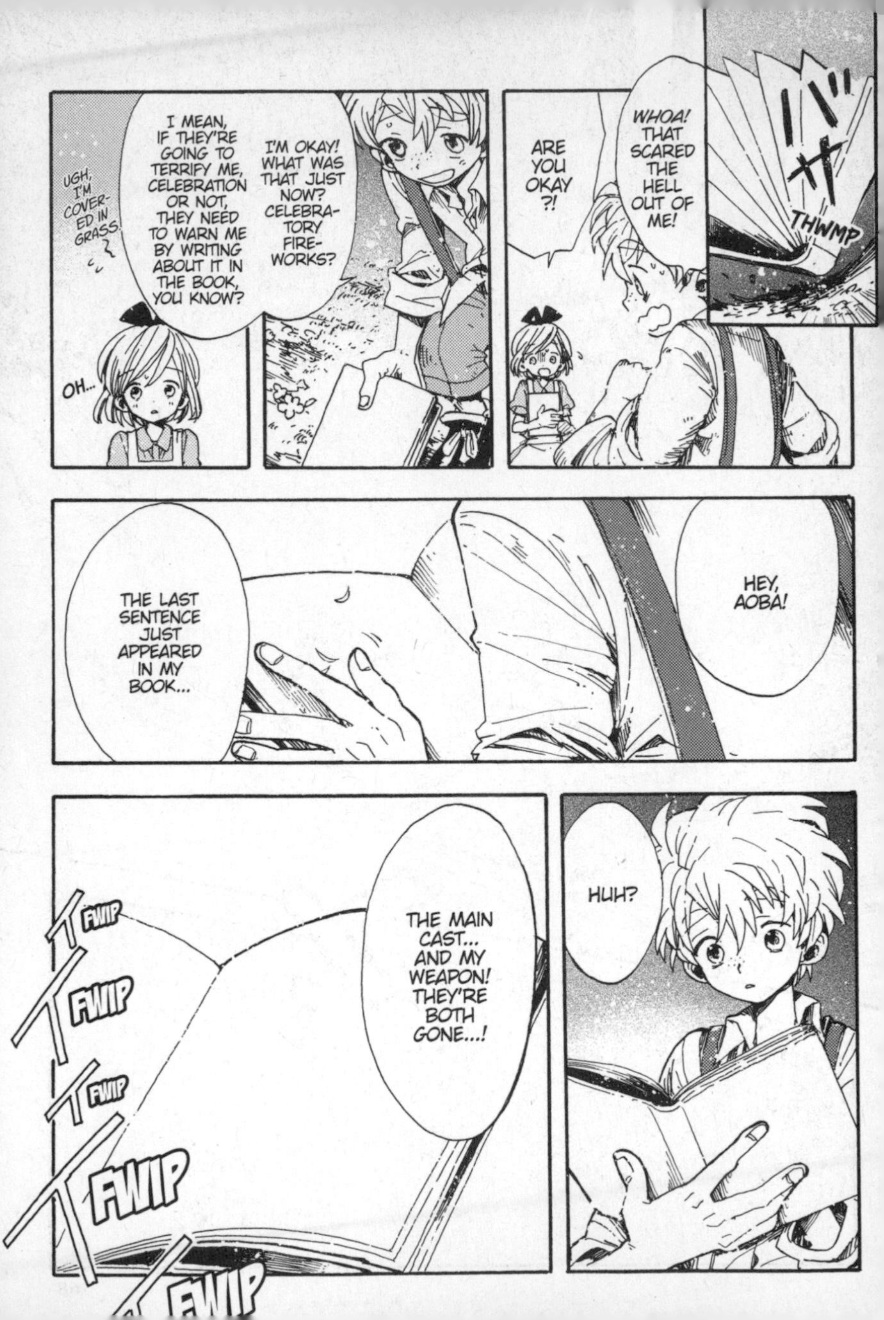
THWMP
WHOA! THAT SCARED THE HELL OUT OF ME!
ARE YOU OKAY?!
I'M OKAY! WHAT WAS THAT JUST NOW? CELEBRATORY FIRE-WORKS?
I MEAN, IF THEY'RE GOING TO TERRIFY ME, CELEBRATION OR NOT, THEY NEED TO WARN ME BY WRITING ABOUT IT IN THE BOOK, YOU KNOW?
UGH, I'M COVER-ED IN GRASS.
OH...
HEY, AOBA!
THE LAST SENTENCE JUST APPEARED IN MY BOOK...
HUH?
THE MAIN CAST... AND MY WEAPON! THEY'RE BOTH GONE...!
FWIP
FWIP
FWIP
FWIP
FWIP

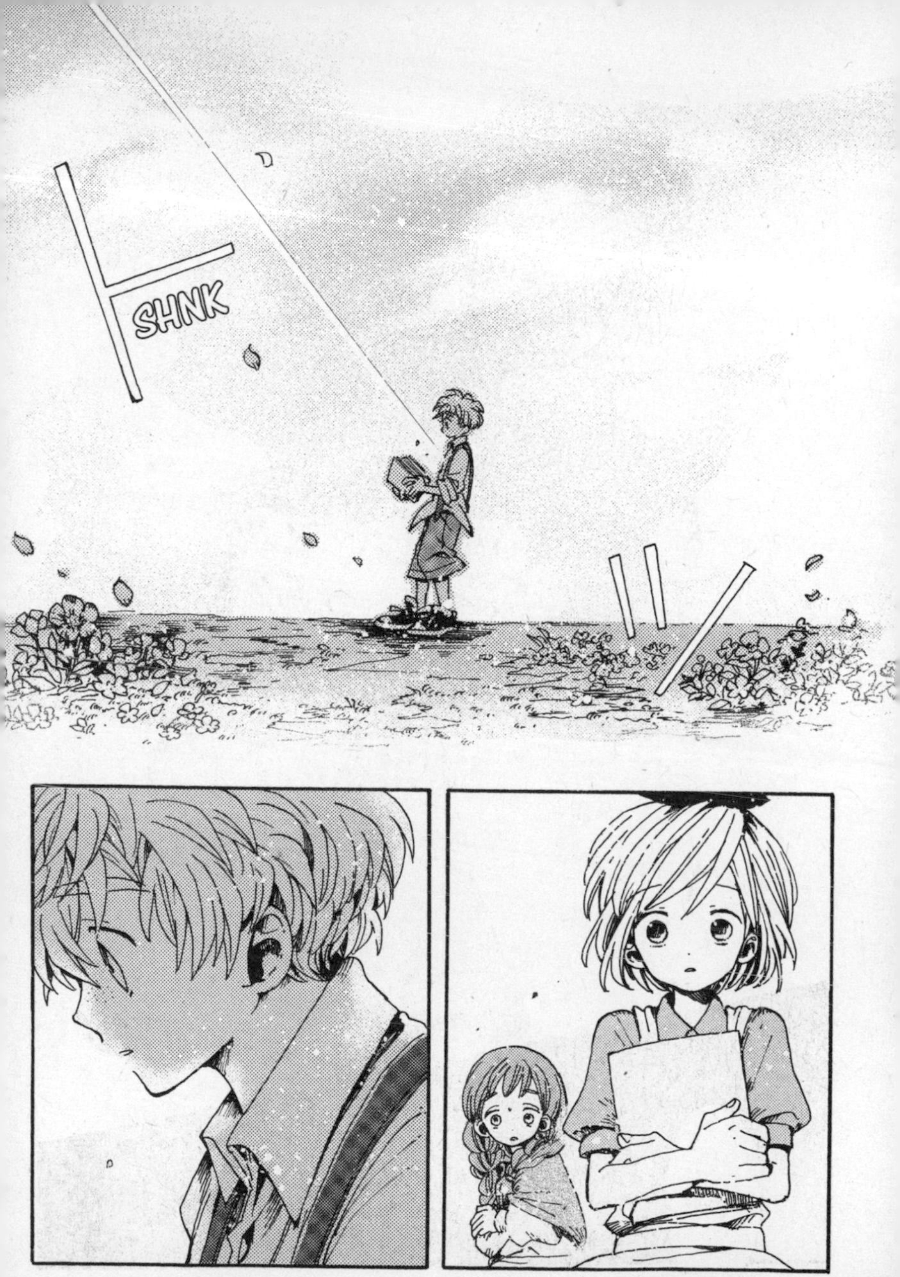
SHNK

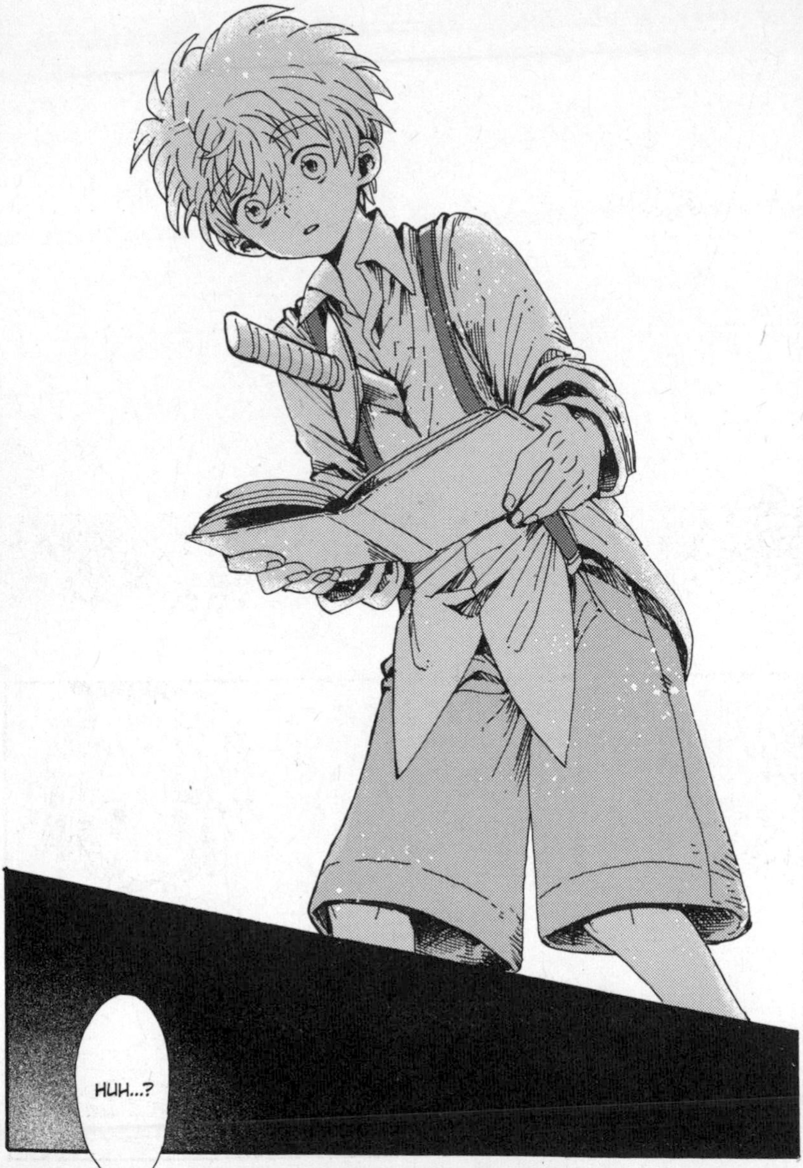
HUH...?

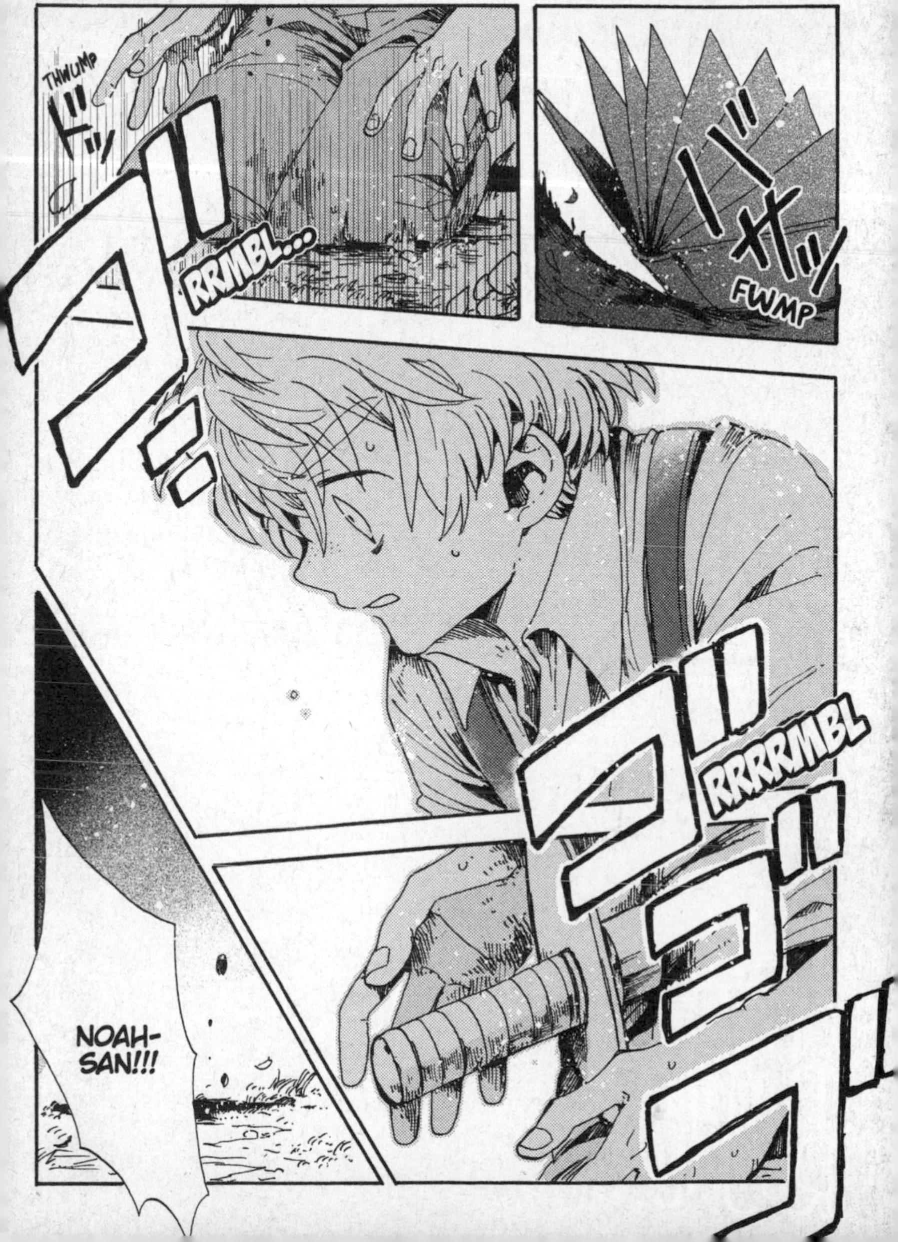
FWMP
THWUMP
RRMBL...
RRRRMBL
NOAH-SAN!!!

FAIRY
TALE
BATTLE
ROYALE

FAIRY
TALE
BATTLE
ROYALE

Chapter 7: Parting

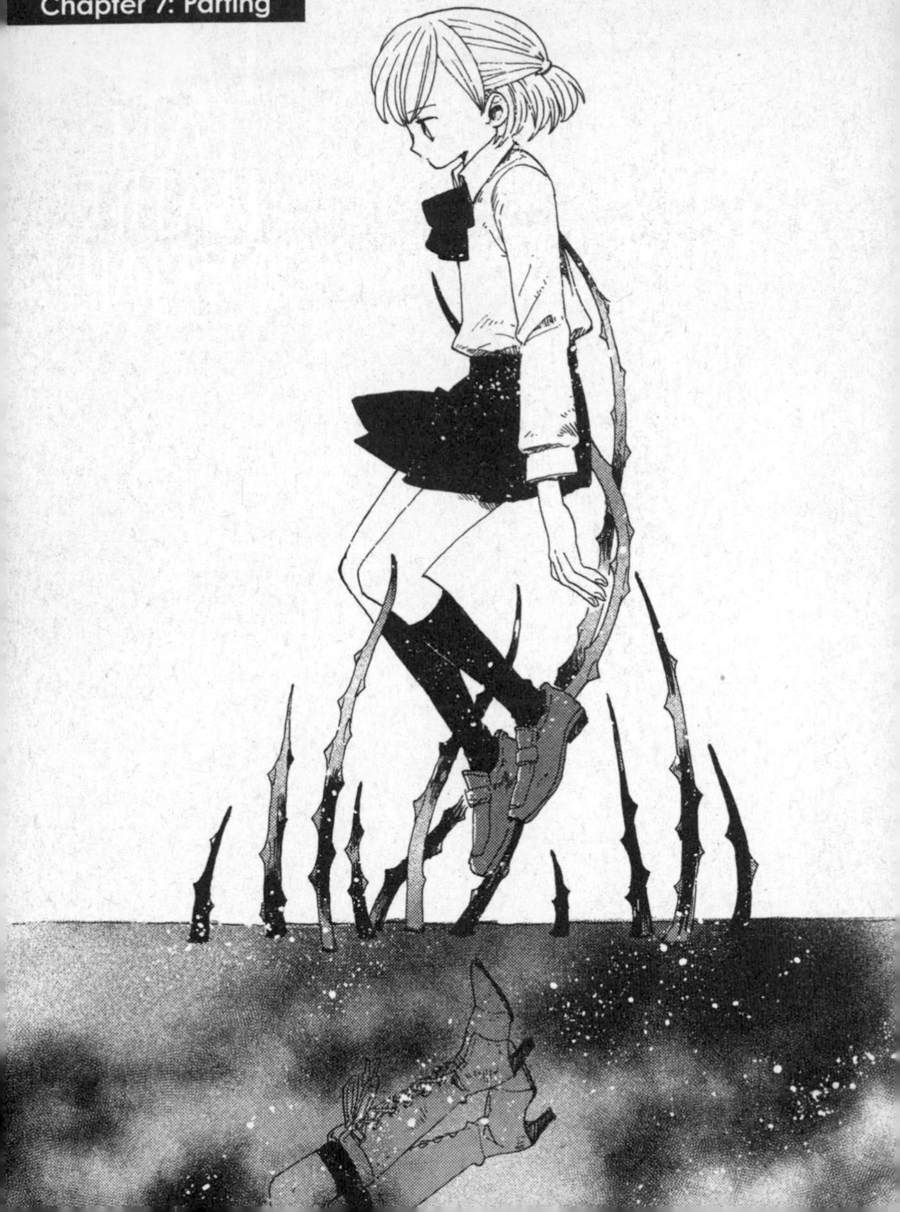

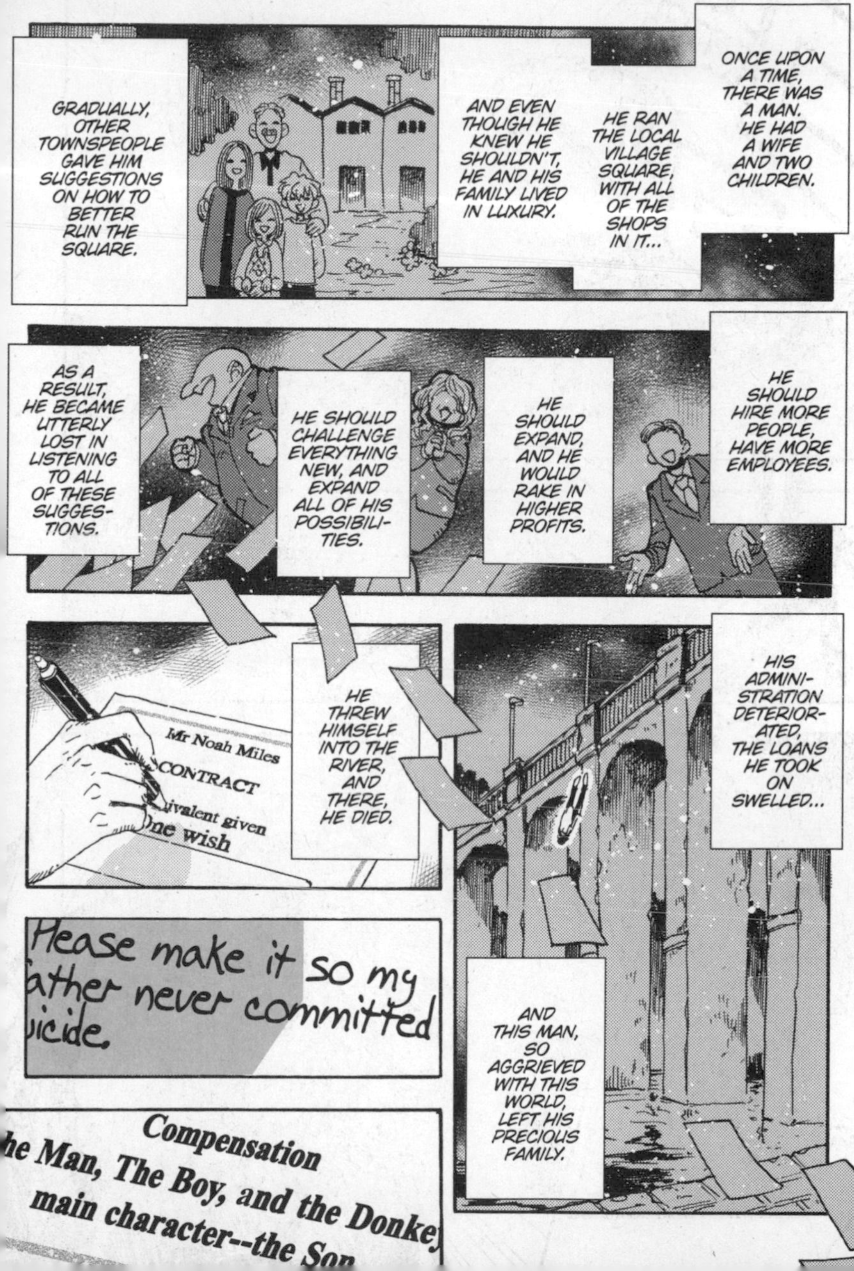
ONCE UPON A TIME, THERE WAS A MAN. HE HAD A WIFE AND TWO CHILDREN.
HE RAN THE LOCAL VILLAGE SQUARE, WITH ALL OF THE SHOPS IN IT...
AND EVEN THOUGH HE KNEW HE SHOULDN'T, HE AND HIS FAMILY LIVED IN LUXURY.
GRADUALLY, OTHER TOWNSPEOPLE GAVE HIM SUGGESTIONS ON HOW TO BETTER RUN THE SQUARE.
HE SHOULD HIRE MORE PEOPLE, HAVE MORE EMPLOYEES.
HE SHOULD EXPAND, AND HE WOULD RAKE IN HIGHER PROFITS.
HE SHOULD CHALLENGE EVERYTHING NEW, AND EXPAND ALL OF HIS POSSIBILI-TIES.
AS A RESULT, HE BECAME UTTERLY LOST IN LISTENING TO ALL OF THESE SUGGES-TIONS.
HIS ADMINI-STRATION DETERIOR-ATED, THE LOANS HE TOOK ON SWELLED...
AND THIS MAN, SO AGGRIEVED WITH THIS WORLD, LEFT HIS PRECIOUS FAMILY.
HE THREW HIMSELF INTO THE RIVER, AND THERE, HE DIED.
Mr Noah Miles
CONTRACT
uivalent given
ne wish
Please make it so my
ather never committed
icide.
Compensation
he Man, The Boy, and the Donke
main character--the Son

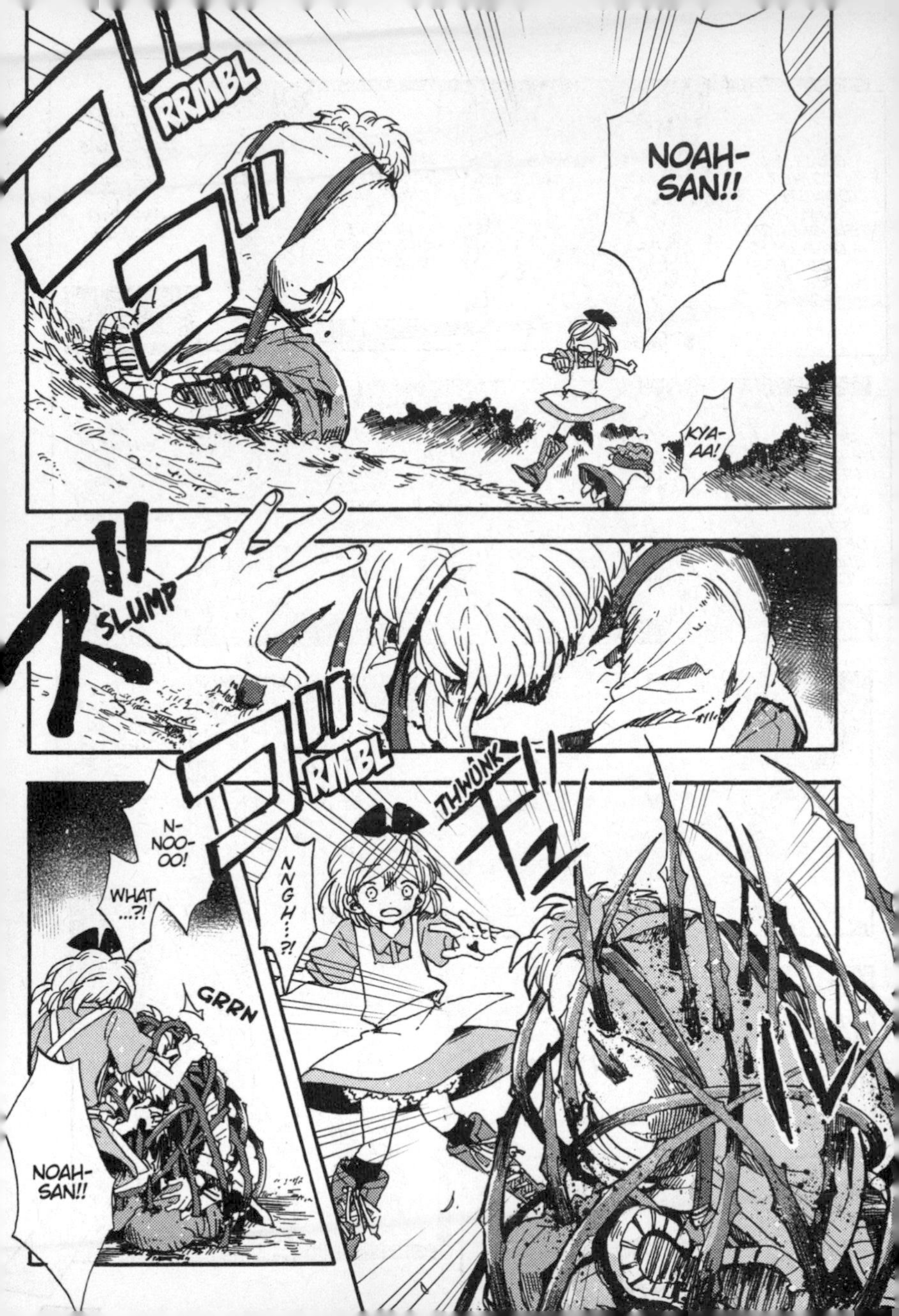
NOAH-SAN!!
KYA-AA!
RRMBL
SLUMP
RMBL
THWUNK
NNGH...?!
N-NOO-OO!
WHAT ...?!
GRRN
NOAH-SAN!!

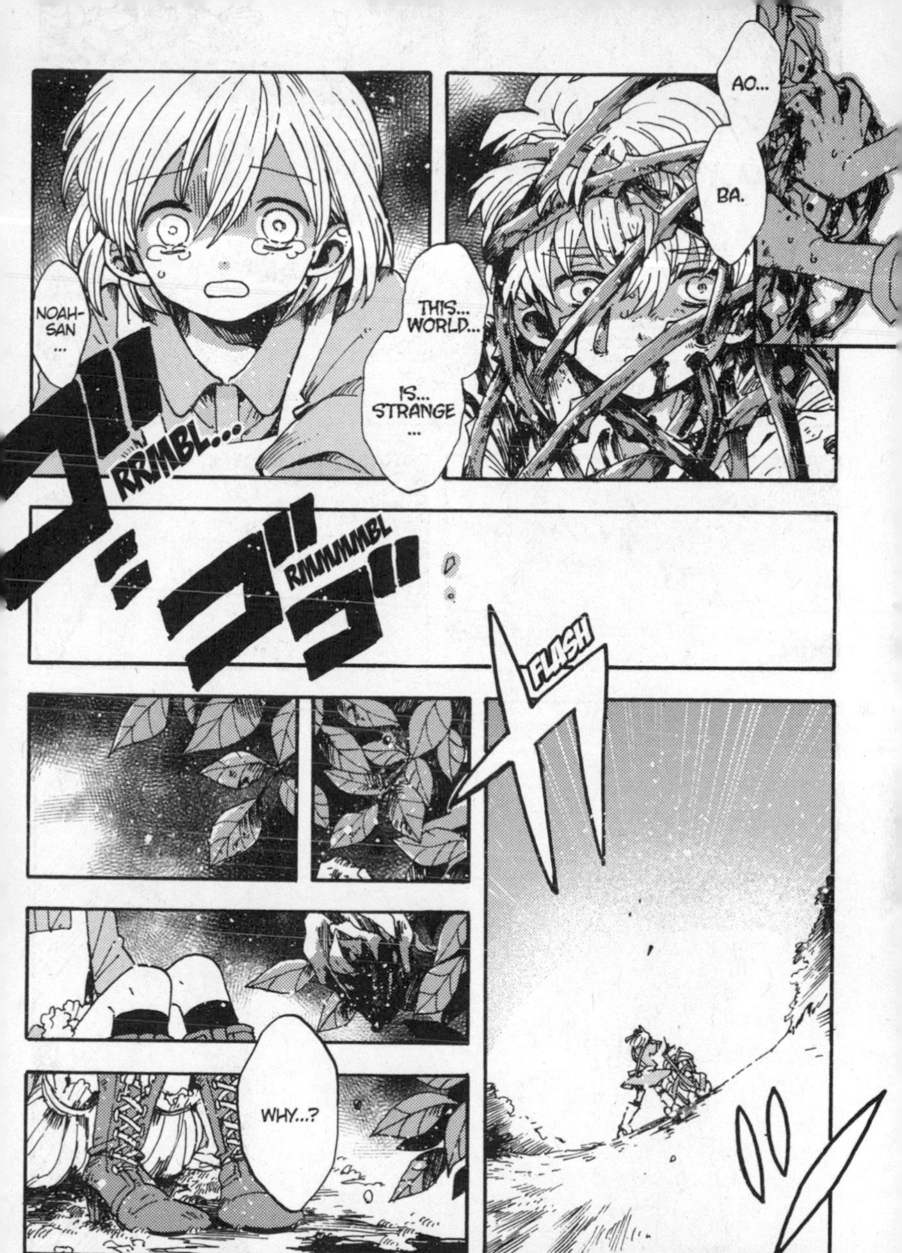
AO...
BA.
THIS... WORLD...
IS... STRANGE ...
NOAH-SAN ...
RRMBL...
RMMMMBL
FLASH
WHY...?

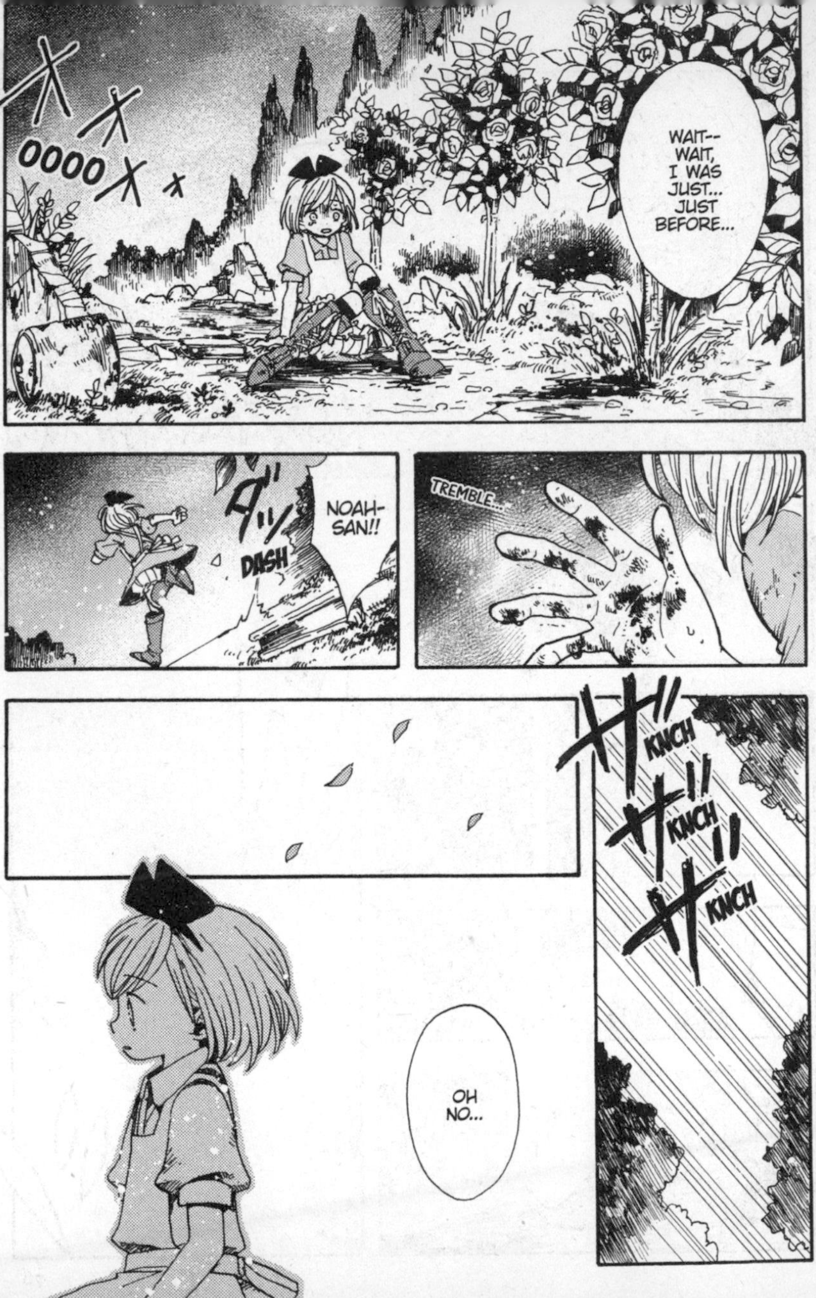
OOOO
WAIT-- WAIT, I WAS JUST... JUST BEFORE...
TREMBLE...
NOAH-SAN!!
DASH
KNCH
KNCH
KNCH
OH NO...

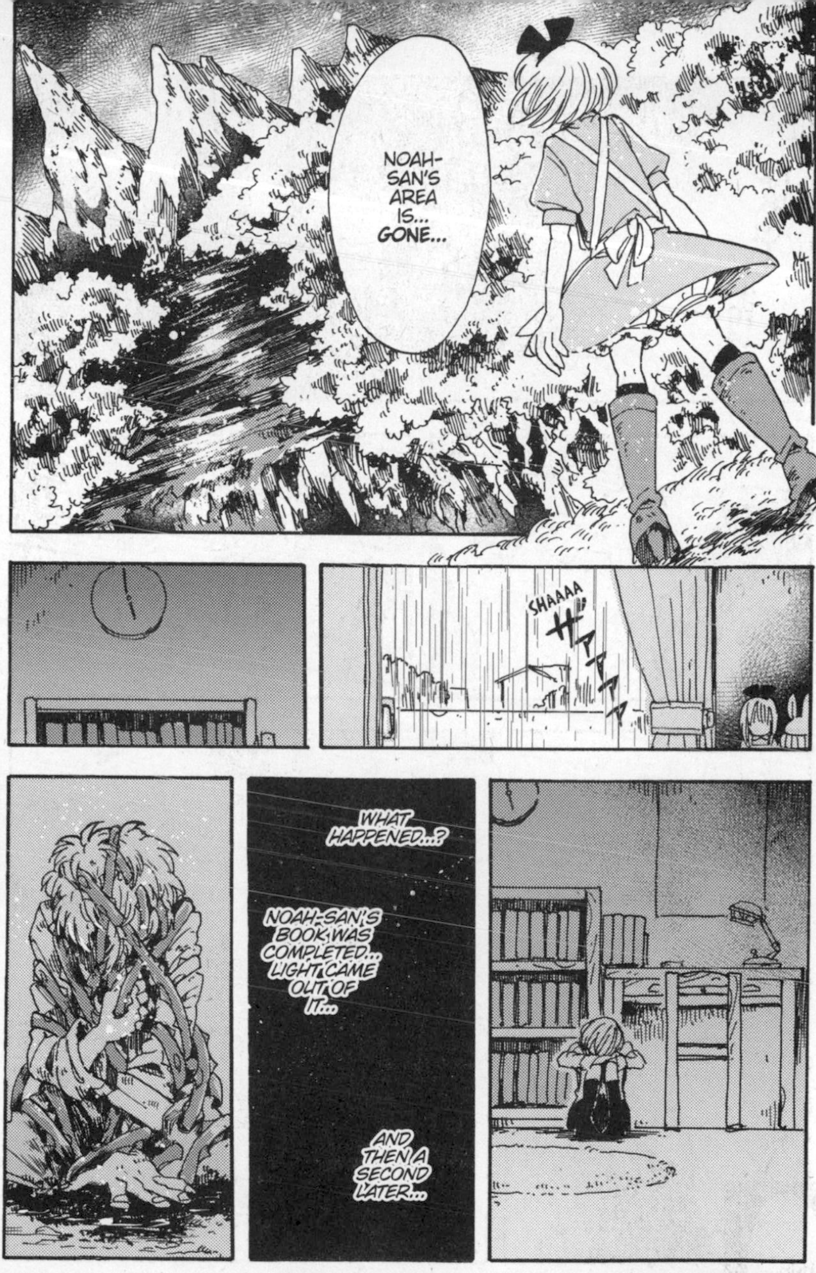
NOAH-SAN'S AREA IS... GONE...
SHAAAA
WHAT HAPPENED...?
NOAH-SAN'S BOOK WAS COMPLETED... LIGHT CAME OUT OF IT...
AND THEN A SECOND LATER...

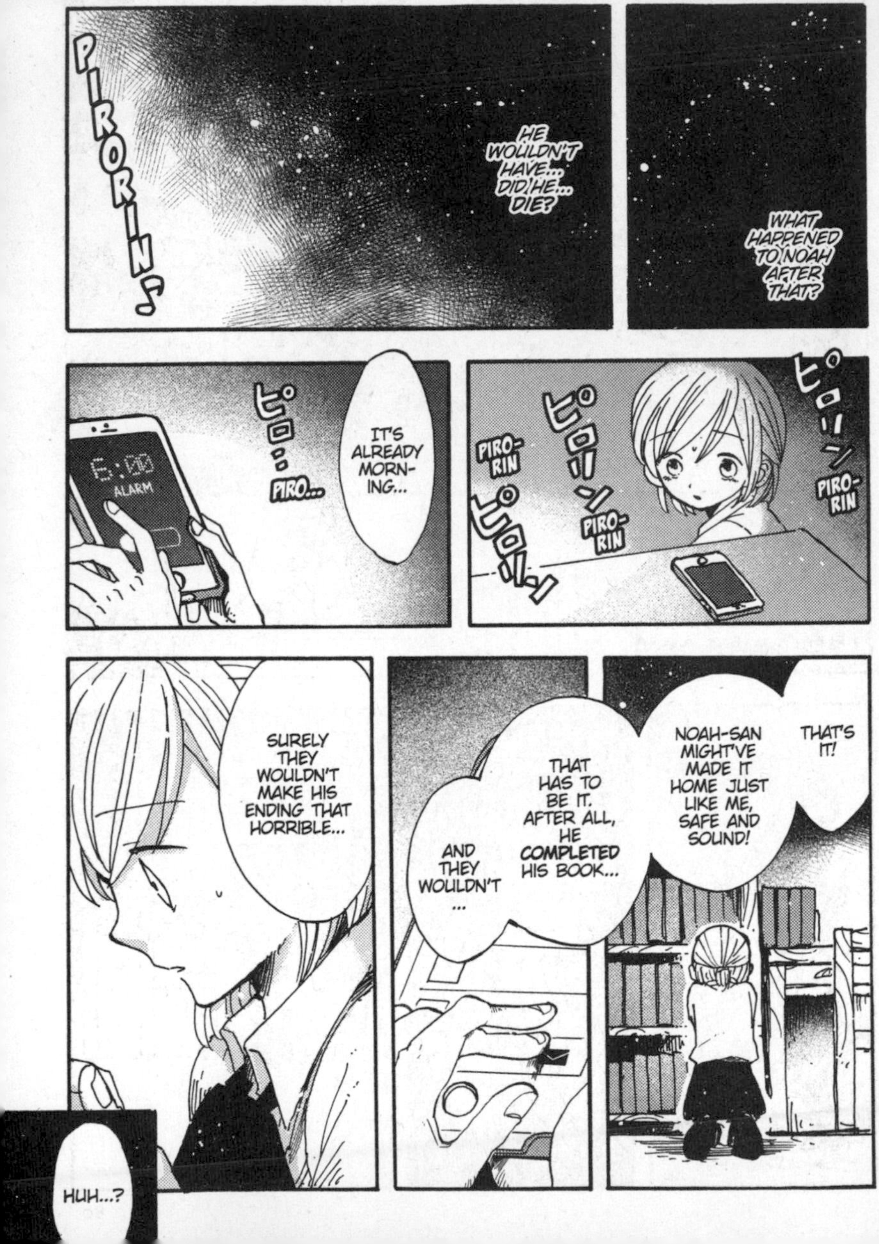
WHAT HAPPENED TO NOAH AFTER THAT?
HE WOULDN'T HAVE... DID HE... DIE?
PIRORIN♪
ピロリン
PIRO-RIN
ピロリン
PIRO-RIN
ピロリン
PIRO-RIN
IT'S ALREADY MORNING...
ピロ。。
PIRO...
6:00
ALARM
THAT'S IT!
NOAH-SAN MIGHT'VE MADE IT HOME JUST LIKE ME, SAFE AND SOUND!
THAT HAS TO BE IT. AFTER ALL, HE COMPLETED HIS BOOK...
AND THEY WOULDN'T ...
SURELY THEY WOULDN'T MAKE HIS ENDING THAT HORRIBLE...
HUH...?

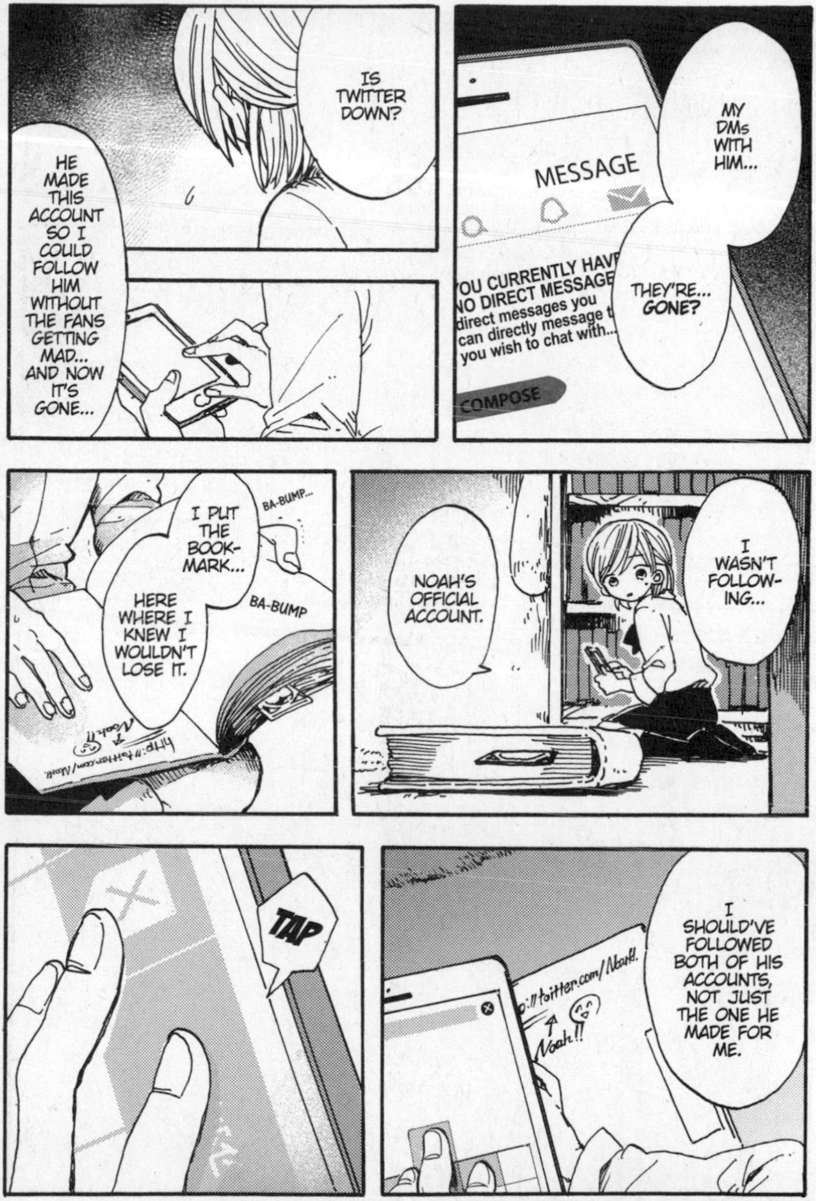
MESSAGE
YOU CURRENTLY HAVE NO DIRECT MESSAGE
direct messages you can directly message t you wish to chat with...
COMPOSE
MY DMs WITH HIM...
THEY'RE... GONE?
IS TWITTER DOWN?
HE MADE THIS ACCOUNT SO I COULD FOLLOW HIM WITHOUT THE FANS GETTING MAD... AND NOW IT'S GONE...
I WASN'T FOLLOWING...
NOAH'S OFFICIAL ACCOUNT.
BA-BUMP...
I PUT THE BOOKMARK...
BA-BUMP
HERE WHERE I KNEW I WOULDN'T LOSE IT.
I SHOULD'VE FOLLOWED BOTH OF HIS ACCOUNTS, NOT JUST THE ONE HE MADE FOR ME.
TAP

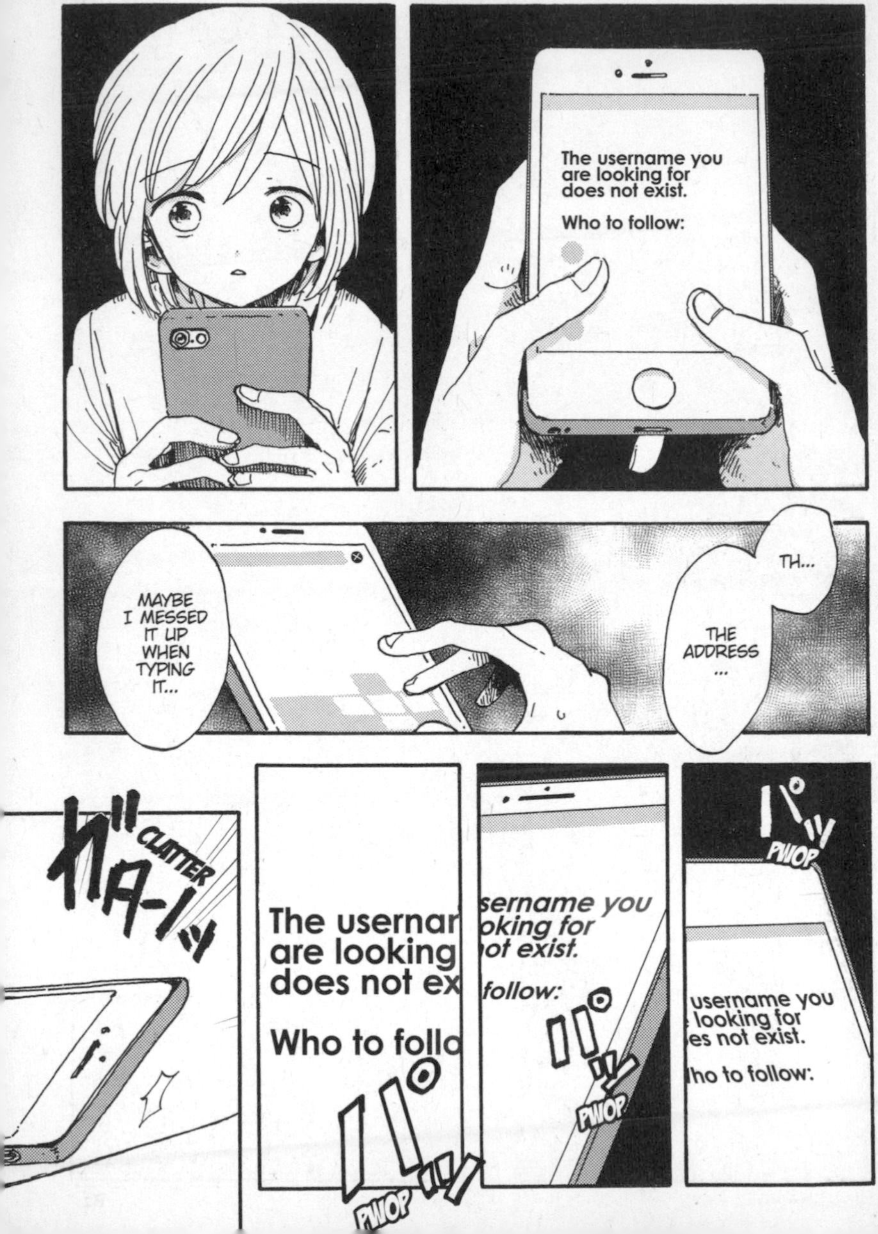
The username you are looking for does not exist.
Who to follow:
TH...
THE ADDRESS...
MAYBE I MESSED IT UP WHEN TYPING IT...
PWOP
username you
looking for
es not exist.
ho to follow:
sername you
oking for
ot exist.
follow:
PWOP
The usernar
are looking
does not ex
Who to follo
PWOP
CLATTER

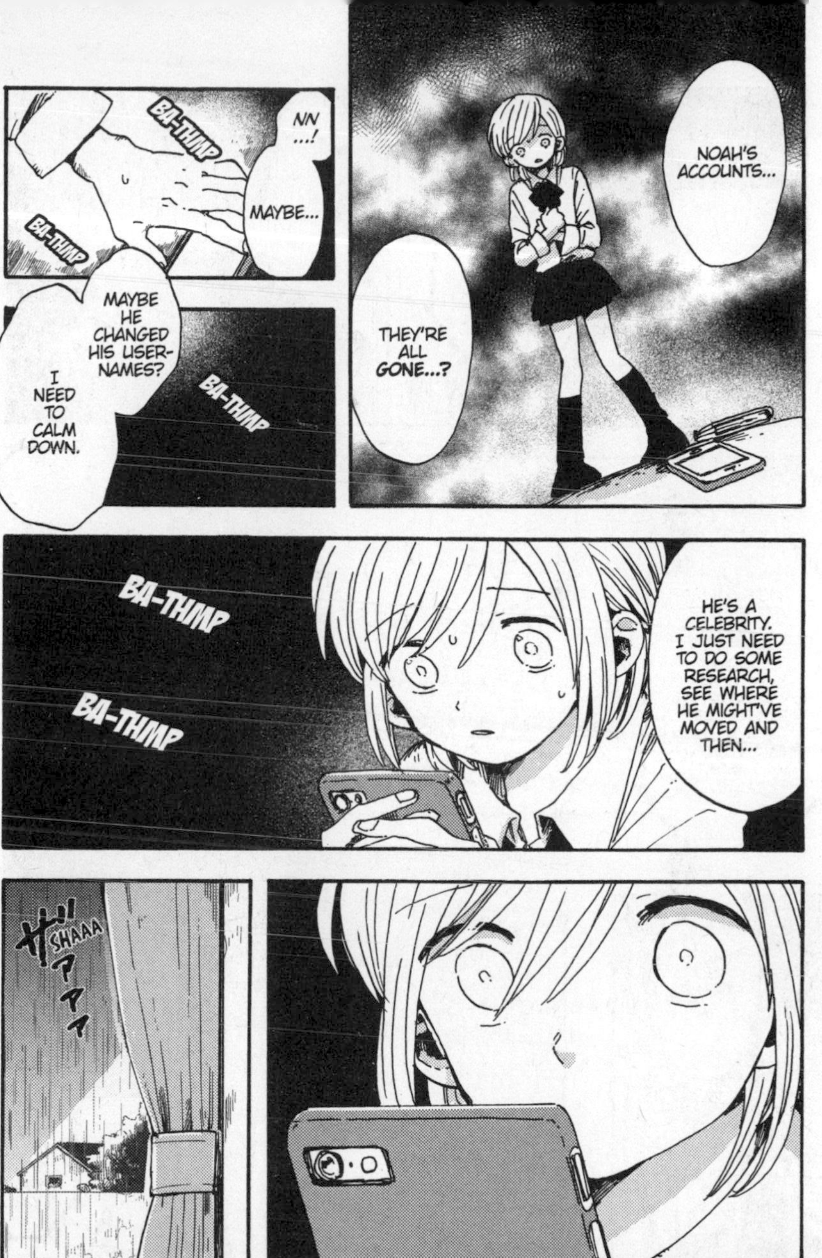
NOAH'S ACCOUNTS...
THEY'RE ALL GONE...?
NN ...!
BA-THMP
MAYBE...
BA-THMP
MAYBE HE CHANGED HIS USER-NAMES?
I NEED TO CALM DOWN.
BA-THMP
HE'S A CELEBRITY. I JUST NEED TO DO SOME RESEARCH, SEE WHERE HE MIGHT'VE MOVED AND THEN...
BA-THMP
BA-THMP
SHAAA

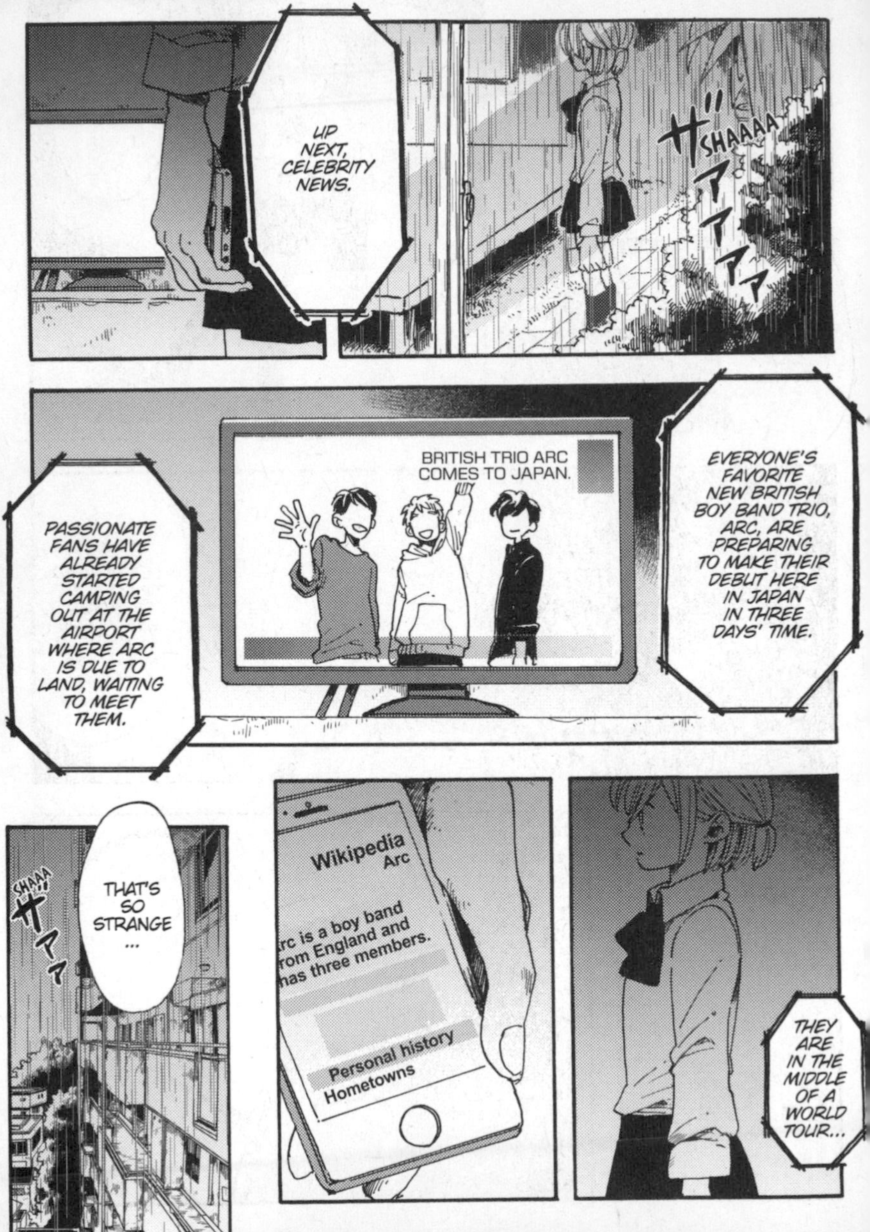
SHAAAA
UP NEXT, CELEBRITY NEWS.
EVERYONE'S FAVORITE NEW BRITISH BOY BAND TRIO, ARC, ARE PREPARING TO MAKE THEIR DEBUT HERE IN JAPAN IN THREE DAYS' TIME.
BRITISH TRIO ARC COMES TO JAPAN.
PASSIONATE FANS HAVE ALREADY STARTED CAMPING OUT AT THE AIRPORT WHERE ARC IS DUE TO LAND, WAITING TO MEET THEM.
THEY ARE IN THE MIDDLE OF A WORLD TOUR...
Wikipedia
Arc
rc is a boy band
rom England and
has three members.
Personal history
Hometowns
THAT'S SO STRANGE...
SHAAA

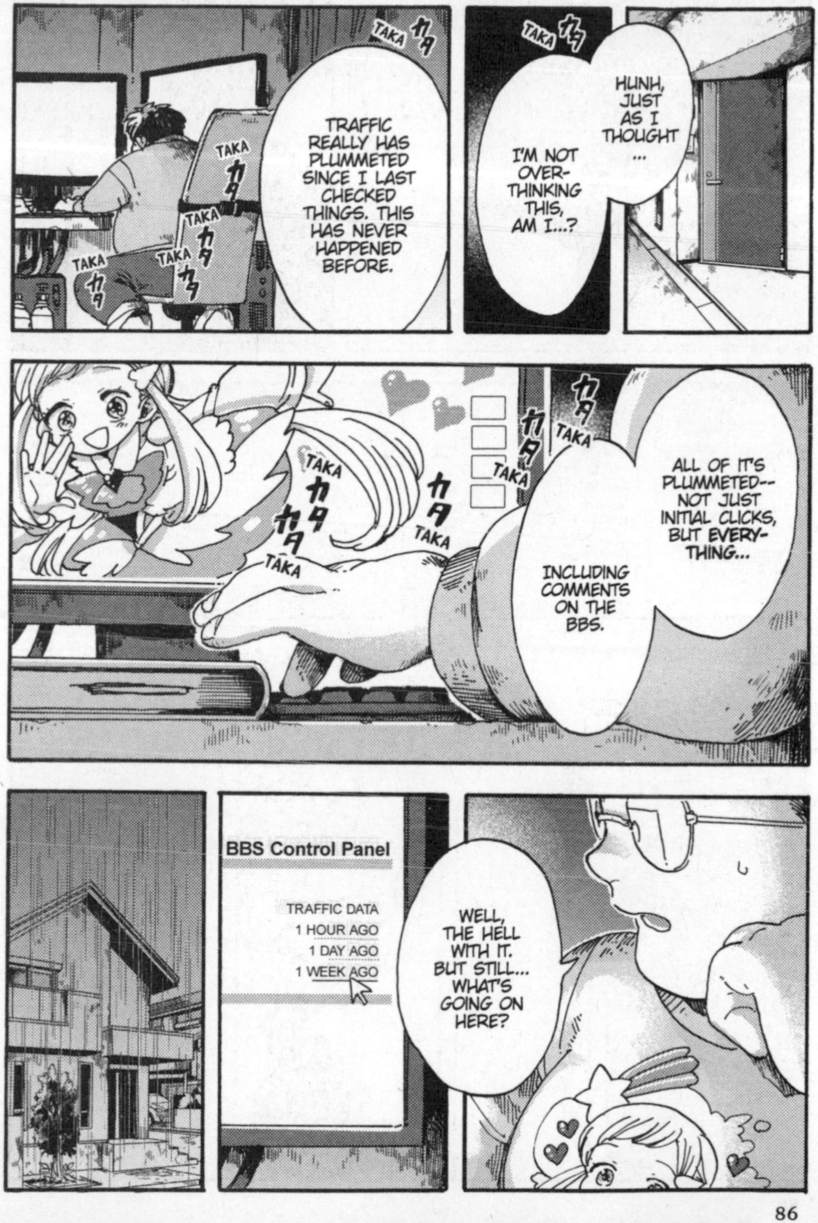
HUNH, JUST AS I THOUGHT ...
TAKA カタ
I'M NOT OVER-THINKING THIS, AM I...?
TAKA カタ
TRAFFIC REALLY HAS PLUMMETED SINCE I LAST CHECKED THINGS. THIS HAS NEVER HAPPENED BEFORE.
TAKA カタ
TAKA カタ
TAKA カタ
TAKA カタ
カタ TAKA
カタ TAKA
ALL OF IT'S PLUMMETED-- NOT JUST INITIAL CLICKS, BUT EVERY-THING...
INCLUDING COMMENTS ON THE BBS.
カタ TAKA
TAKA カタ
カタ TAKA
WELL, THE HELL WITH IT. BUT STILL... WHAT'S GOING ON HERE?
BBS Control Panel
TRAFFIC DATA
1 HOUR AGO
1 DAY AGO
1 WEEK AGO

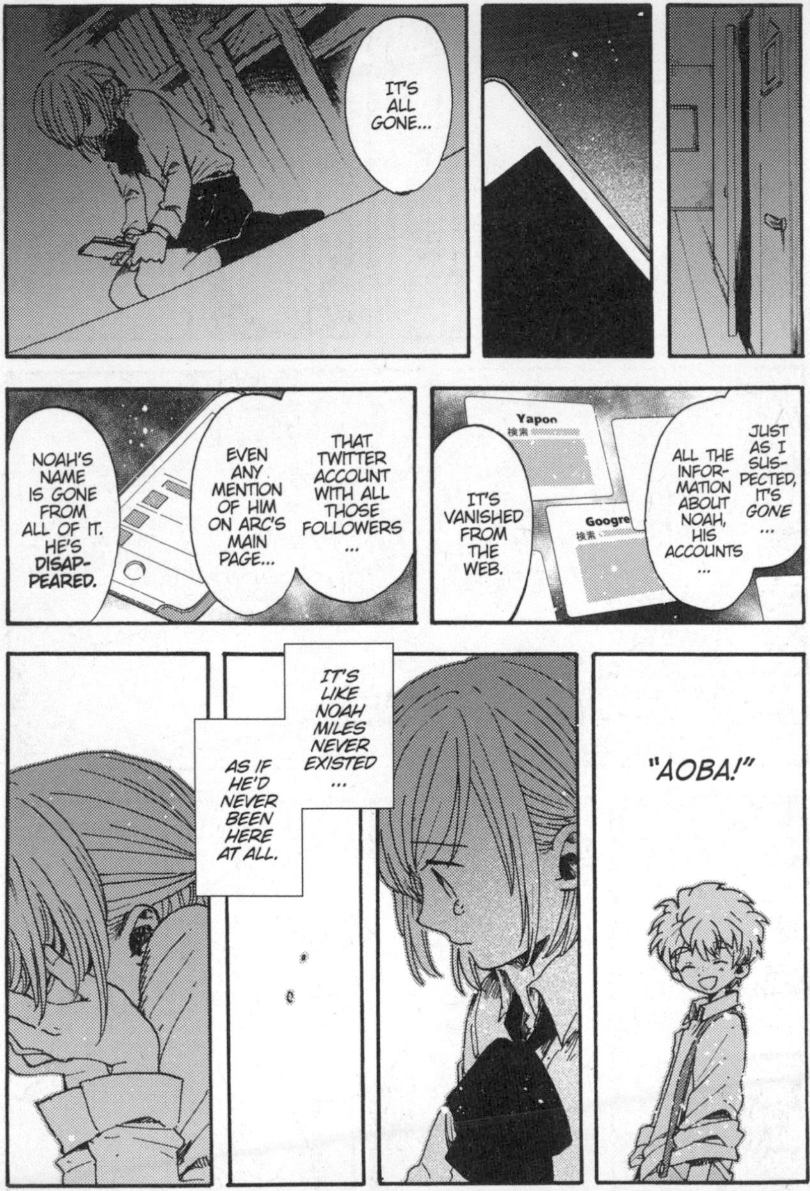
IT'S ALL GONE...
Yapon
検索
Googre
検索
JUST AS I SUSPECTED, IT'S GONE...
ALL THE INFORMATION ABOUT NOAH, HIS ACCOUNTS...
IT'S VANISHED FROM THE WEB.
THAT TWITTER ACCOUNT WITH ALL THOSE FOLLOWERS...
EVEN ANY MENTION OF HIM ON ARC'S MAIN PAGE...
NOAH'S NAME IS GONE FROM ALL OF IT. HE'S DISAPPEARED.
"AOBA!"
IT'S LIKE NOAH MILES NEVER EXISTED...
AS IF HE'D NEVER BEEN HERE AT ALL.

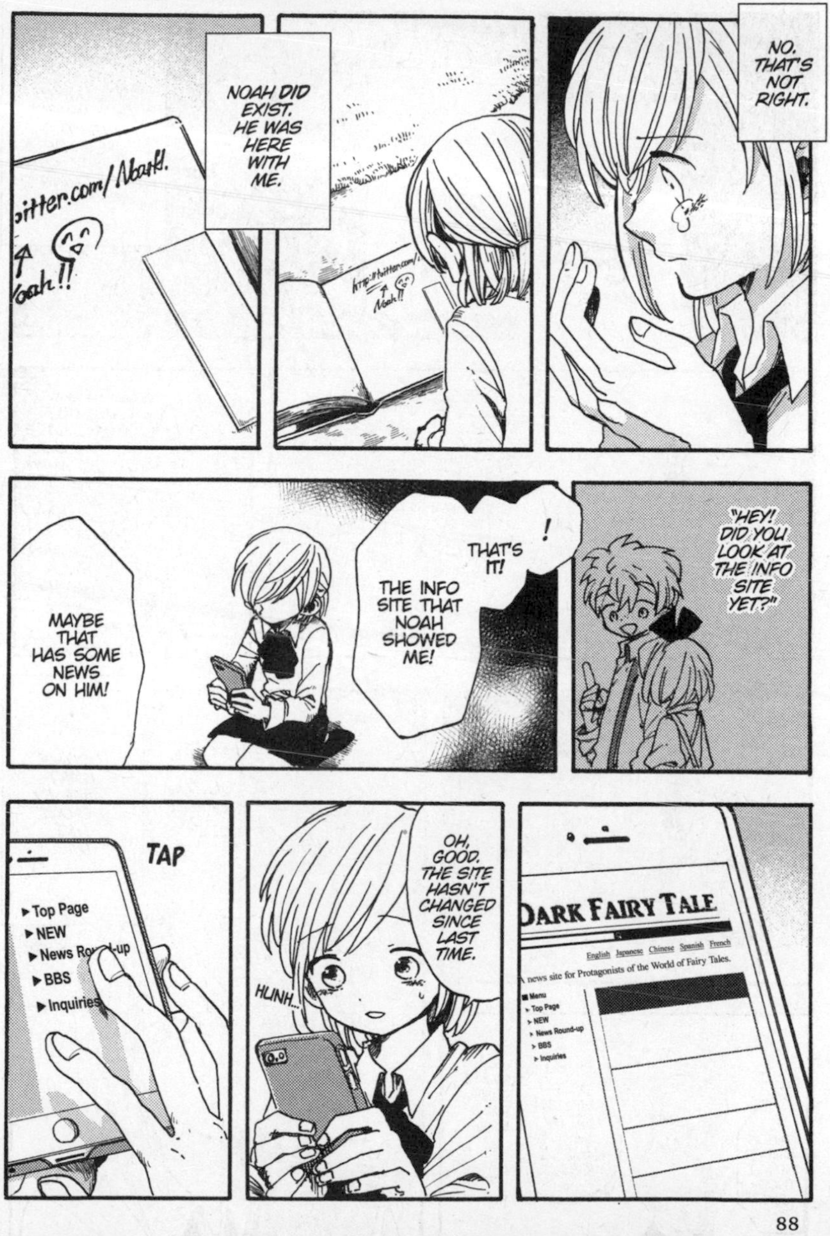
NO. THAT'S NOT RIGHT.
NOAH DID EXIST. HE WAS HERE WITH ME.
"HEY! DID YOU LOOK AT THE INFO SITE YET?"
!
THAT'S IT!
THE INFO SITE THAT NOAH SHOWED ME!
MAYBE THAT HAS SOME NEWS ON HIM!
DARK FAIRY TALE
English Japanese Chinese Spanish French
A news site for Protagonists of the World of Fairy Tales.
Menu
Top Page
NEW
News Round-up
BBS
Inquiries
OH, GOOD. THE SITE HASN'T CHANGED SINCE LAST TIME.
HUNH...
TAP
Top Page
NEW
BBS
Inquiries

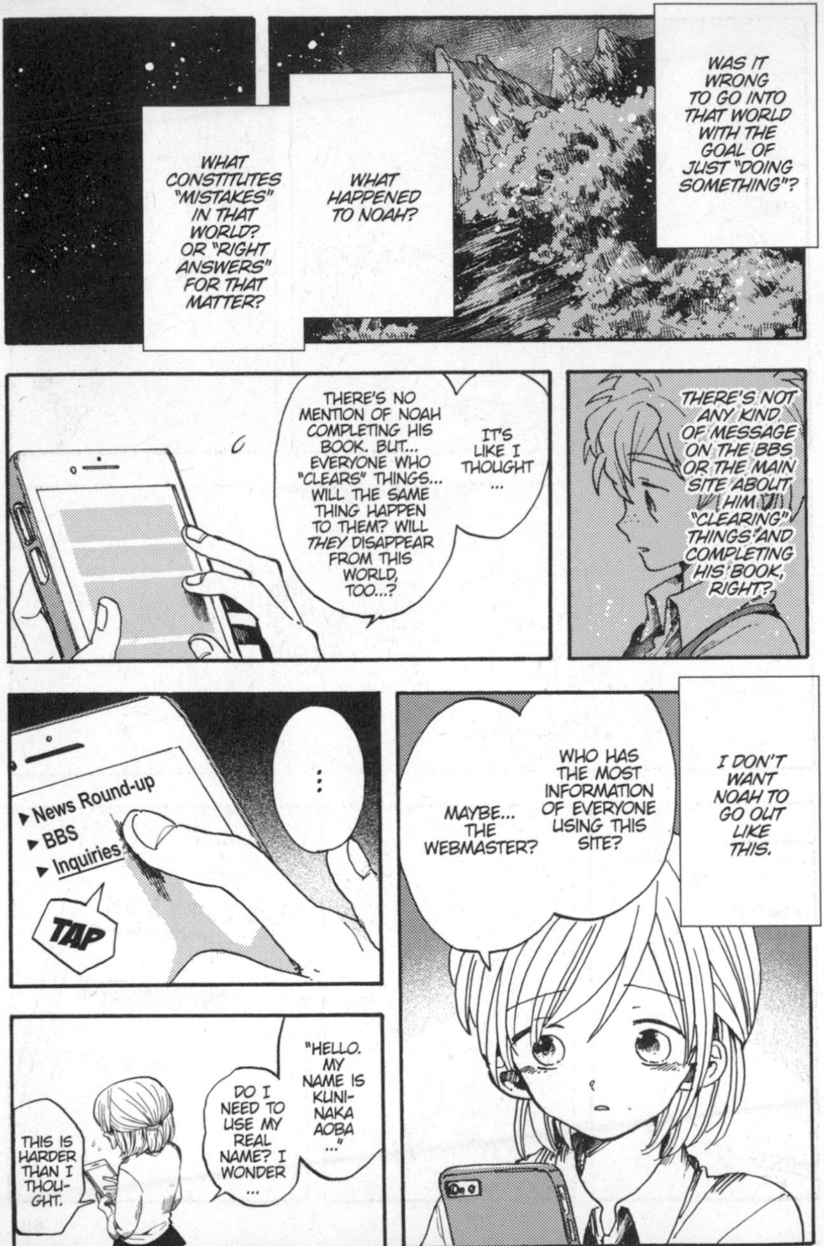
WAS IT WRONG TO GO INTO THAT WORLD WITH THE GOAL OF JUST "DOING SOMETHING"?
WHAT HAPPENED TO NOAH?
WHAT CONSTITUTES "MISTAKES" IN THAT WORLD? OR "RIGHT ANSWERS" FOR THAT MATTER?
THERE'S NOT ANY KIND OF MESSAGE ON THE BBS OR THE MAIN SITE ABOUT HIM "CLEARING" THINGS AND COMPLETING HIS BOOK, RIGHT?
IT'S LIKE I THOUGHT...
THERE'S NO MENTION OF NOAH COMPLETING HIS BOOK. BUT... EVERYONE WHO "CLEARS" THINGS... WILL THE SAME THING HAPPEN TO THEM? WILL THEY DISAPPEAR FROM THIS WORLD, TOO...?
I DON'T WANT NOAH TO GO OUT LIKE THIS.
WHO HAS THE MOST INFORMATION OF EVERYONE USING THIS SITE?
MAYBE... THE WEBMASTER?
...
▸ News Round-up
▸ BBS
▸ Inquiries
TAP
"HELLO. MY NAME IS KUNINAKA AOBA..."
DO I NEED TO USE MY REAL NAME? I WONDER...
THIS IS HARDER THAN I THOUGHT.

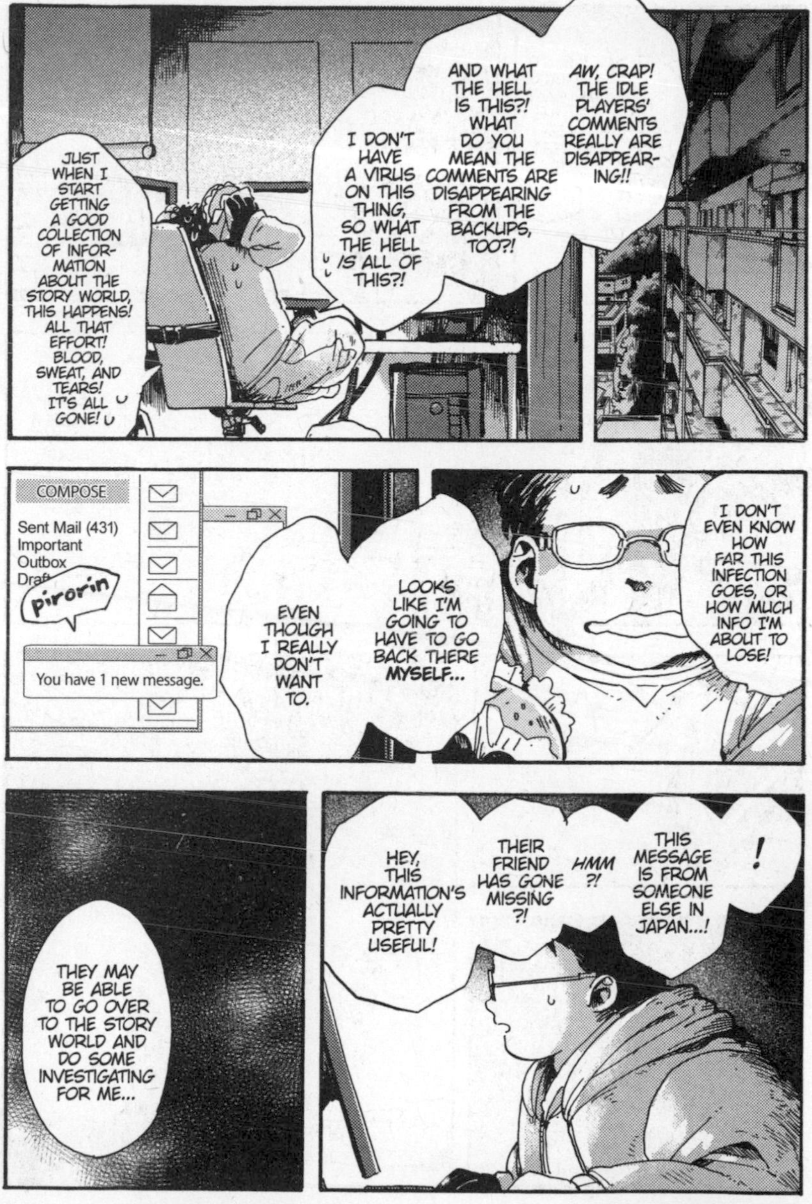
AW, CRAP! THE IDLE PLAYERS' COMMENTS REALLY ARE DISAPPEARING!!
AND WHAT THE HELL IS THIS?! WHAT DO YOU MEAN THE COMMENTS ARE DISAPPEARING FROM THE BACKUPS, TOO?!
I DON'T HAVE A VIRUS ON THIS THING, SO WHAT THE HELL IS ALL OF THIS?!
JUST WHEN I START GETTING A GOOD COLLECTION OF INFORMATION ABOUT THE STORY WORLD, THIS HAPPENS! ALL THAT EFFORT! BLOOD, SWEAT, AND TEARS! IT'S ALL GONE!
I DON'T EVEN KNOW HOW FAR THIS INFECTION GOES, OR HOW MUCH INFO I'M ABOUT TO LOSE!
LOOKS LIKE I'M GOING TO HAVE TO GO BACK THERE MYSELF...
EVEN THOUGH I REALLY DON'T WANT TO.
COMPOSE
Sent Mail (431)
Important
Outbox
Draf
pirorin
You have 1 new message.
!
THIS MESSAGE IS FROM SOMEONE ELSE IN JAPAN...!
HMM?!
THEIR FRIEND HAS GONE MISSING?!
HEY, THIS INFORMATION'S ACTUALLY PRETTY USEFUL!
THEY MAY BE ABLE TO GO OVER TO THE STORY WORLD AND DO SOME INVESTIGATING FOR ME...

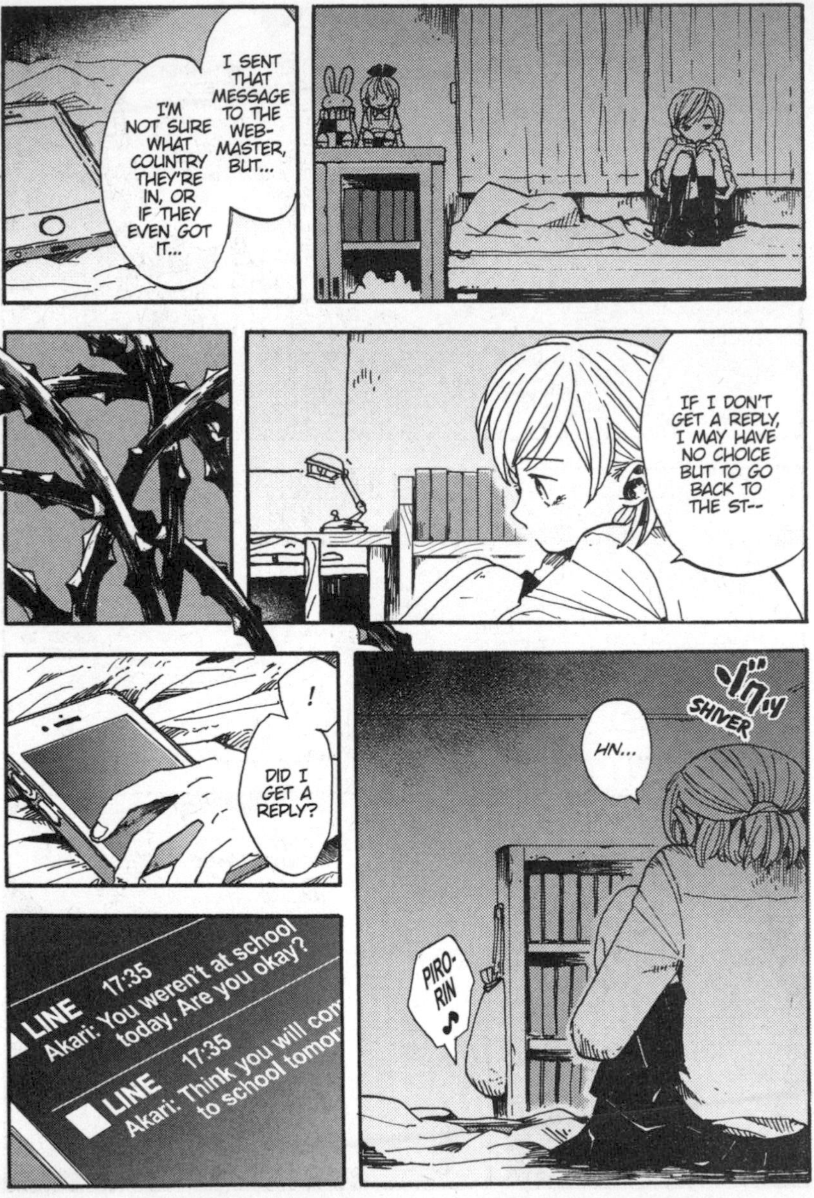
I SENT THAT MESSAGE TO THE WEB-MASTER, BUT...
I'M NOT SURE WHAT COUNTRY THEY'RE IN, OR IF THEY EVEN GOT IT...
IF I DON'T GET A REPLY, I MAY HAVE NO CHOICE BUT TO GO BACK TO THE ST--
SHIVER
HN...
PIRO-RIN ♪
!
DID I GET A REPLY?
LINE 17:35
Akari: You weren't at school today. Are you okay?
LINE 17:35
Akari: Think you will com
to school tomor

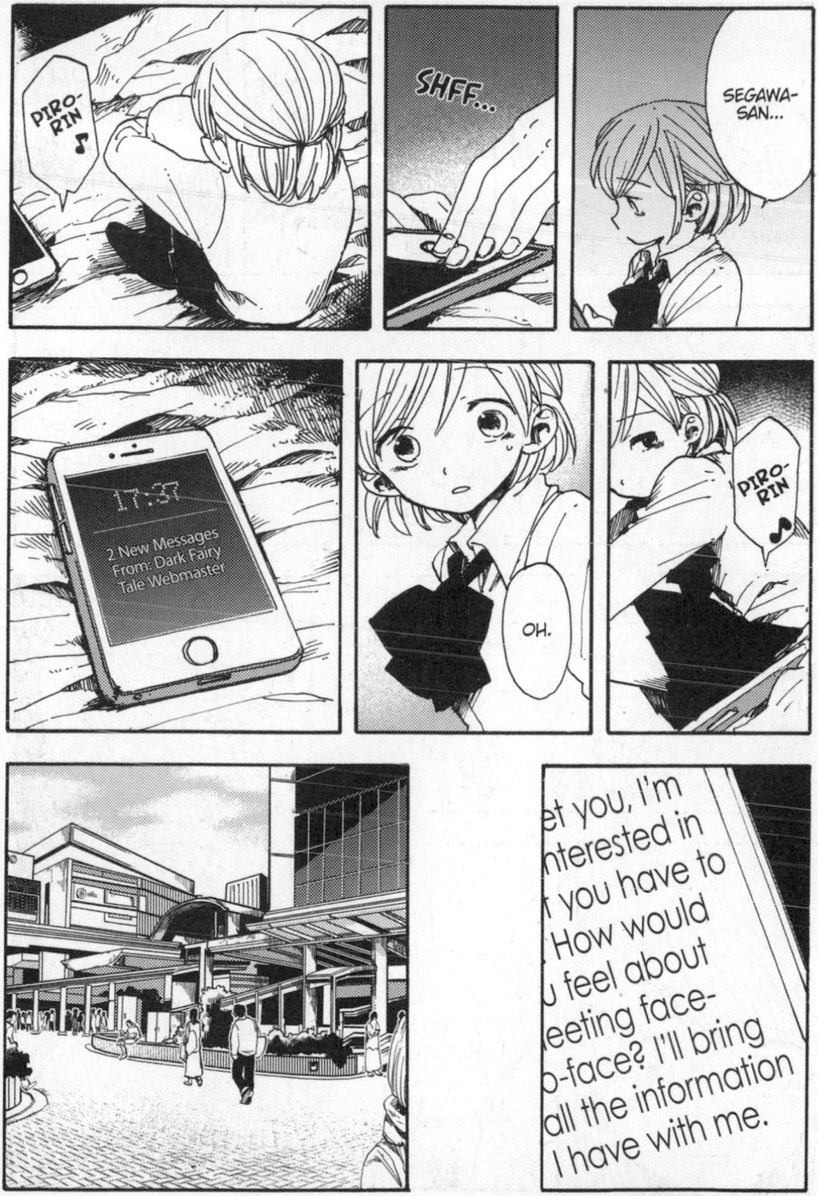
SEGAWA-SAN...
SHFF...
PIRO-RIN ♪
PIRO-RIN ♪
OH.
17:37
2 New Messages From: Dark Fairy Tale Webmaster
et you, I'm nterested in t you have to . How would u feel about eeting face- o-face? I'll bring all the information I have with me.

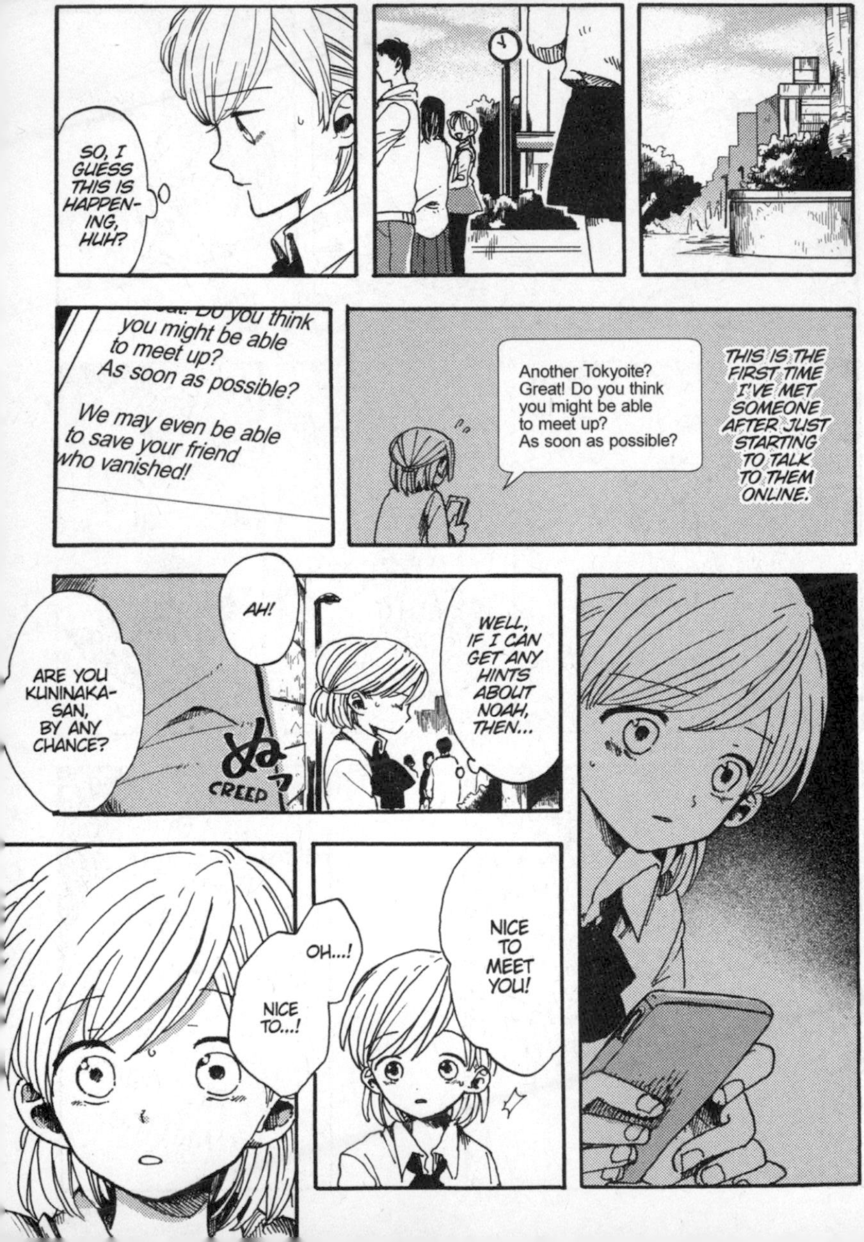

SO, I GUESS THIS IS HAPPENING, HUH?
THIS IS THE FIRST TIME I'VE MET SOMEONE AFTER JUST STARTING TO TALK TO THEM ONLINE.
Another Tokyoite? Great! Do you think you might be able to meet up? As soon as possible?
Do you think you might be able to meet up? As soon as possible?
We may even be able to save your friend who vanished!
WELL, IF I CAN GET ANY HINTS ABOUT NOAH, THEN...
AH!
ARE YOU KUNINAKA-SAN, BY ANY CHANCE?
CREEP
NICE TO MEET YOU!
OH...!
NICE TO...!

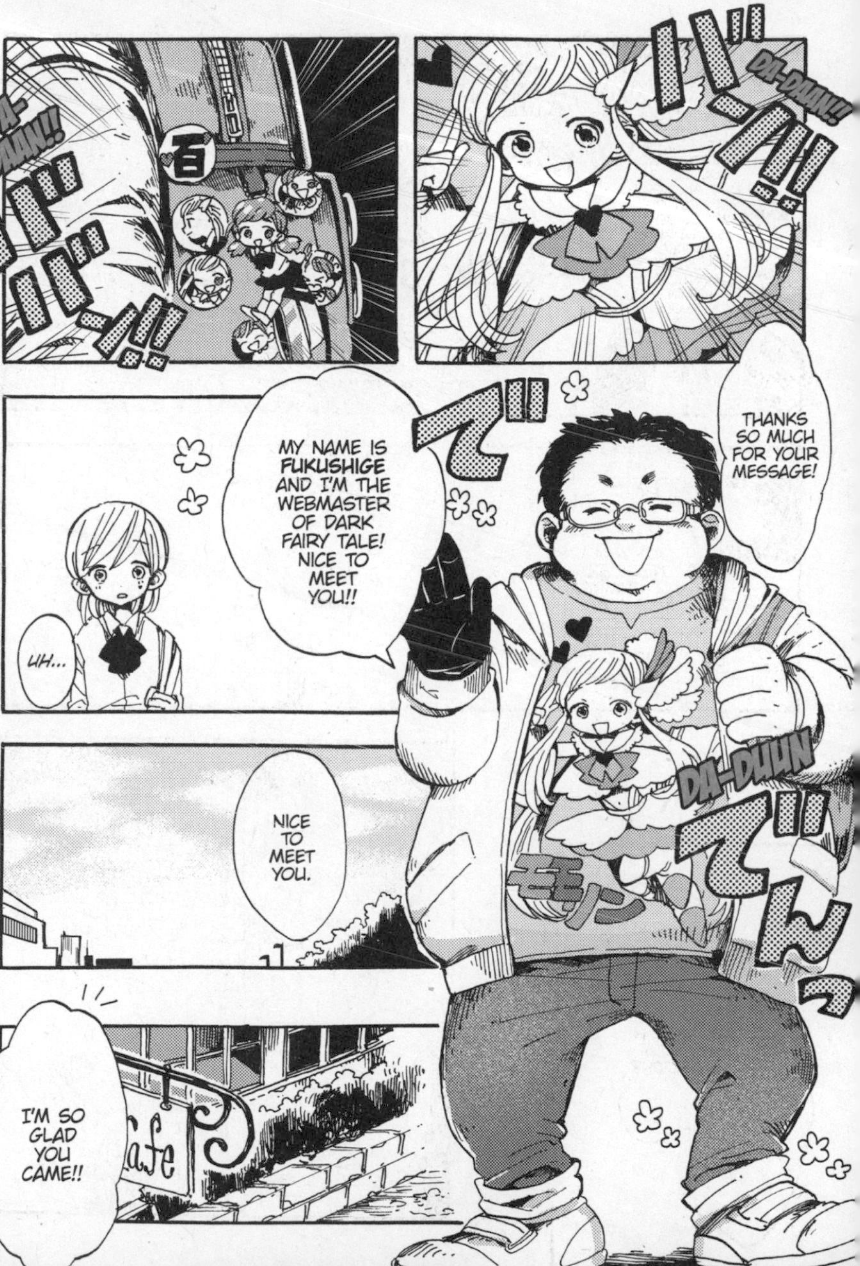
DA-DAAN!!
DA-DAAN!!
THANKS SO MUCH FOR YOUR MESSAGE!
MY NAME IS FUKUSHIGE AND I'M THE WEBMASTER OF DARK FAIRY TALE! NICE TO MEET YOU!!
DA-DUUN
UH...
NICE TO MEET YOU.
I'M SO GLAD YOU CAME!!

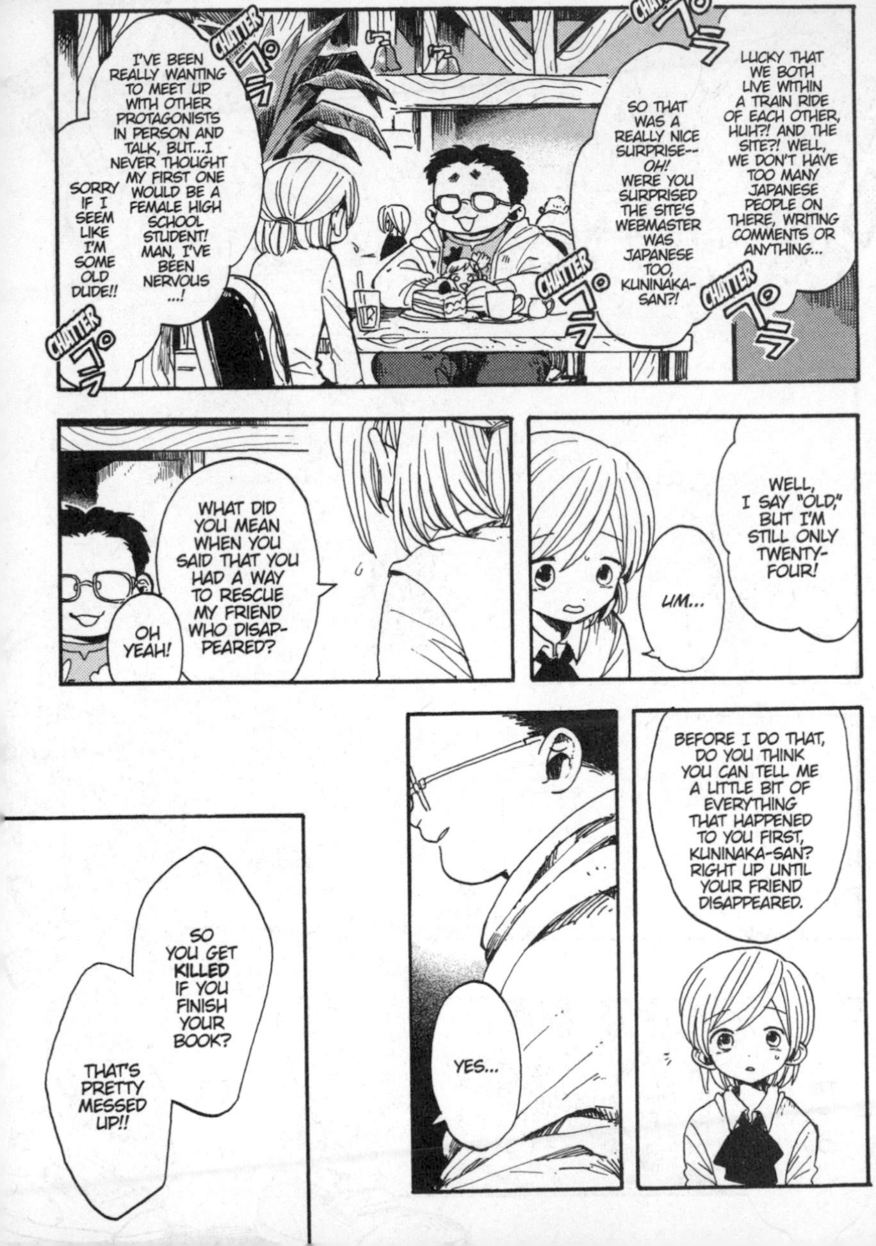
CHATTER
LUCKY THAT WE BOTH LIVE WITHIN A TRAIN RIDE OF EACH OTHER, HUH?! AND THE SITE?! WELL, WE DON'T HAVE TOO MANY JAPANESE PEOPLE ON THERE, WRITING COMMENTS OR ANYTHING...
SO THAT WAS A REALLY NICE SURPRISE--OH! WERE YOU SURPRISED THE SITE'S WEBMASTER WAS JAPANESE TOO, KUNINAKA-SAN?!
CHATTER
CHATTER
CHATTER
I'VE BEEN REALLY WANTING TO MEET UP WITH OTHER PROTAGONISTS IN PERSON AND TALK, BUT...I NEVER THOUGHT MY FIRST ONE WOULD BE A FEMALE HIGH SCHOOL STUDENT! MAN, I'VE BEEN NERVOUS ...!
SORRY IF I SEEM LIKE I'M SOME OLD DUDE!!
CHATTER
WELL, I SAY "OLD," BUT I'M STILL ONLY TWENTY-FOUR!
UM...
WHAT DID YOU MEAN WHEN YOU SAID THAT YOU HAD A WAY TO RESCUE MY FRIEND WHO DISAPPEARED?
OH YEAH!
BEFORE I DO THAT, DO YOU THINK YOU CAN TELL ME A LITTLE BIT OF EVERYTHING THAT HAPPENED TO YOU FIRST, KUNINAKA-SAN? RIGHT UP UNTIL YOUR FRIEND DISAPPEARED.
YES...
SO YOU GET KILLED IF YOU FINISH YOUR BOOK?
THAT'S PRETTY MESSED UP!!

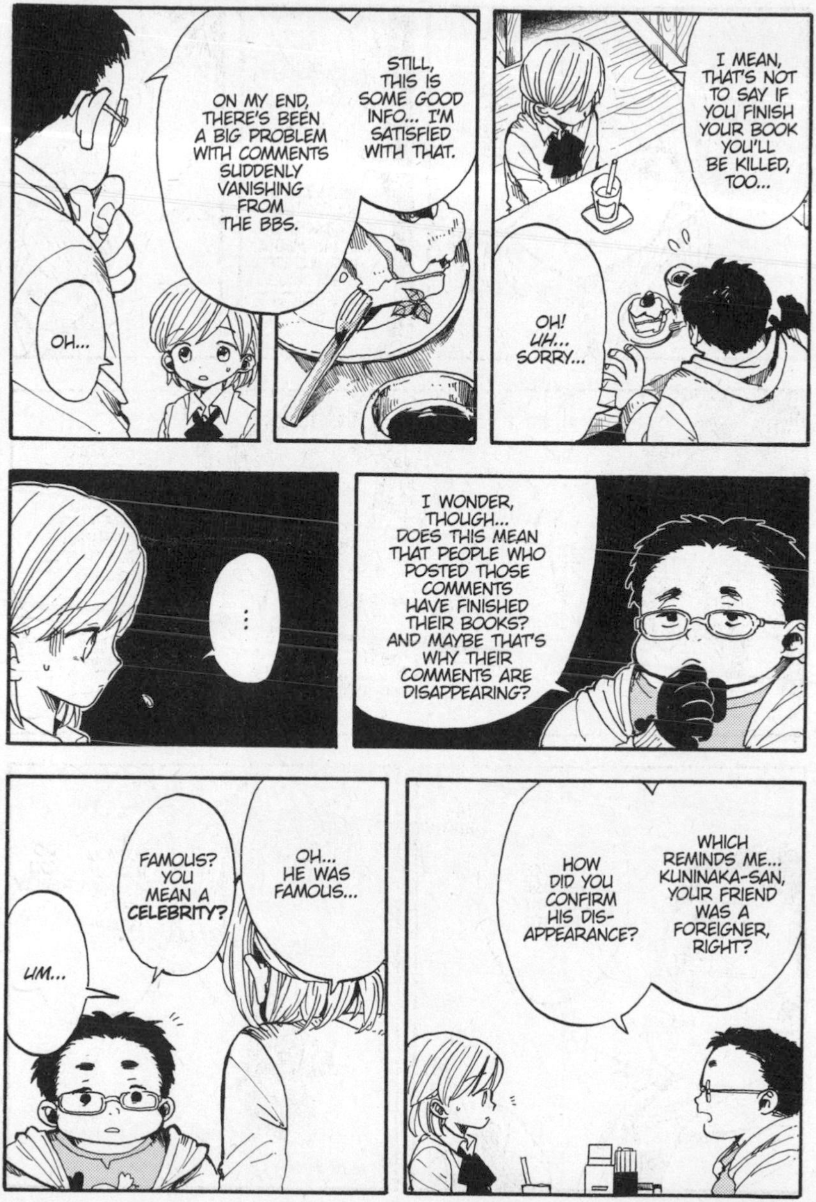
I MEAN, THAT'S NOT TO SAY IF YOU FINISH YOUR BOOK YOU'LL BE KILLED, TOO...
OH! UH... SORRY...
STILL, THIS IS SOME GOOD INFO... I'M SATISFIED WITH THAT.
ON MY END, THERE'S BEEN A BIG PROBLEM WITH COMMENTS SUDDENLY VANISHING FROM THE BBS.
OH...
I WONDER, THOUGH... DOES THIS MEAN THAT PEOPLE WHO POSTED THOSE COMMENTS HAVE FINISHED THEIR BOOKS? AND MAYBE THAT'S WHY THEIR COMMENTS ARE DISAPPEARING?
...
WHICH REMINDS ME... KUNINAKA-SAN, YOUR FRIEND WAS A FOREIGNER, RIGHT?
HOW DID YOU CONFIRM HIS DIS-APPEARANCE?
OH... HE WAS FAMOUS...
FAMOUS? YOU MEAN A CELEBRITY?
UM...

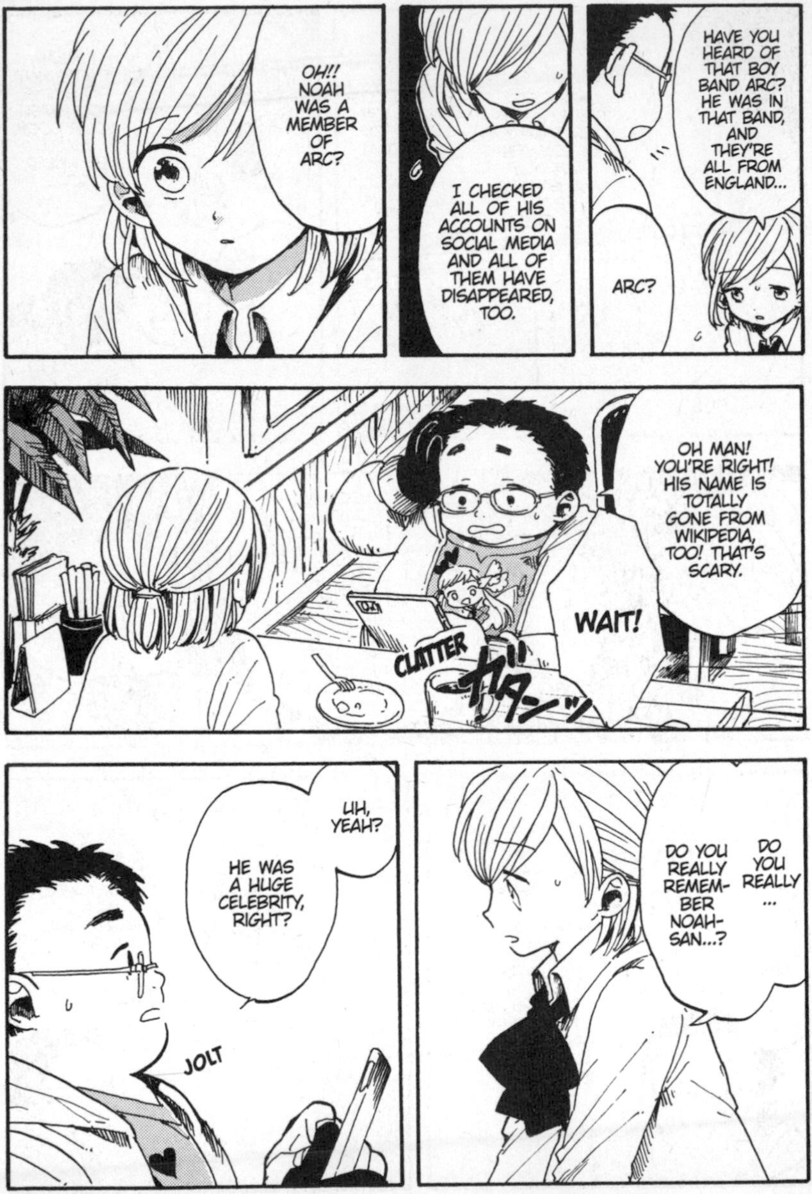
HAVE YOU HEARD OF THAT BOY BAND ARC? HE WAS IN THAT BAND, AND THEY'RE ALL FROM ENGLAND...
ARC?
I CHECKED ALL OF HIS ACCOUNTS ON SOCIAL MEDIA AND ALL OF THEM HAVE DISAPPEARED, TOO.
OH!! NOAH WAS A MEMBER OF ARC?
OH MAN! YOU'RE RIGHT! HIS NAME IS TOTALLY GONE FROM WIKIPEDIA, TOO! THAT'S SCARY.
WAIT!
CLATTER
DO YOU REALLY ...
DO YOU REALLY REMEM-BER NOAH-SAN...?
UH, YEAH?
HE WAS A HUGE CELEBRITY, RIGHT?
JOLT

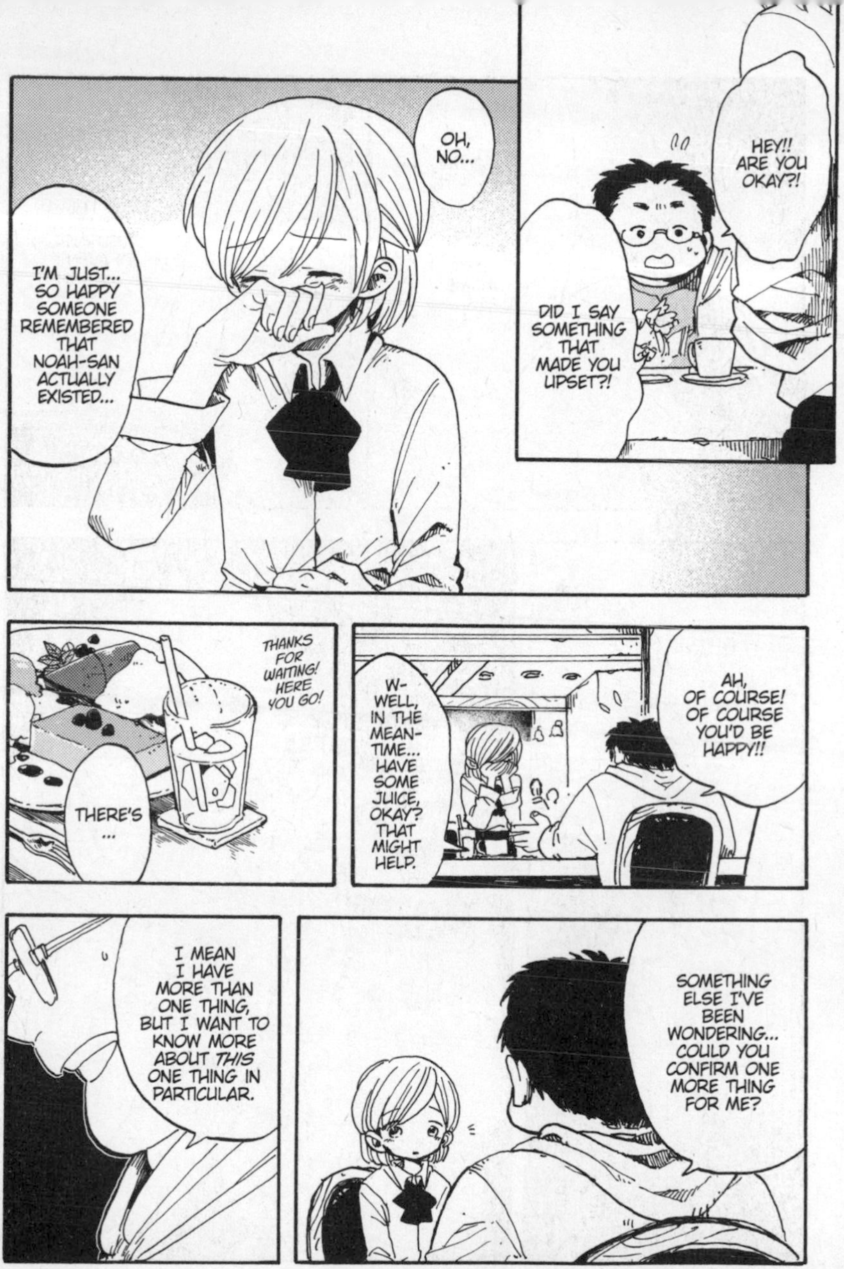
HEY!! ARE YOU OKAY?!
DID I SAY SOMETHING THAT MADE YOU UPSET?!
OH, NO...
I'M JUST... SO HAPPY SOMEONE REMEMBERED THAT NOAH-SAN ACTUALLY EXISTED...
AH, OF COURSE! OF COURSE YOU'D BE HAPPY!!
W-WELL, IN THE MEAN-TIME... HAVE SOME JUICE, OKAY? THAT MIGHT HELP.
THANKS FOR WAITING! HERE YOU GO!
THERE'S ...
SOMETHING ELSE I'VE BEEN WONDERING... COULD YOU CONFIRM ONE MORE THING FOR ME?
I MEAN I HAVE MORE THAN ONE THING, BUT I WANT TO KNOW MORE ABOUT *THIS* ONE THING IN PARTICULAR.

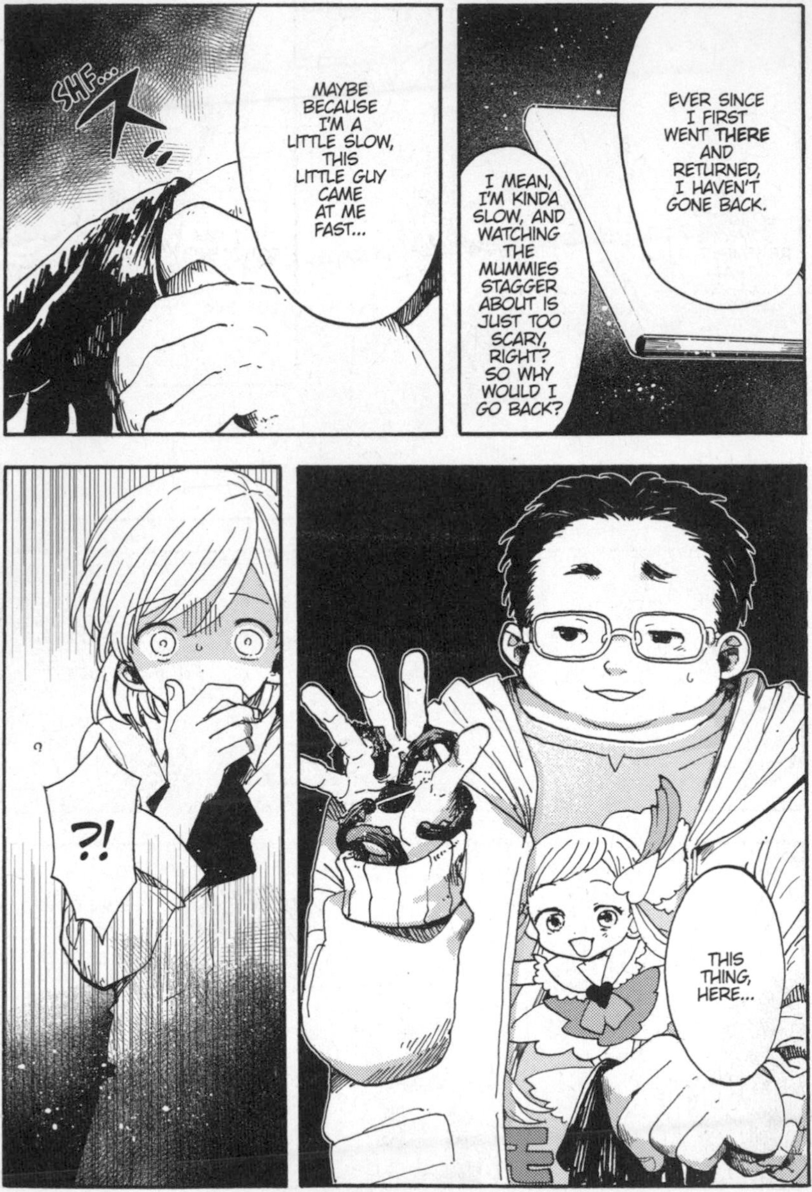
EVER SINCE I FIRST WENT THERE AND RETURNED, I HAVEN'T GONE BACK.
I MEAN, I'M KINDA SLOW, AND WATCHING THE MUMMIES STAGGER ABOUT IS JUST TOO SCARY, RIGHT? SO WHY WOULD I GO BACK?
MAYBE BECAUSE I'M A LITTLE SLOW, THIS LITTLE GUY CAME AT ME FAST...
SHF...
THIS THING, HERE...
?!

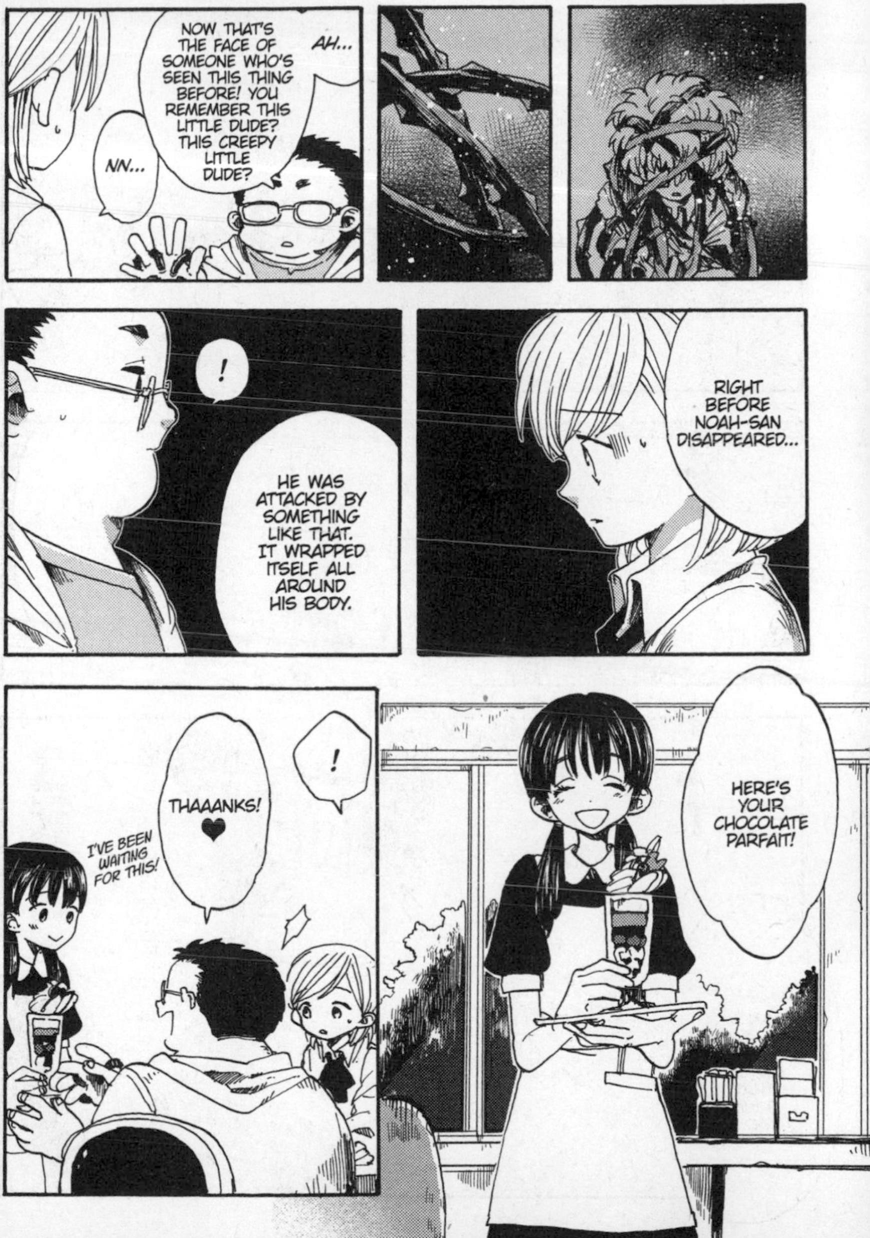
AH...
NOW THAT'S THE FACE OF SOMEONE WHO'S SEEN THIS THING BEFORE! YOU REMEMBER THIS LITTLE DUDE? THIS CREEPY LITTLE DUDE?
NN...
RIGHT BEFORE NOAH-SAN DISAPPEARED...
HE WAS ATTACKED BY SOMETHING LIKE THAT. IT WRAPPED ITSELF ALL AROUND HIS BODY.
!
HERE'S YOUR CHOCOLATE PARFAIT!
!
THAAANKS! ♥
I'VE BEEN WAITING FOR THIS!

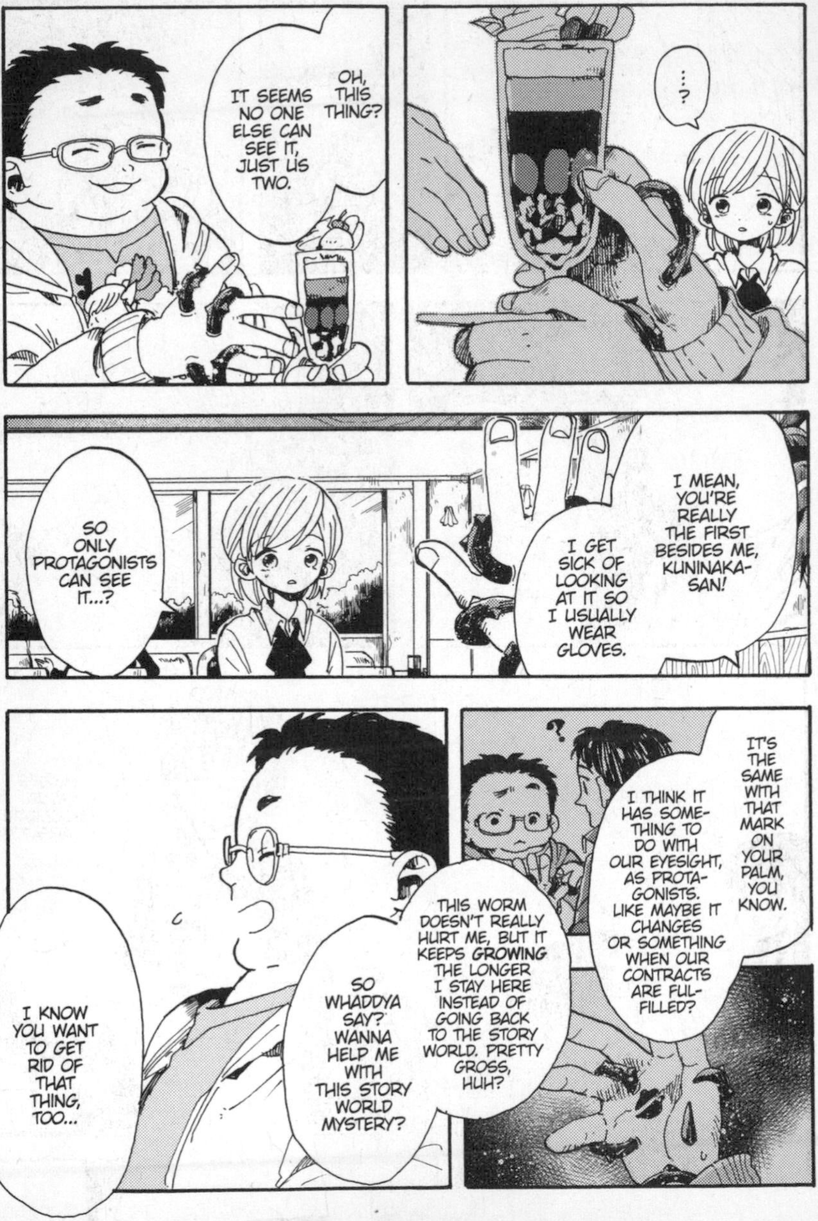
...?
OH, THIS THING? IT SEEMS NO ONE ELSE CAN SEE IT, JUST US TWO.
I MEAN, YOU'RE REALLY THE FIRST BESIDES ME, KUNINAKA-SAN!
I GET SICK OF LOOKING AT IT SO I USUALLY WEAR GLOVES.
SO ONLY PROTAGONISTS CAN SEE IT...?
?
IT'S THE SAME WITH THAT MARK ON YOUR PALM, YOU KNOW.
I THINK IT HAS SOME-THING TO DO WITH OUR EYESIGHT, AS PROTA-GONISTS. LIKE MAYBE IT CHANGES OR SOMETHING WHEN OUR CONTRACTS ARE FUL-FILLED?
THIS WORM DOESN'T REALLY HURT ME, BUT IT KEEPS **GROWING** THE LONGER I STAY HERE INSTEAD OF GOING BACK TO THE STORY WORLD. PRETTY GROSS, HUH?
SO WHADDYA SAY? WANNA HELP ME WITH THIS STORY WORLD MYSTERY?
I KNOW YOU WANT TO GET RID OF THAT THING, TOO...

THAT **WORM** YOU HAVE AROUND YOUR HAND.

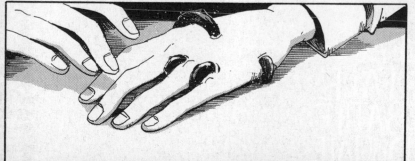

FAIRU
TALE
BATTLE
ROYALE

FAIRY
TALE
BATTLE
ROYALE

Chapter 8: Binding Spell

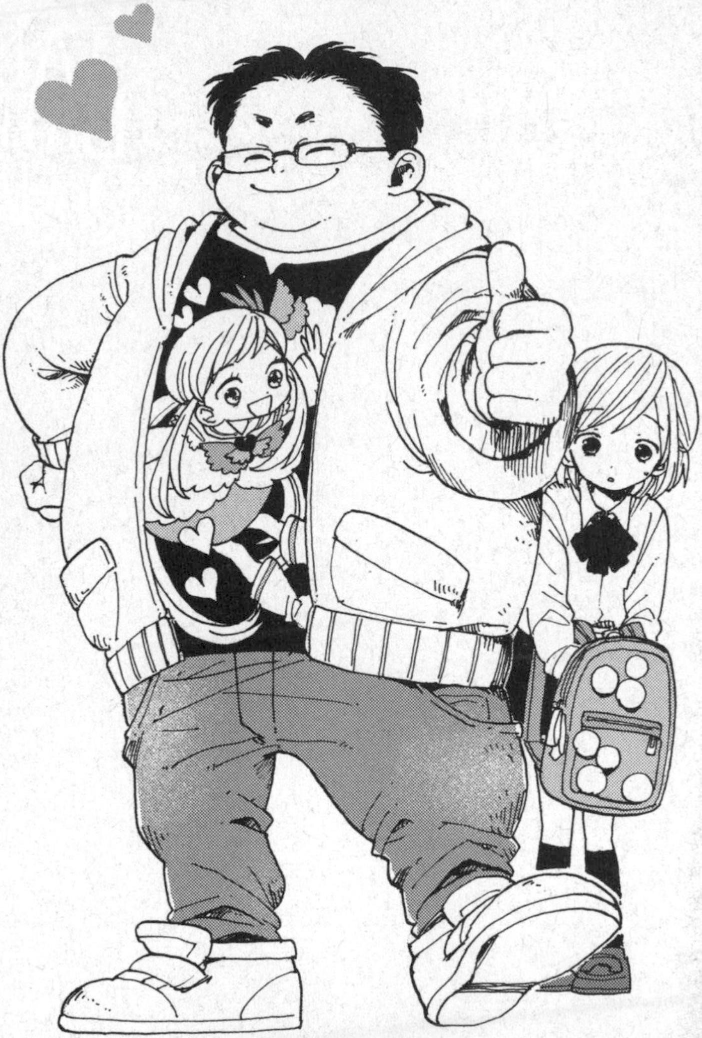

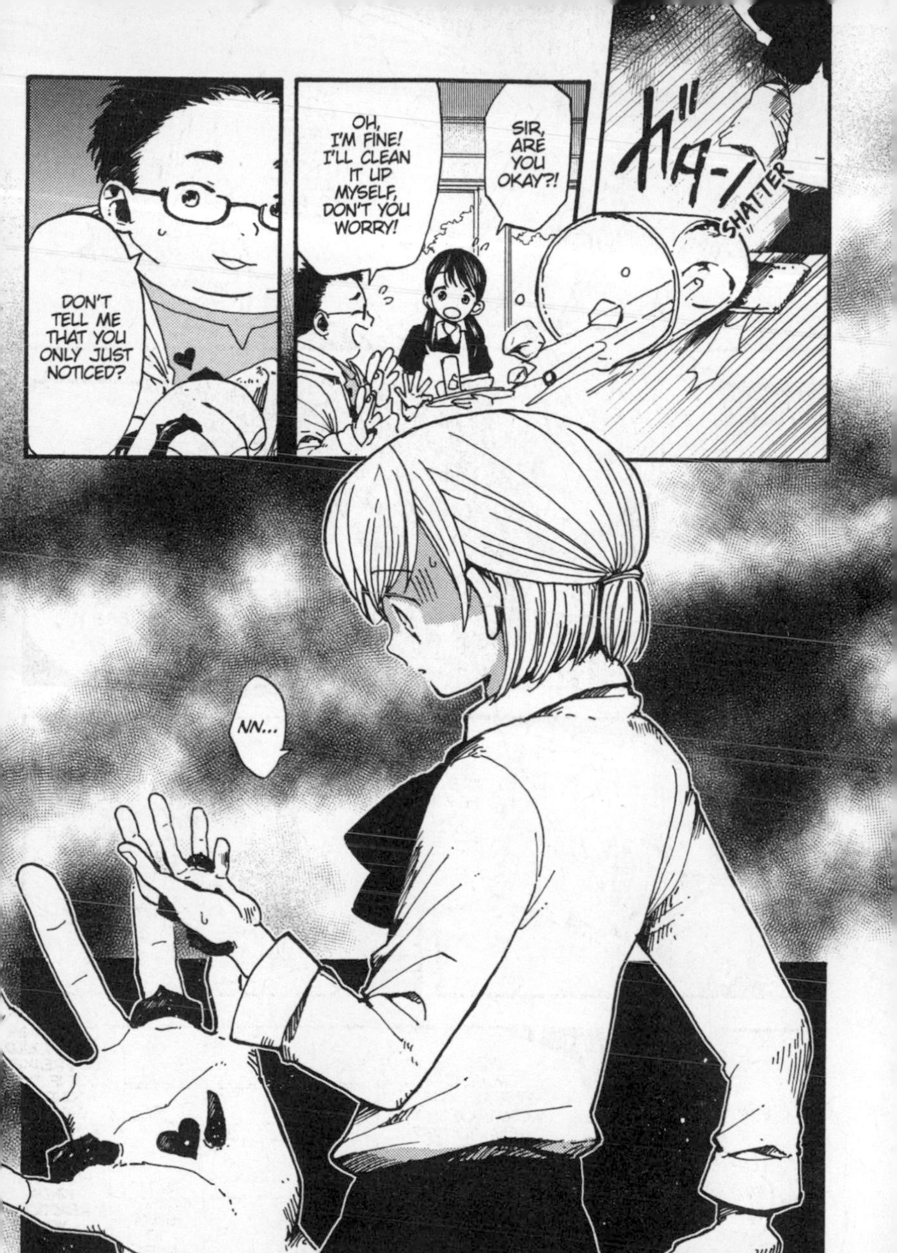
SHATTER
SIR, ARE YOU OKAY?!
OH, I'M FINE! I'LL CLEAN IT UP MYSELF, DON'T YOU WORRY!
DON'T TELL ME THAT YOU ONLY JUST NOTICED?
NN...

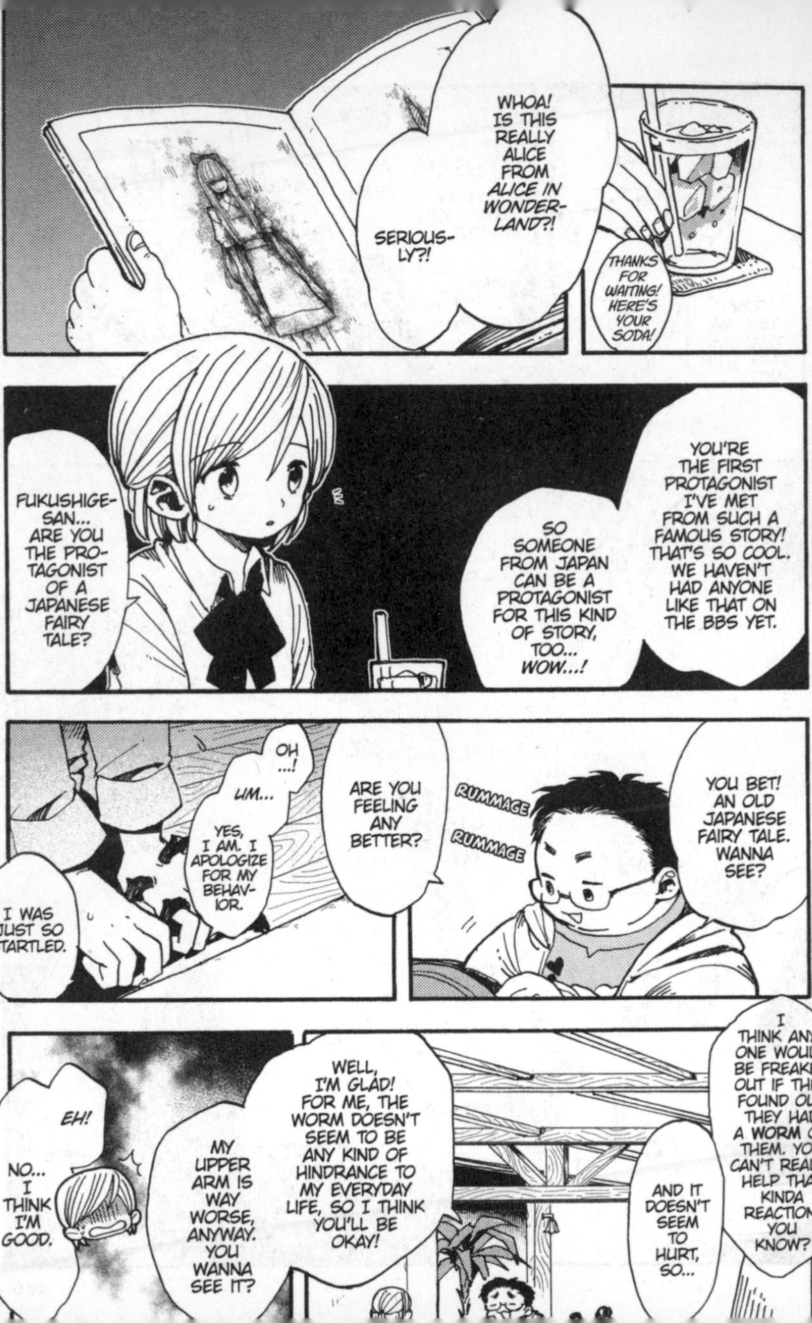
THANKS FOR WAITING! HERE'S YOUR SODA!
WHOA! IS THIS REALLY ALICE FROM ALICE IN WONDERLAND?!
SERIOUSLY?!
YOU'RE THE FIRST PROTAGONIST I'VE MET FROM SUCH A FAMOUS STORY! THAT'S SO COOL. WE HAVEN'T HAD ANYONE LIKE THAT ON THE BBS YET.
SO SOMEONE FROM JAPAN CAN BE A PROTAGONIST FOR THIS KIND OF STORY, TOO... WOW...!
FUKUSHIGE-SAN... ARE YOU THE PROTAGONIST OF A JAPANESE FAIRY TALE?
YOU BET! AN OLD JAPANESE FAIRY TALE. WANNA SEE?
RUMMAGE
RUMMAGE
ARE YOU FEELING ANY BETTER?
OH ...!
UM...
YES, I AM. I APOLOGIZE FOR MY BEHAVIOR.
I WAS JUST SO STARTLED.
I THINK ANYONE WOULD BE FREAKED OUT IF THEY FOUND OUT THEY HAD A WORM ON THEM. YOU CAN'T REALLY HELP THAT KINDA REACTION, YOU KNOW?
AND IT DOESN'T SEEM TO HURT, SO...
WELL, I'M GLAD! FOR ME, THE WORM DOESN'T SEEM TO BE ANY KIND OF HINDRANCE TO MY EVERYDAY LIFE, SO I THINK YOU'LL BE OKAY!
MY UPPER ARM IS WAY WORSE, ANYWAY. YOU WANNA SEE IT?
EH!
NO... I THINK I'M GOOD.

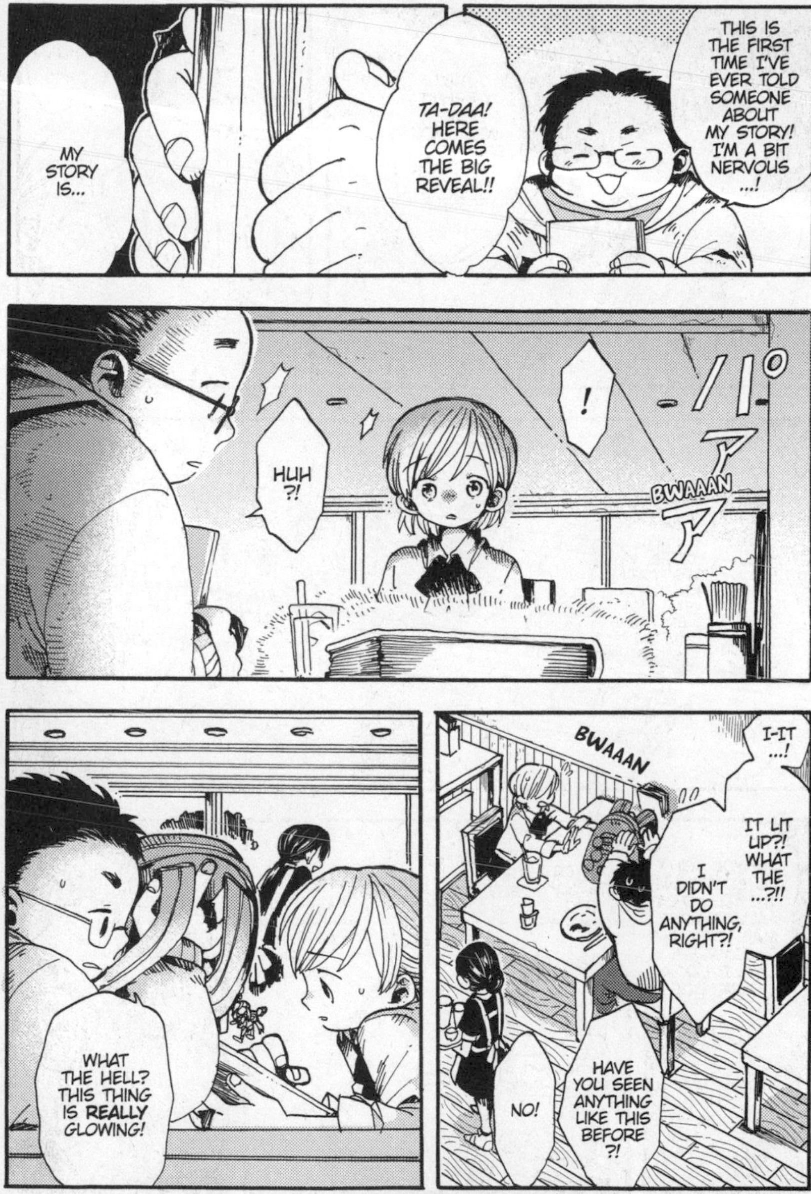
THIS IS THE FIRST TIME I'VE EVER TOLD SOMEONE ABOUT MY STORY! I'M A BIT NERVOUS ...!
TA-DAA! HERE COMES THE BIG REVEAL!!
MY STORY IS...
!
BWAAAN
HUH ?!
I-IT ...!
IT LIT UP?! WHAT THE ...?!!
I DIDN'T DO ANYTHING, RIGHT?!
BWAAAN
HAVE YOU SEEN ANYTHING LIKE THIS BEFORE ?!
NO!
WHAT THE HELL? THIS THING IS REALLY GLOWING!

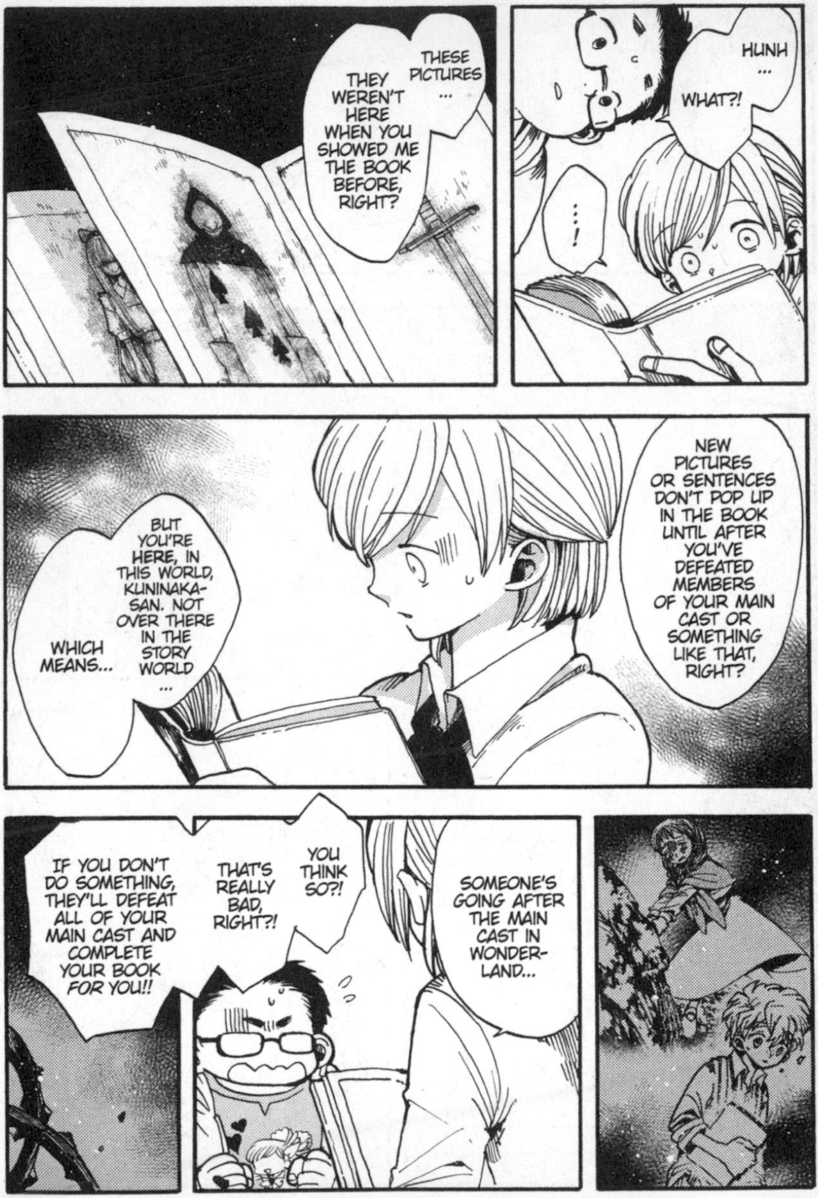
HUNH ... WHAT?!
...!
THESE PICTURES ...
THEY WEREN'T HERE WHEN YOU SHOWED ME THE BOOK BEFORE, RIGHT?
NEW PICTURES OR SENTENCES DON'T POP UP IN THE BOOK UNTIL AFTER YOU'VE DEFEATED MEMBERS OF YOUR MAIN CAST OR SOMETHING LIKE THAT, RIGHT?
BUT YOU'RE HERE, IN THIS WORLD, KUNINAKA-SAN. NOT OVER THERE IN THE STORY WORLD ...
WHICH MEANS...
SOMEONE'S GOING AFTER THE MAIN CAST IN WONDER-LAND...
YOU THINK SO?!
THAT'S REALLY BAD, RIGHT?!
IF YOU DON'T DO SOMETHING, THEY'LL DEFEAT ALL OF YOUR MAIN CAST AND COMPLETE YOUR BOOK FOR YOU!!

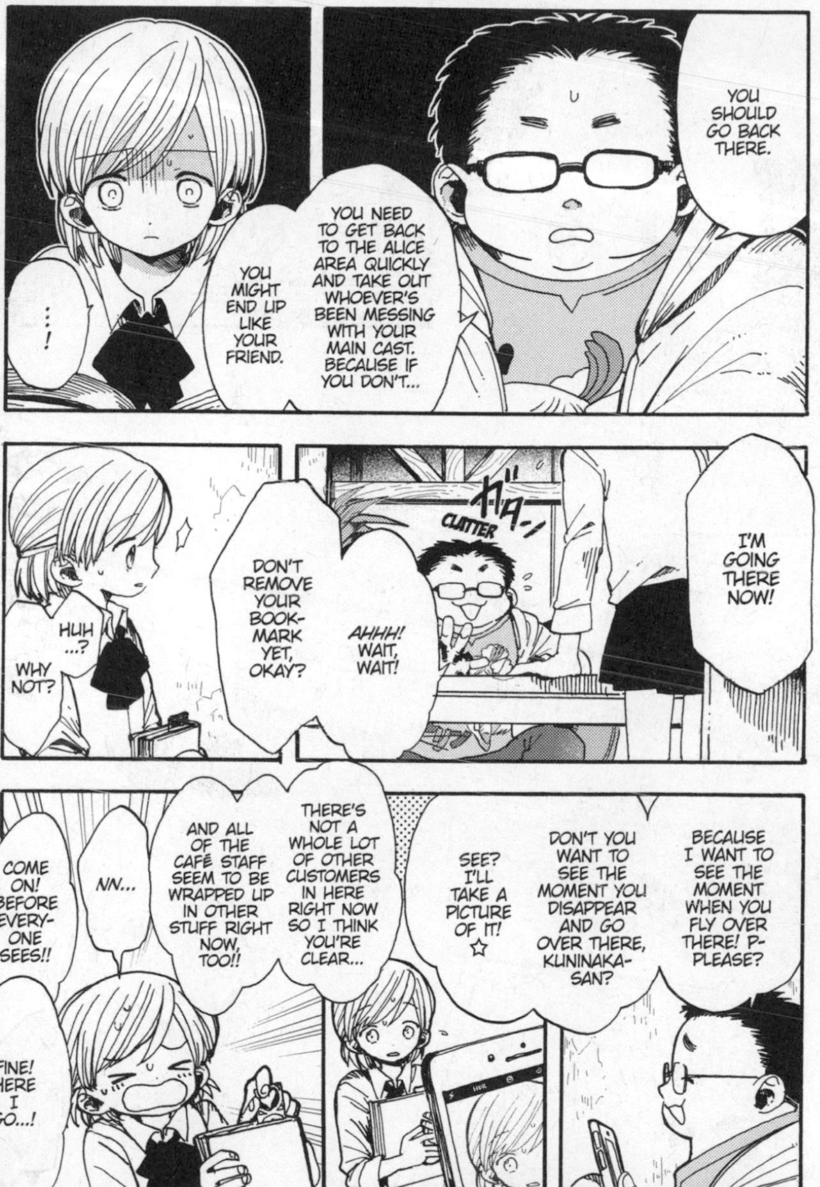
YOU SHOULD GO BACK THERE.
YOU NEED TO GET BACK TO THE ALICE AREA QUICKLY AND TAKE OUT WHOEVER'S BEEN MESSING WITH YOUR MAIN CAST. BECAUSE IF YOU DON'T...
YOU MIGHT END UP LIKE YOUR FRIEND.
...!
I'M GOING THERE NOW!
CLATTER
AHHH! WAIT, WAIT!
DON'T REMOVE YOUR BOOK-MARK YET, OKAY?
HUH ...?
WHY NOT?
BECAUSE I WANT TO SEE THE MOMENT WHEN YOU FLY OVER THERE! P-PLEASE?
DON'T YOU WANT TO SEE THE MOMENT YOU DISAPPEAR AND GO OVER THERE, KUNINAKA-SAN?
SEE? I'LL TAKE A PICTURE OF IT! ☆
THERE'S NOT A WHOLE LOT OF OTHER CUSTOMERS IN HERE RIGHT NOW SO I THINK YOU'RE CLEAR...
AND ALL OF THE CAFÉ STAFF SEEM TO BE WRAPPED UP IN OTHER STUFF RIGHT NOW, TOO!!
NN...
COME ON! BEFORE EVERY-ONE SEES!!
FINE! HERE I GO...!

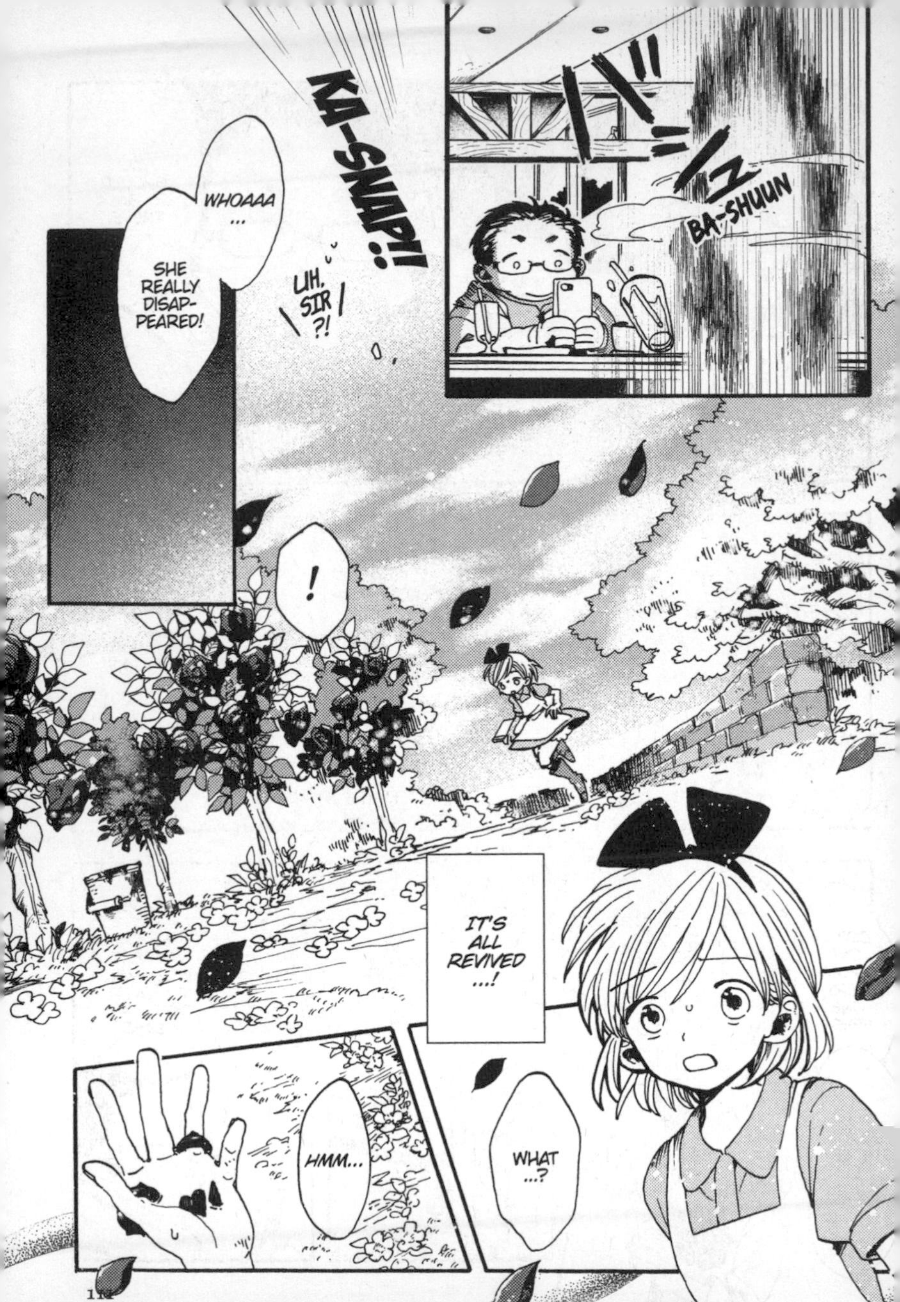
BA-SHUUN
KA-SNAP!!
UH, SIR ?!
WHOAAA ... SHE REALLY DISAPPEARED!
!
IT'S ALL REVIVED ...!
WHAT ...?
HMM...

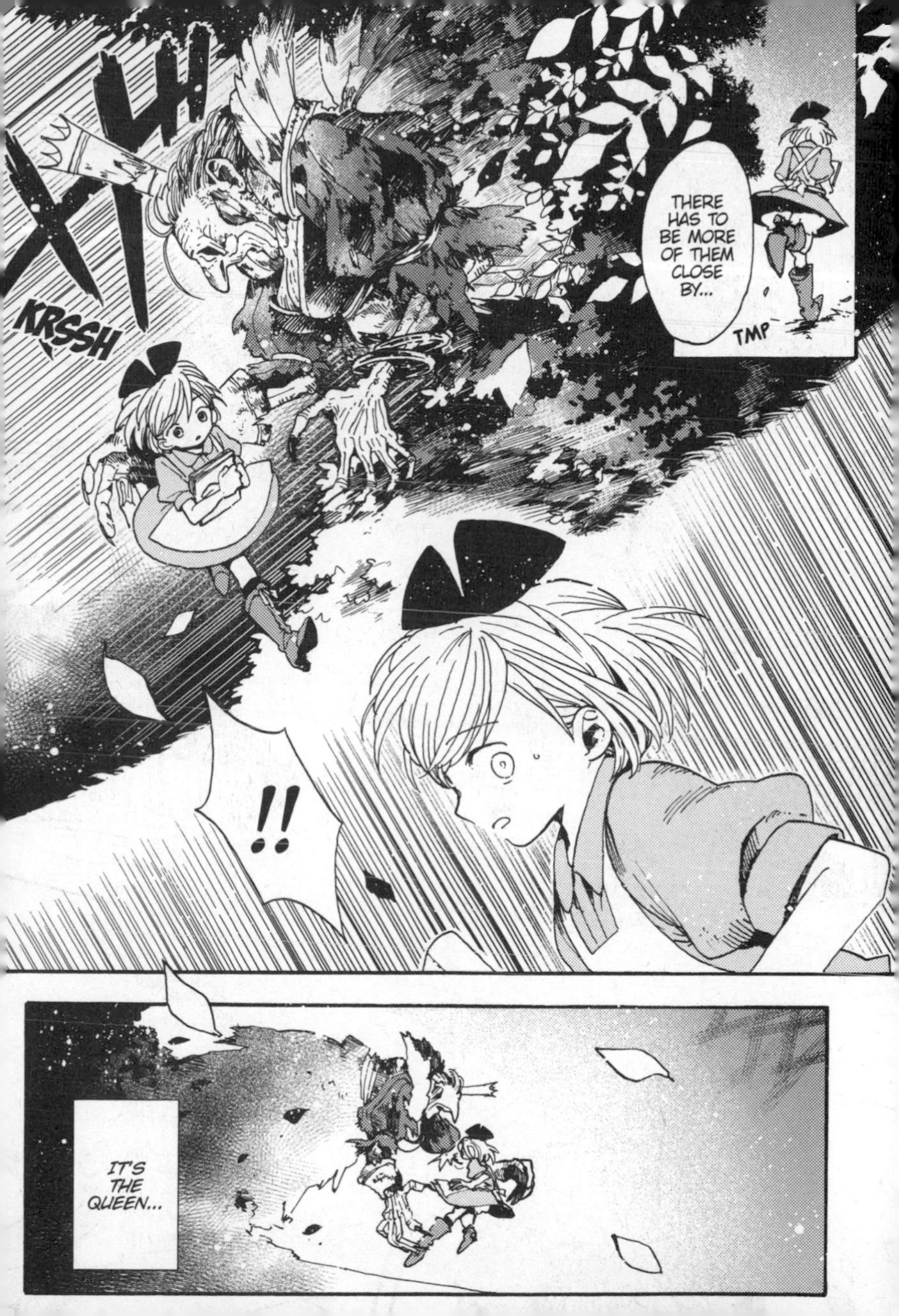
THERE HAS TO BE MORE OF THEM CLOSE BY...
TMP
KRSSH
!!
IT'S THE QUEEN...

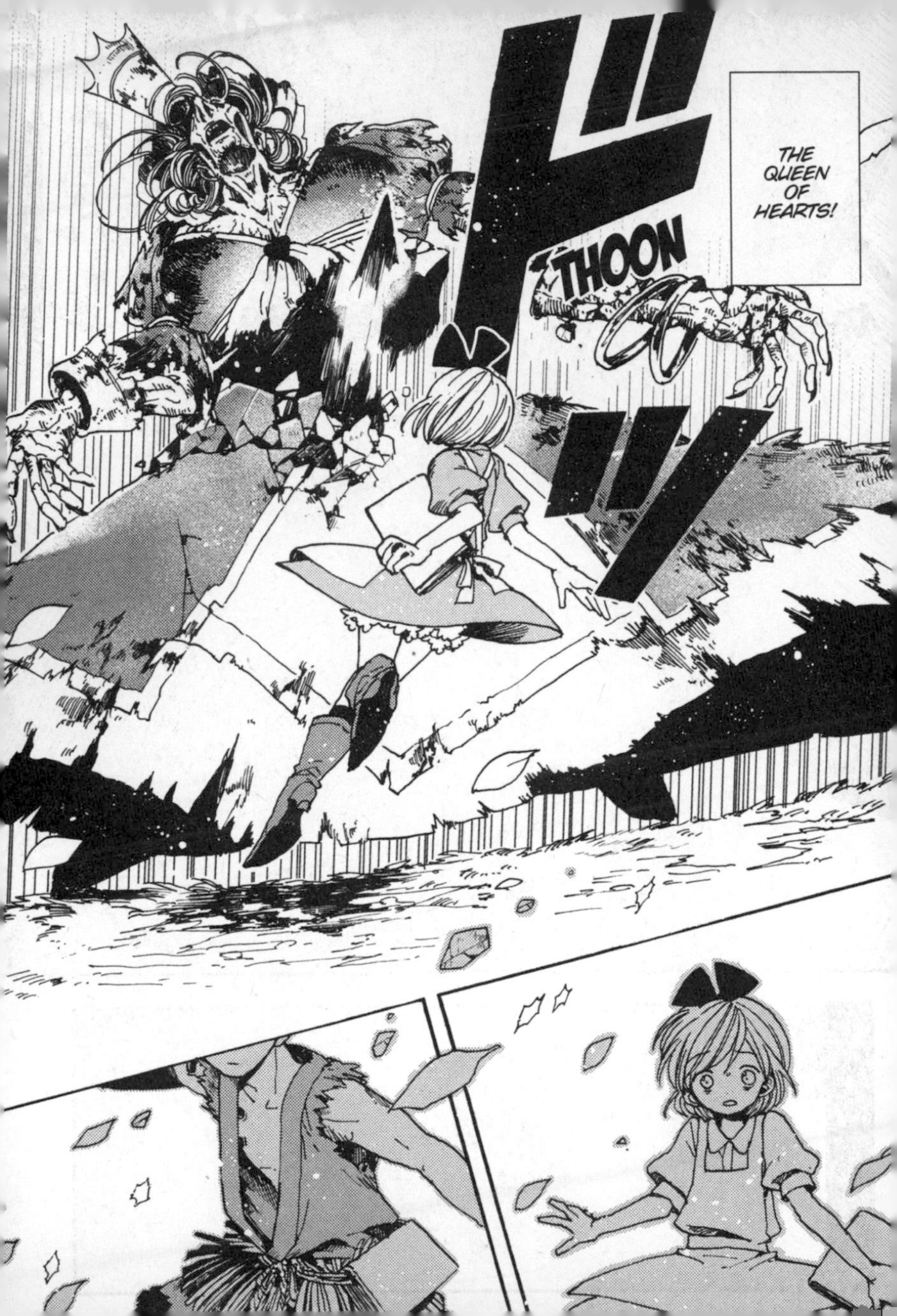
THE QUEEN OF HEARTS!
THOON

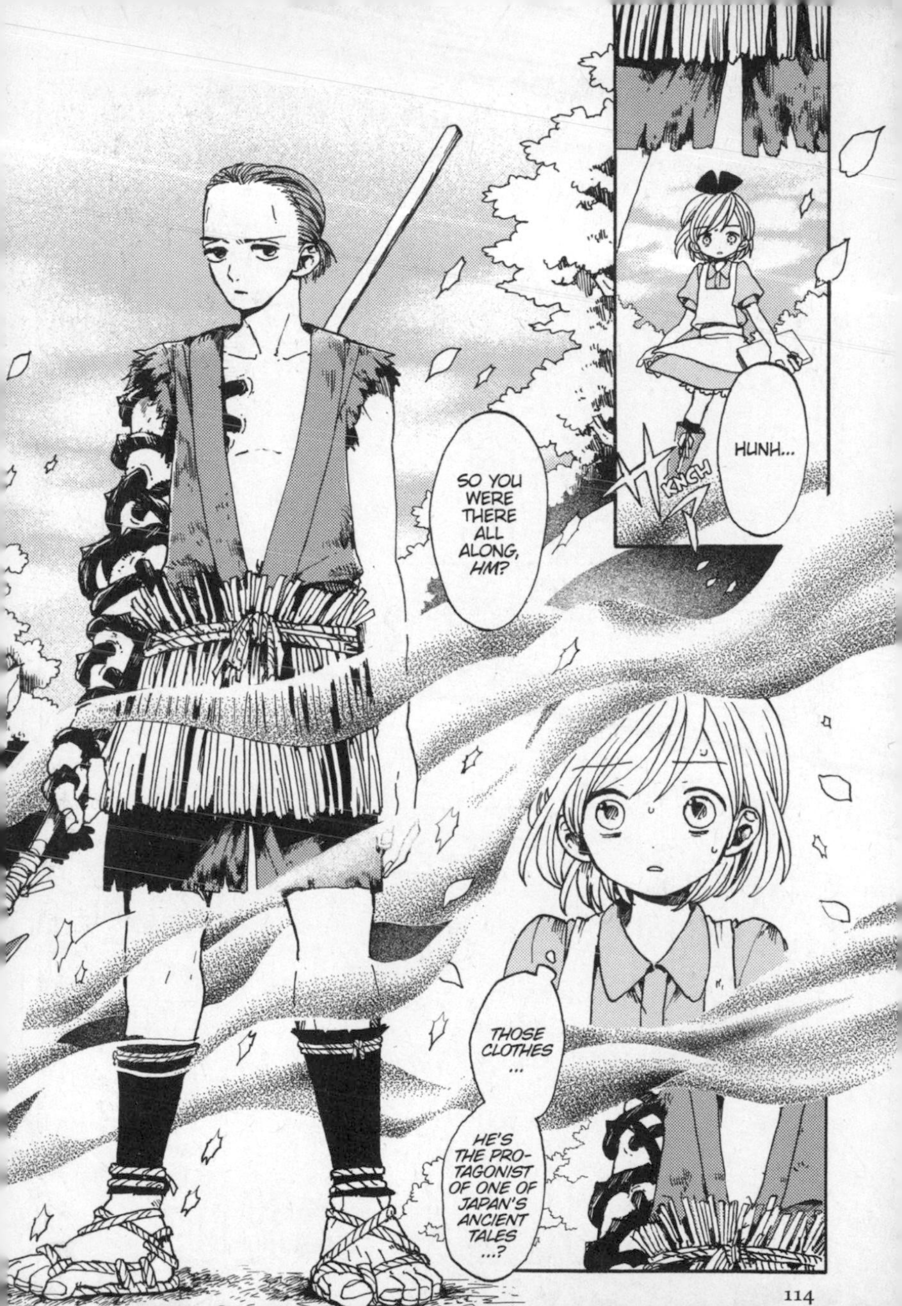
HUNH...
KNGH
THOSE CLOTHES ...
HE'S THE PRO-TAGONIST OF ONE OF JAPAN'S ANCIENT TALES ...?
SO YOU WERE THERE ALL ALONG, HM?

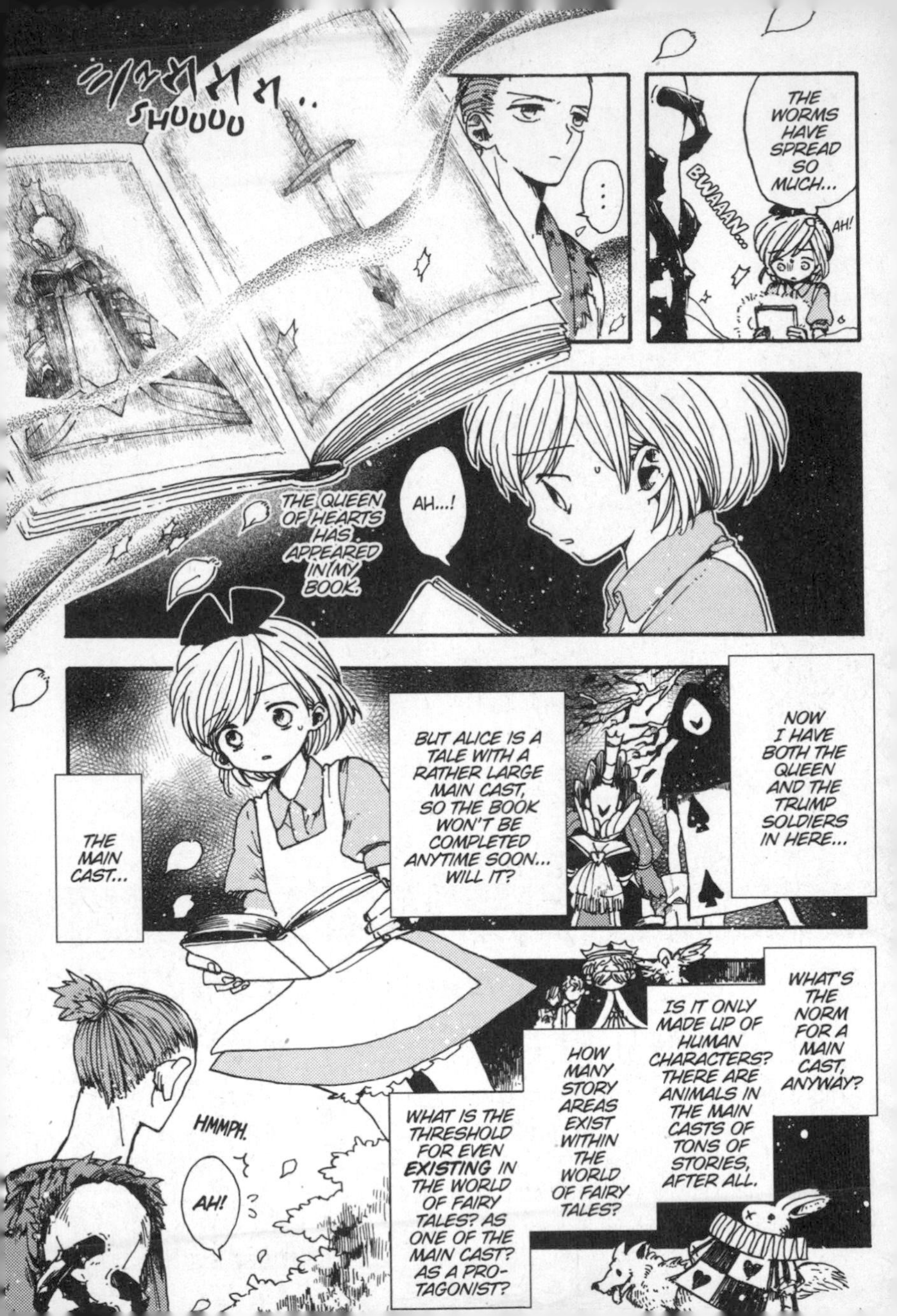
THE WORMS HAVE SPREAD SO MUCH...
BWAAAN...
AH!
...
SHUUUU
AH...!
THE QUEEN OF HEARTS HAS APPEARED IN MY BOOK.
NOW I HAVE BOTH THE QUEEN AND THE TRUMP SOLDIERS IN HERE...
BUT ALICE IS A TALE WITH A RATHER LARGE MAIN CAST, SO THE BOOK WON'T BE COMPLETED ANYTIME SOON... WILL IT?
THE MAIN CAST...
WHAT'S THE NORM FOR A MAIN CAST, ANYWAY?
IS IT ONLY MADE UP OF HUMAN CHARACTERS? THERE ARE ANIMALS IN THE MAIN CASTS OF TONS OF STORIES, AFTER ALL.
HOW MANY STORY AREAS EXIST WITHIN THE WORLD OF FAIRY TALES?
WHAT IS THE THRESHOLD FOR EVEN EXISTING IN THE WORLD OF FAIRY TALES? AS ONE OF THE MAIN CAST? AS A PROTAGONIST?
HMMPH.
AH!

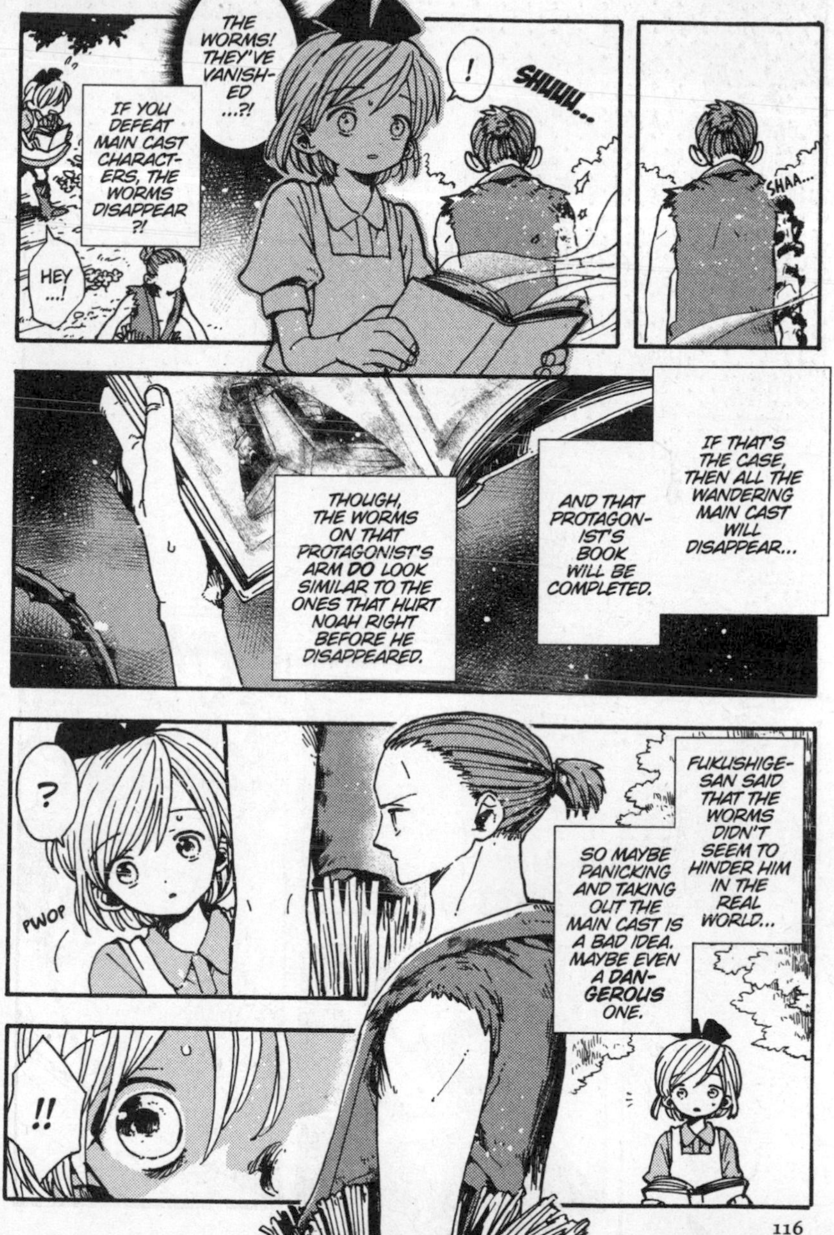
SHAA...
SHUUU...
!
THE WORMS! THEY'VE VANISH-ED ...?!
IF YOU DEFEAT MAIN CAST CHARACT-ERS, THE WORMS DISAPPEAR ?!
HEY ...!
IF THAT'S THE CASE, THEN ALL THE WANDERING MAIN CAST WILL DISAPPEAR...
AND THAT PROTAGON-IST'S BOOK WILL BE COMPLETED.
THOUGH, THE WORMS ON THAT PROTAGONIST'S ARM DO LOOK SIMILAR TO THE ONES THAT HURT NOAH RIGHT BEFORE HE DISAPPEARED.
FUKUSHIGE-SAN SAID THAT THE WORMS DIDN'T SEEM TO HINDER HIM IN THE REAL WORLD...
SO MAYBE PANICKING AND TAKING OUT THE MAIN CAST IS A BAD IDEA. MAYBE EVEN A DAN-GEROUS ONE.
?
PWOP
!!

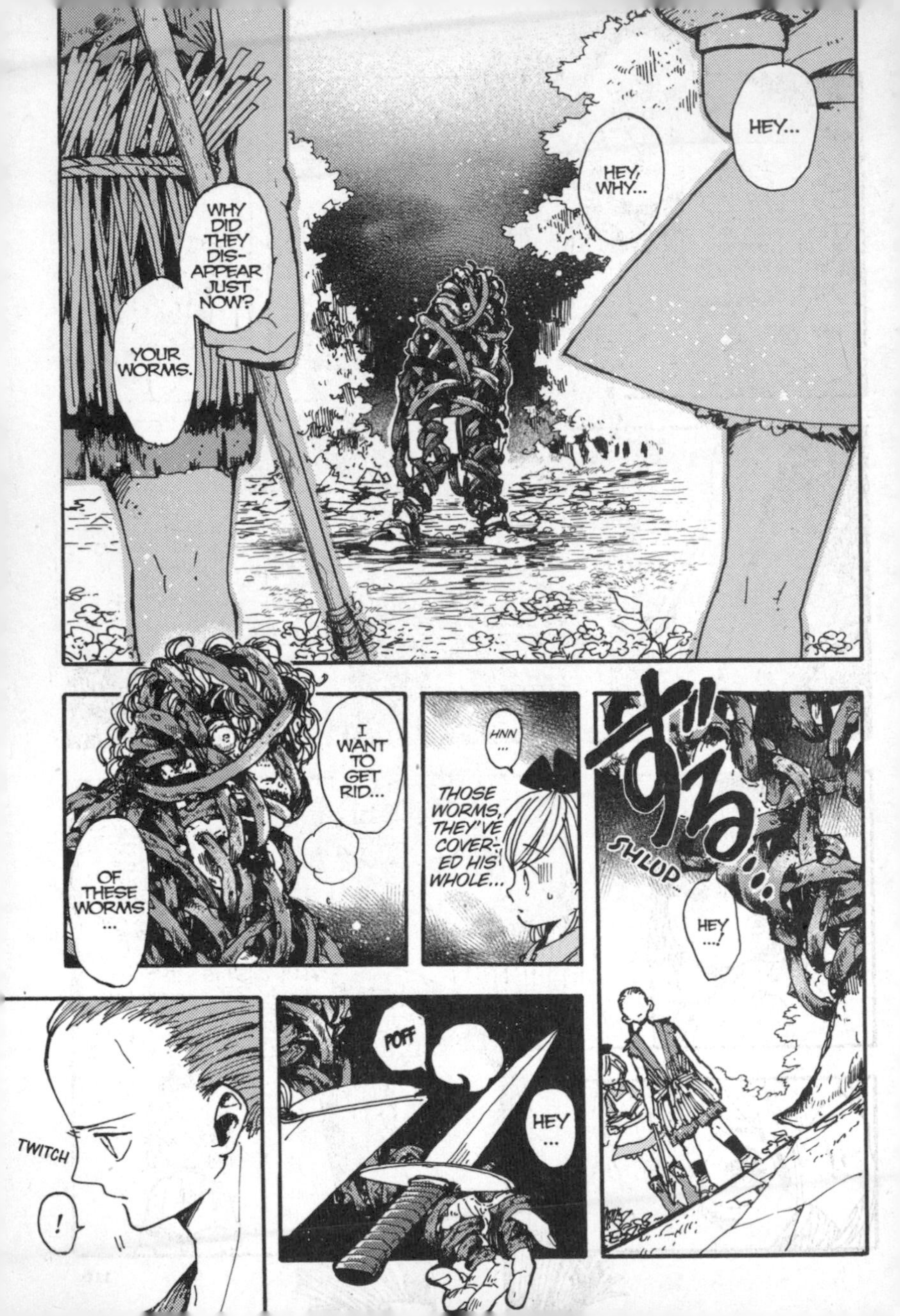
HEY...
HEY, WHY...
WHY DID THEY DIS-APPEAR JUST NOW?
YOUR WORMS.
ずる
SHLUP
HEY ...!
HNN ...
THOSE WORMS, THEY'VE COVER-ED HIS WHOLE...
I WANT TO GET RID...
OF THESE WORMS ...
POFF
HEY ...
TWITCH
!

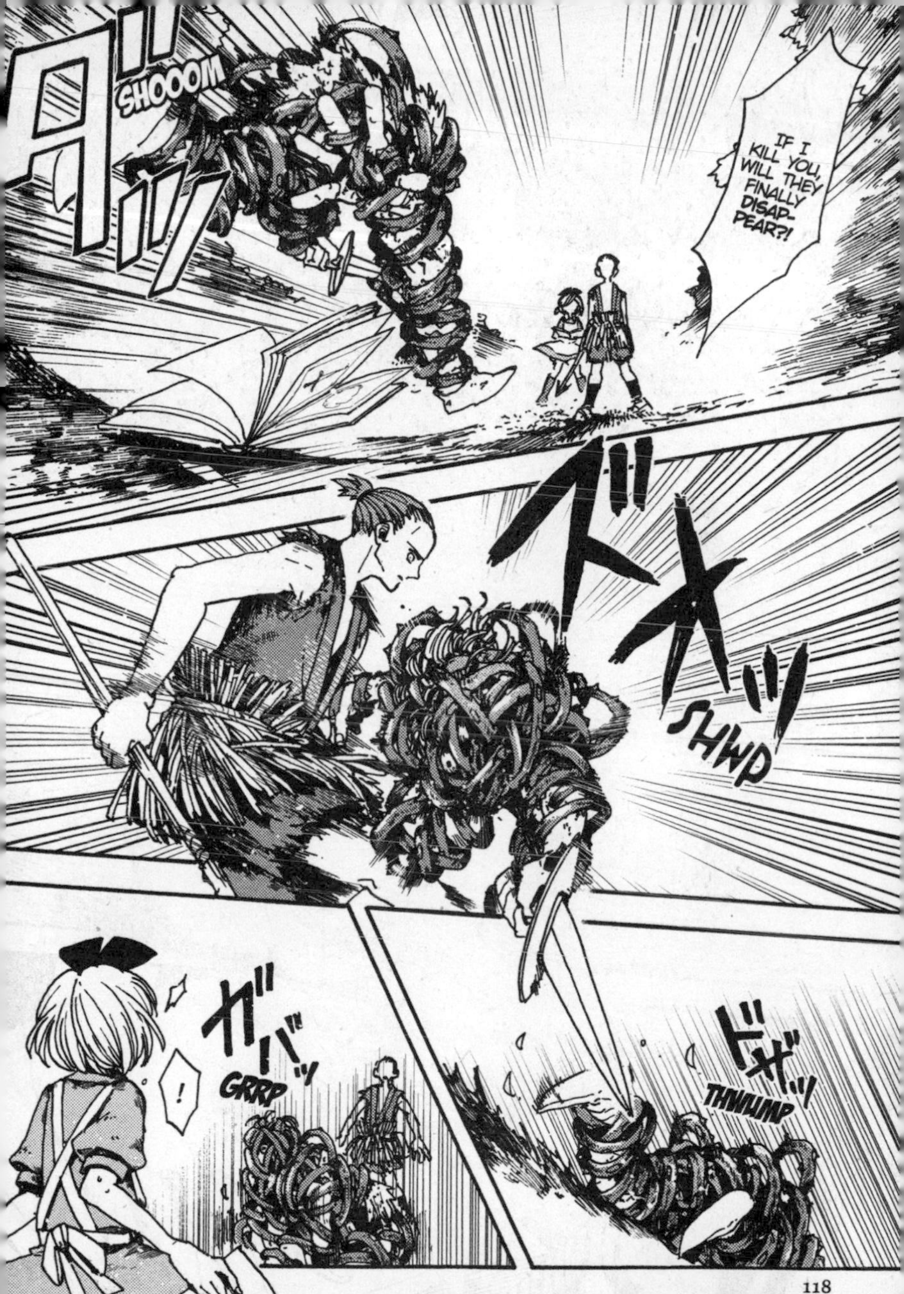
IF I KILL YOU, WILL THEY FINALLY DISAPPEAR?!
SHOOOM
SHWP
THWUMP
GRRP
!

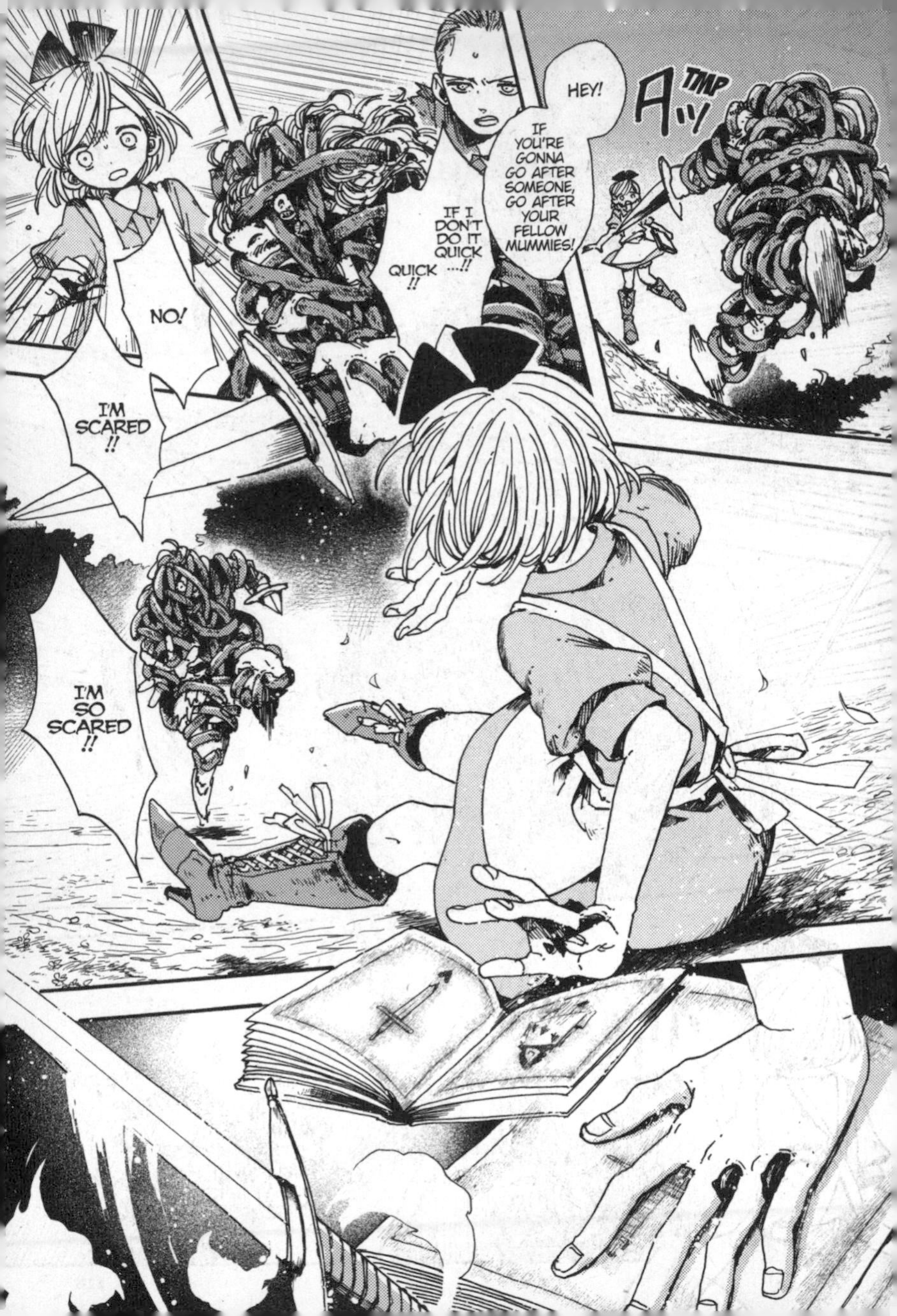
TMP
HEY!
IF YOU'RE GONNA GO AFTER SOMEONE, GO AFTER YOUR FELLOW MUMMIES!
IF I DON'T DO IT QUICK ...!!
QUICK!!
NO!
I'M SCARED!!
I'M SO SCARED!!

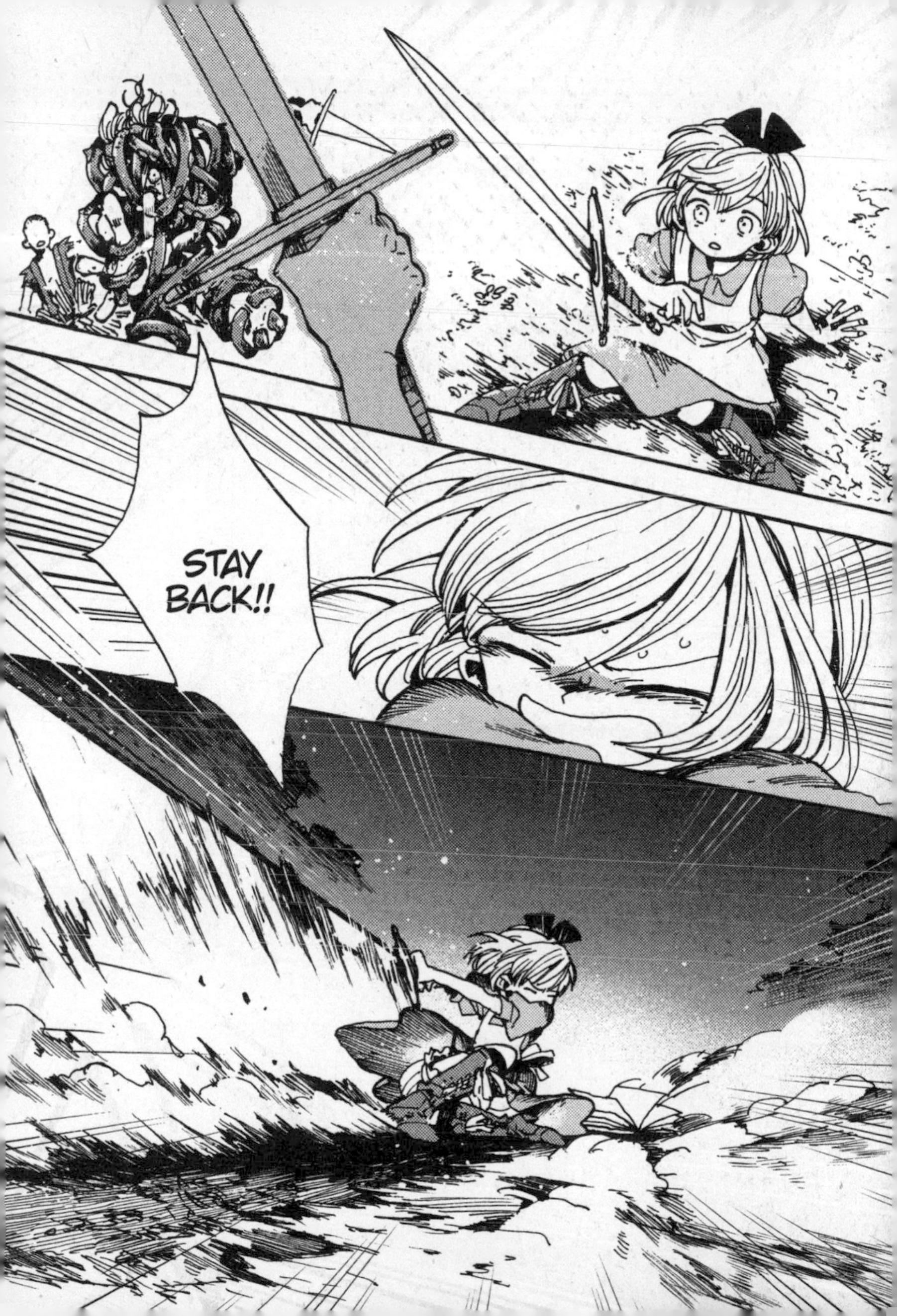
STAY BACK!!

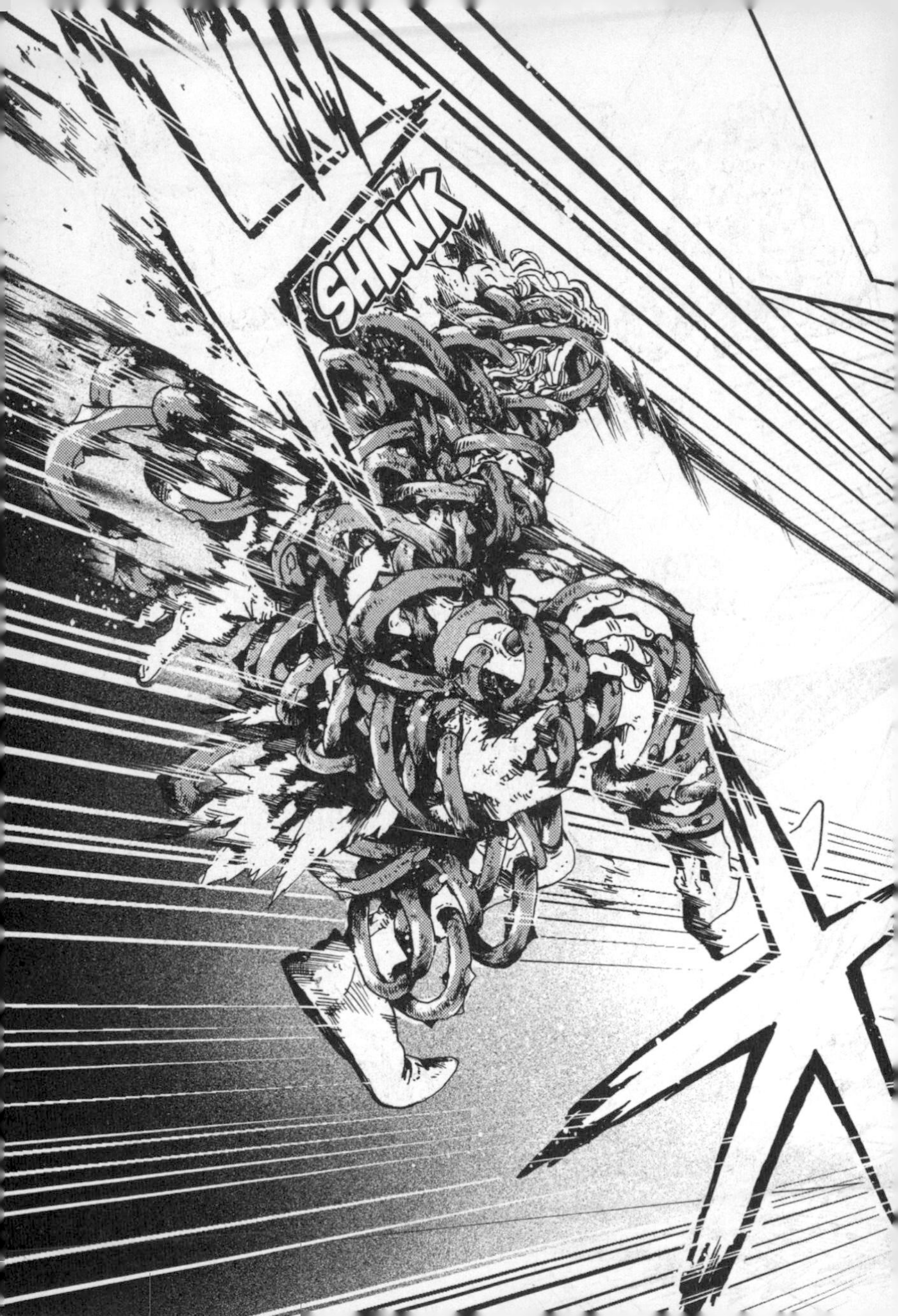
SHNNK

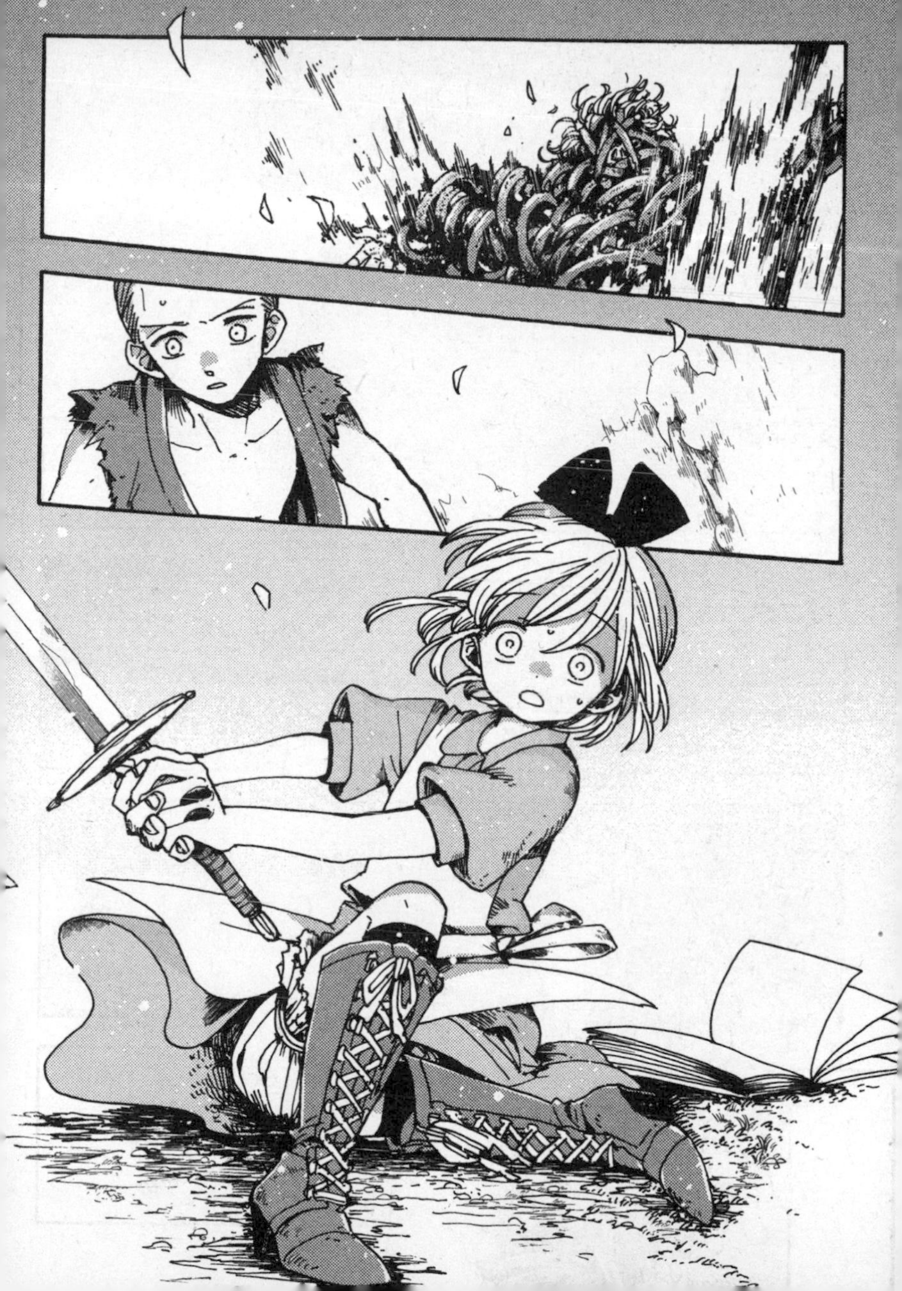

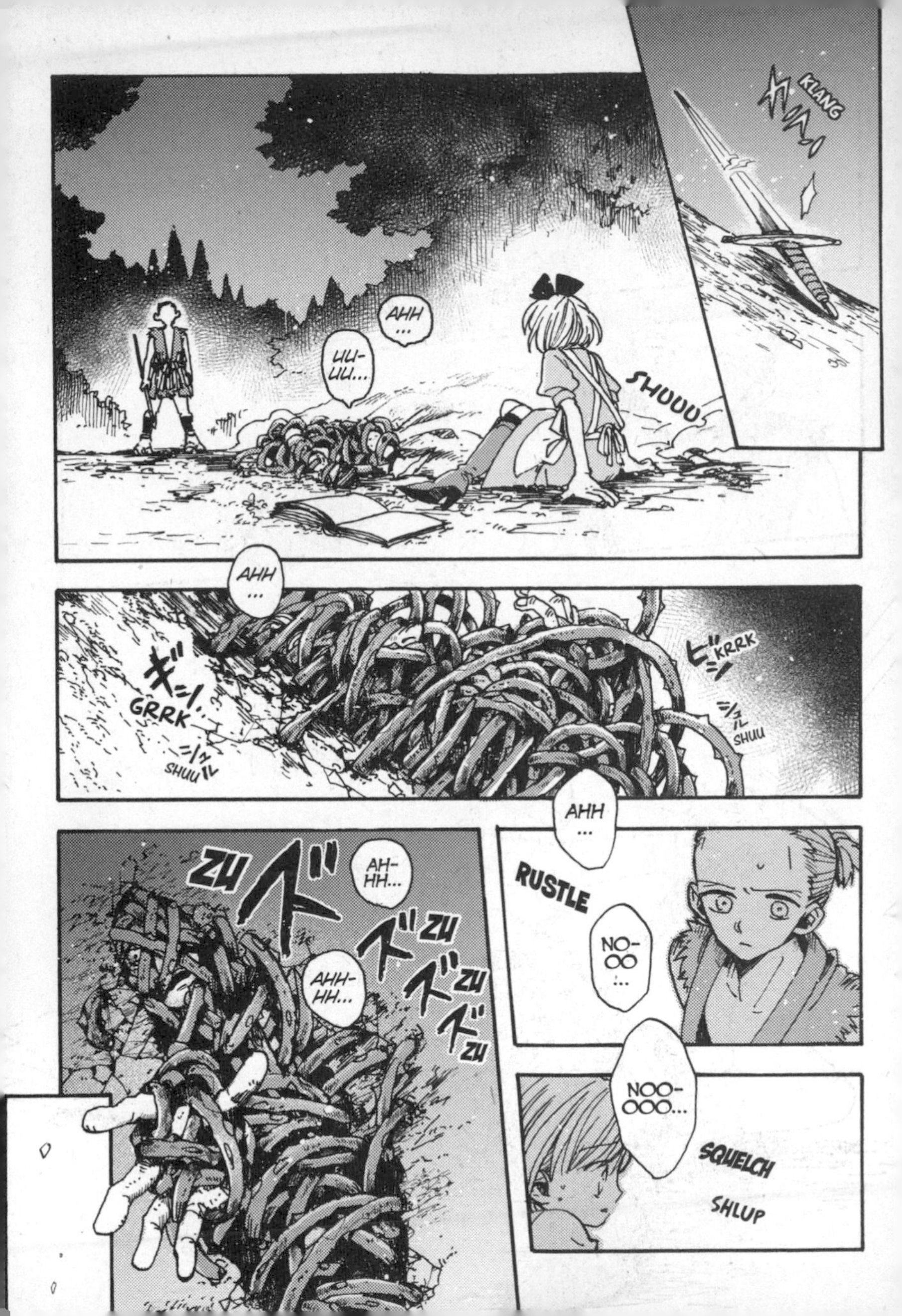

KLANG
AHH ...
UU-UU...
SHUUU
AHH ...
KRRK
SHUU
GRRK
SHUU
AHH ...
RUSTLE
NO-OO !...
NOO-OOO...
SQUELCH
SHLUP
AH-HH...
ZU
AHH-HH...
ZU
ZU
ZU

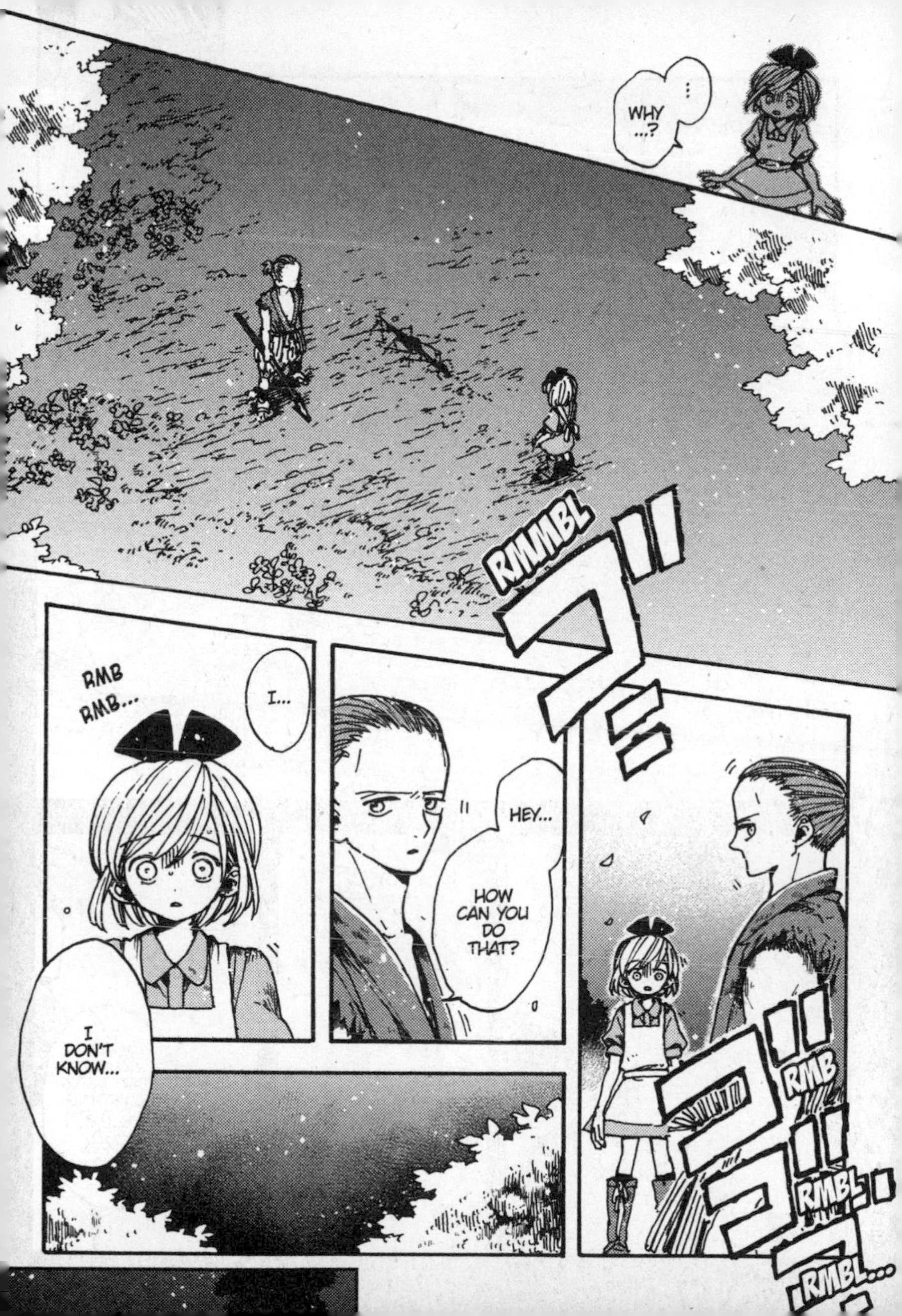
...
WHY ...?
RMMBL
RMB
RMBL
RMBL...
HEY...
HOW CAN YOU DO THAT?
RMB RMB...
I...
I DON'T KNOW...

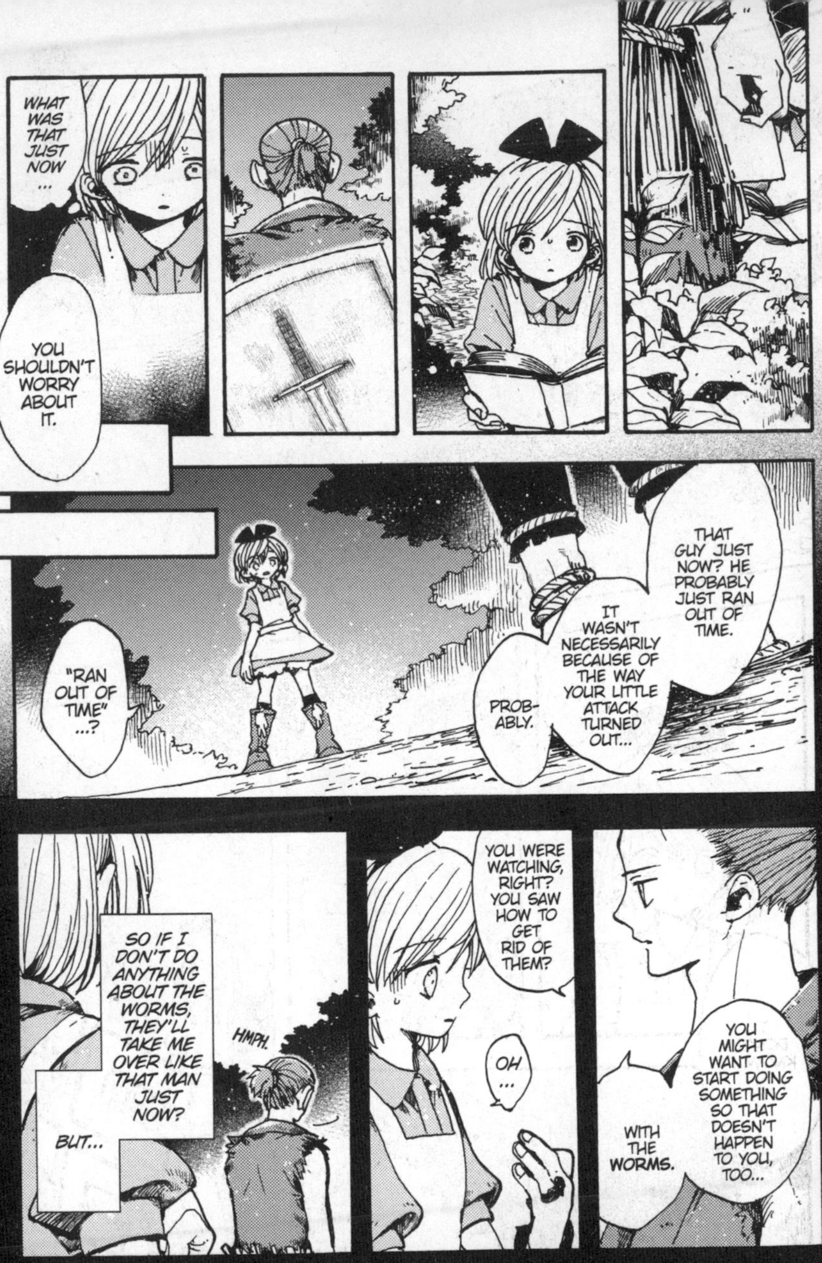
WHAT WAS THAT JUST NOW ...
YOU SHOULDN'T WORRY ABOUT IT.
THAT GUY JUST NOW? HE PROBABLY JUST RAN OUT OF TIME.
IT WASN'T NECESSARILY BECAUSE OF THE WAY YOUR LITTLE ATTACK TURNED OUT...
PROB-ABLY.
"RAN OUT OF TIME" ...?
YOU MIGHT WANT TO START DOING SOMETHING SO THAT DOESN'T HAPPEN TO YOU, TOO...
WITH THE WORMS.
YOU WERE WATCHING, RIGHT? YOU SAW HOW TO GET RID OF THEM?
OH ...
HMPH.
SO IF I DON'T DO ANYTHING ABOUT THE WORMS, THEY'LL TAKE ME OVER LIKE THAT MAN JUST NOW?
BUT...

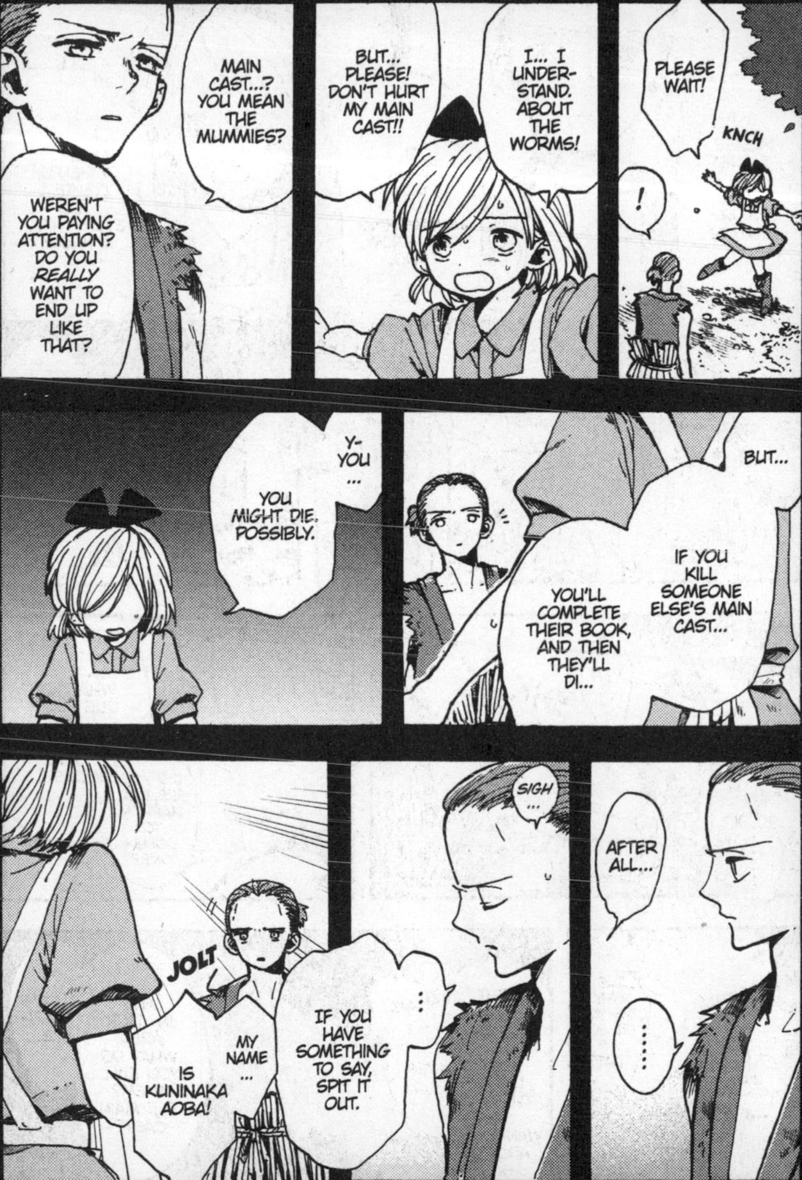
PLEASE WAIT!
KNCH
!
I... I UNDER-STAND. ABOUT THE WORMS!
BUT... PLEASE! DON'T HURT MY MAIN CAST!!
MAIN CAST...? YOU MEAN THE MUMMIES?
WEREN'T YOU PAYING ATTENTION? DO YOU *REALLY* WANT TO END UP LIKE THAT?
BUT...
IF YOU KILL SOMEONE ELSE'S MAIN CAST...
YOU'LL COMPLETE THEIR BOOK, AND THEN THEY'LL DI...
Y-YOU ...
YOU MIGHT DIE. POSSIBLY.
AFTER ALL...
......
SIGH ...
...
IF YOU HAVE SOMETHING TO SAY, SPIT IT OUT.
JOLT
MY NAME ...
IS KUNINAKA AOBA!

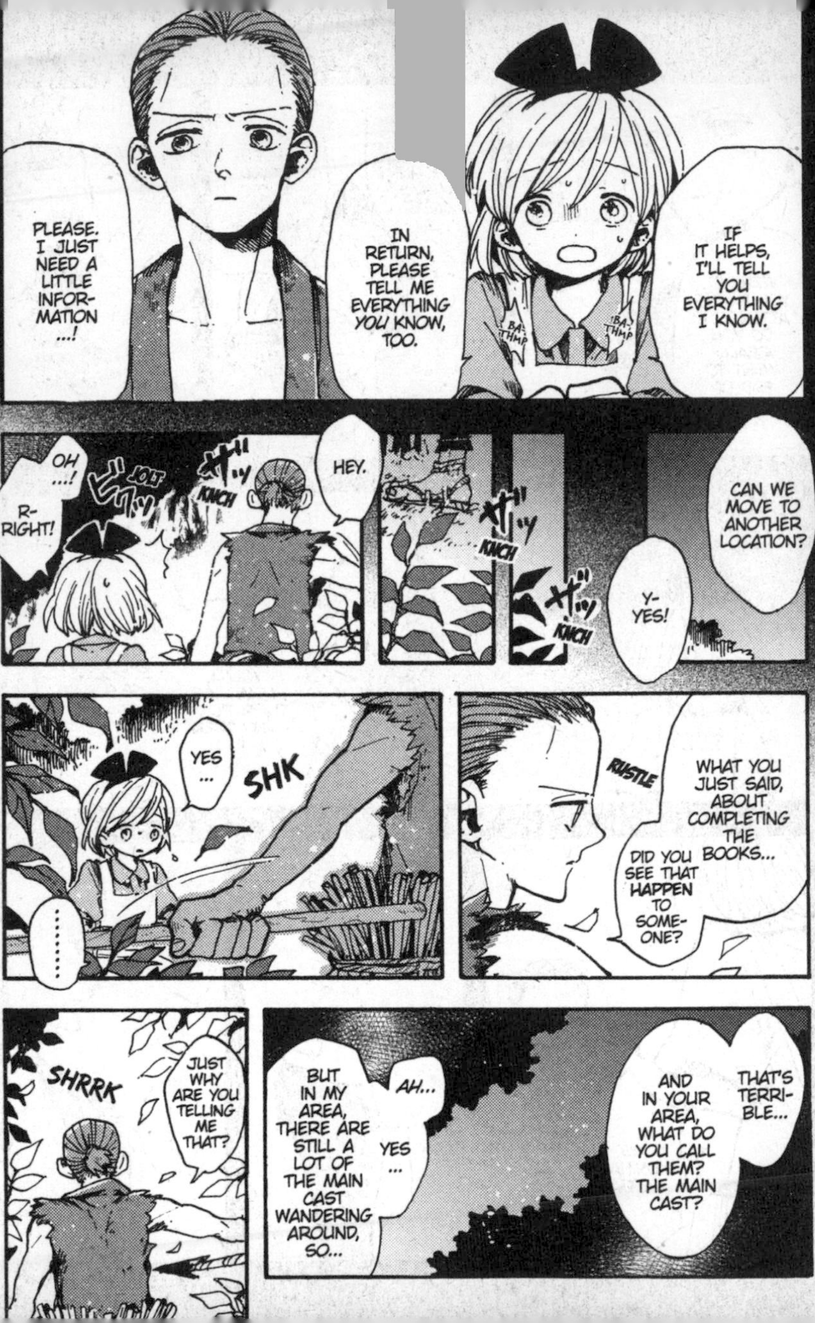
IF IT HELPS, I'LL TELL YOU EVERYTHING I KNOW.
BA-THMP
BA-THMP
IN RETURN, PLEASE TELL ME EVERYTHING YOU KNOW, TOO.
PLEASE. I JUST NEED A LITTLE INFORMATION ...!
CAN WE MOVE TO ANOTHER LOCATION?
Y-YES!
KNCH
KNCH
HEY.
KNCH
JOLT
OH ...!
R-RIGHT!
WHAT YOU JUST SAID, ABOUT COMPLETING THE BOOKS...
RUSTLE
DID YOU SEE THAT HAPPEN TO SOME-ONE?
YES ...
SHK
......
THAT'S TERRI-BLE...
AND IN YOUR AREA, WHAT DO YOU CALL THEM? THE MAIN CAST?
AH...
YES ...
BUT IN MY AREA, THERE ARE STILL A LOT OF THE MAIN CAST WANDERING AROUND, SO...
JUST WHY ARE YOU TELLING ME THAT?
SHRRK

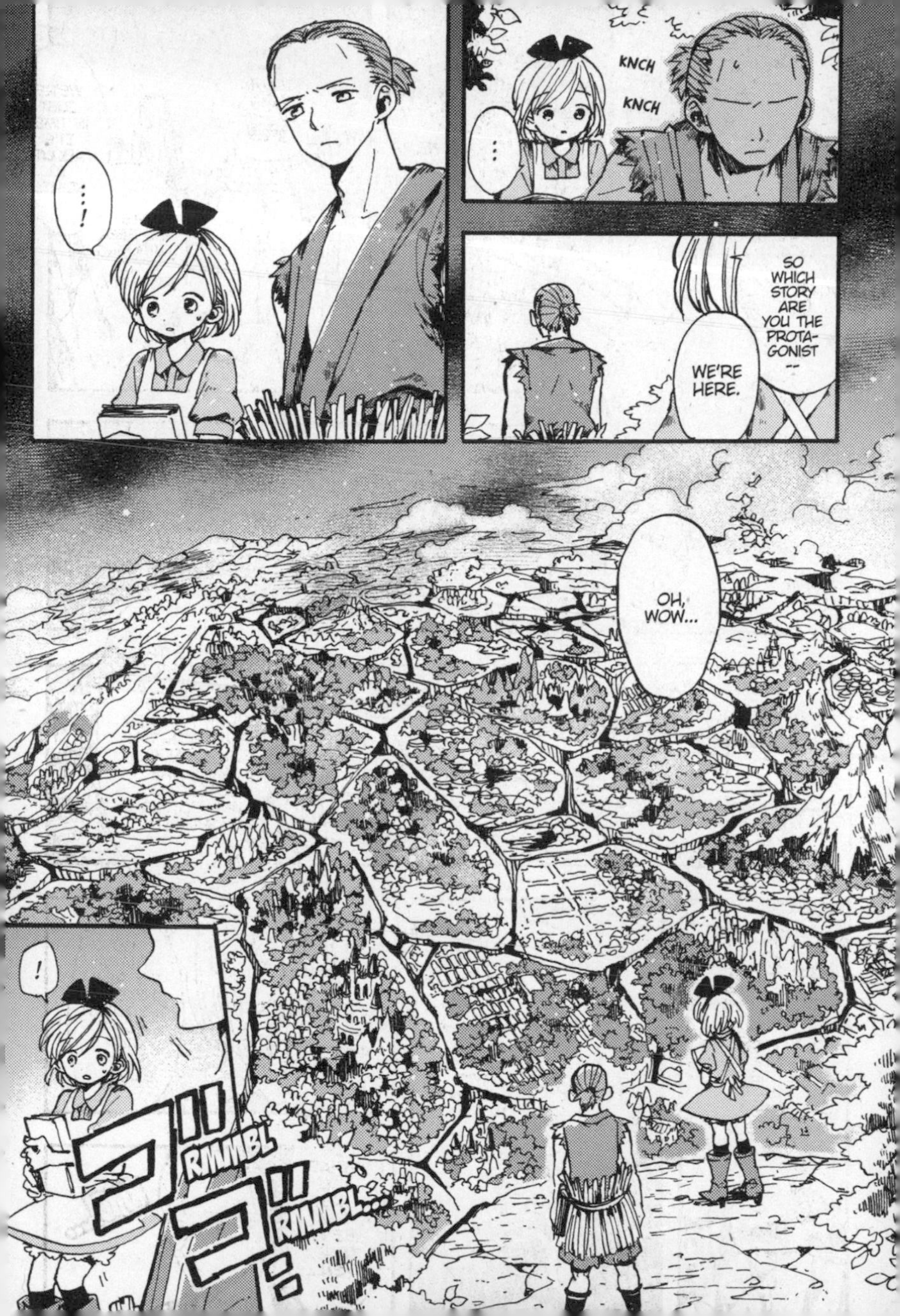
KNCH
KNCH
...
SO WHICH STORY ARE YOU THE PROTAGONIST--
WE'RE HERE.
...!
OH, WOW...
!
RMMBL
RMMBL...

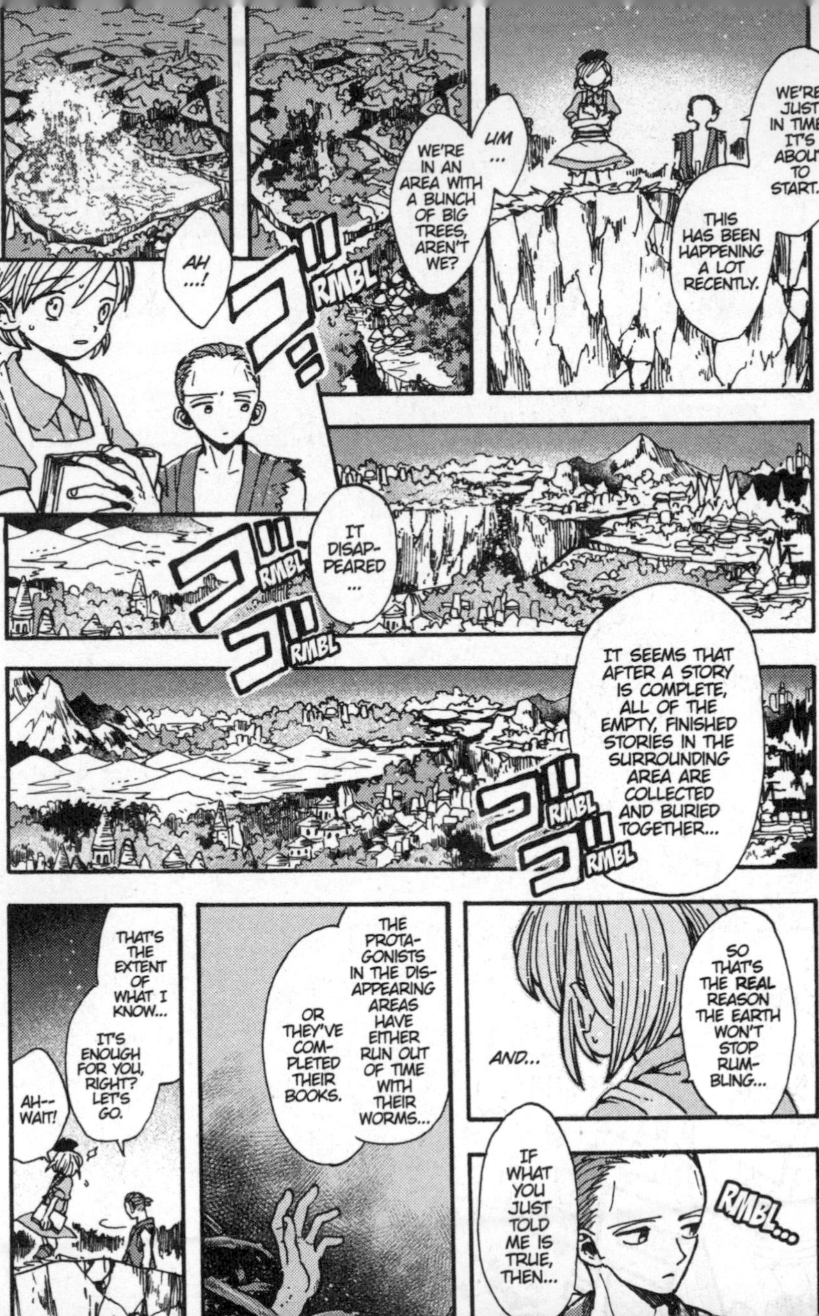

WE'RE JUST IN TIME. IT'S ABOUT TO START...
THIS HAS BEEN HAPPENING A LOT RECENTLY.
UM...
WE'RE IN AN AREA WITH A BUNCH OF BIG TREES, AREN'T WE?
RMBL
AH...!
IT DISAPPEARED...
RMBL
RMBL
IT SEEMS THAT AFTER A STORY IS COMPLETE, ALL OF THE EMPTY, FINISHED STORIES IN THE SURROUNDING AREA ARE COLLECTED AND BURIED TOGETHER...
RMBL
RMBL
SO THAT'S THE REAL REASON THE EARTH WON'T STOP RUMBLING...
AND...
IF WHAT YOU JUST TOLD ME IS TRUE, THEN...
RMBL...
THE PROTAGONISTS IN THE DISAPPEARING AREAS HAVE EITHER RUN OUT OF TIME WITH THEIR WORMS...
OR THEY'VE COMPLETED THEIR BOOKS.
THAT'S THE EXTENT OF WHAT I KNOW...
IT'S ENOUGH FOR YOU, RIGHT? LET'S GO.
AH-- WAIT!

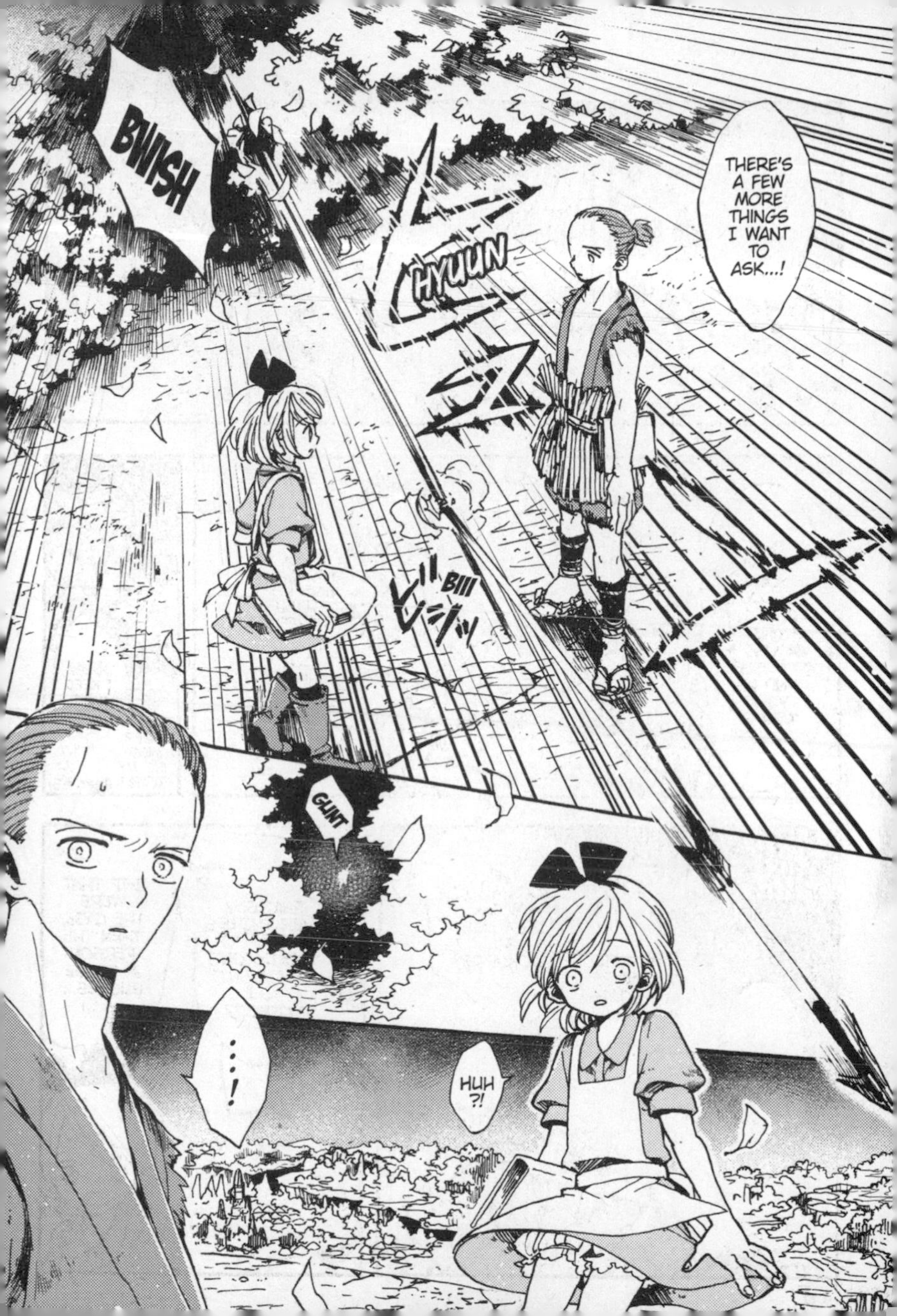
THERE'S A FEW MORE THINGS I WANT TO ASK...!
CHYUUN
BWISH
BIII
HUH ?!
GLINT
...!

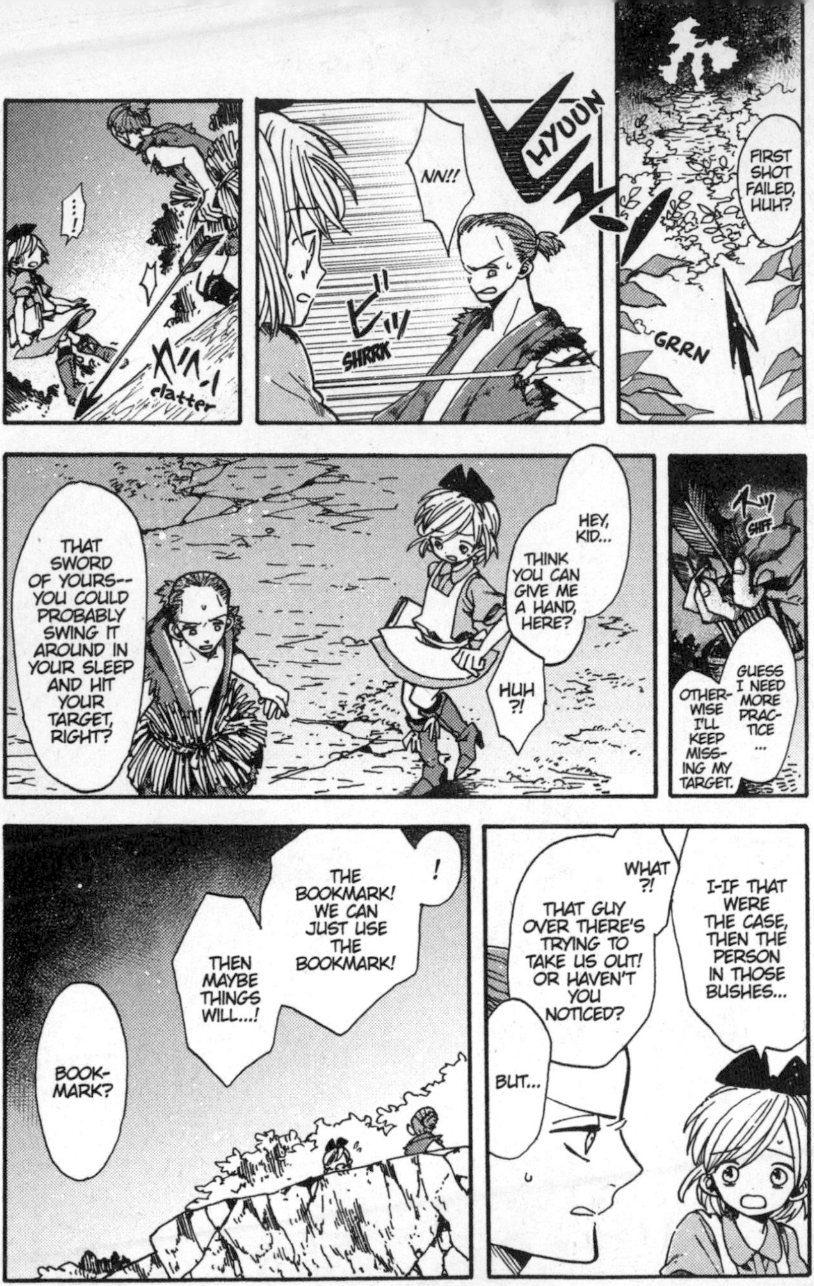
FIRST SHOT FAILED, HUH?
GRRN
HYUUN
NN!!
SHRRK
...!
clatter
SHFF
GUESS I NEED MORE PRAC-TICE ...
OTHER-WISE I'LL KEEP MISS-ING MY TARGET.
HEY, KID...
THINK YOU CAN GIVE ME A HAND, HERE?
HUH ?!
THAT SWORD OF YOURS-- YOU COULD PROBABLY SWING IT AROUND IN YOUR SLEEP AND HIT YOUR TARGET, RIGHT?
I-IF THAT WERE THE CASE, THEN THE PERSON IN THOSE BUSHES...
WHAT ?!
THAT GUY OVER THERE'S TRYING TO TAKE US OUT! OR HAVEN'T YOU NOTICED?
BUT...
!
THE BOOKMARK! WE CAN JUST USE THE BOOKMARK!
THEN MAYBE THINGS WILL...!
BOOK-MARK?

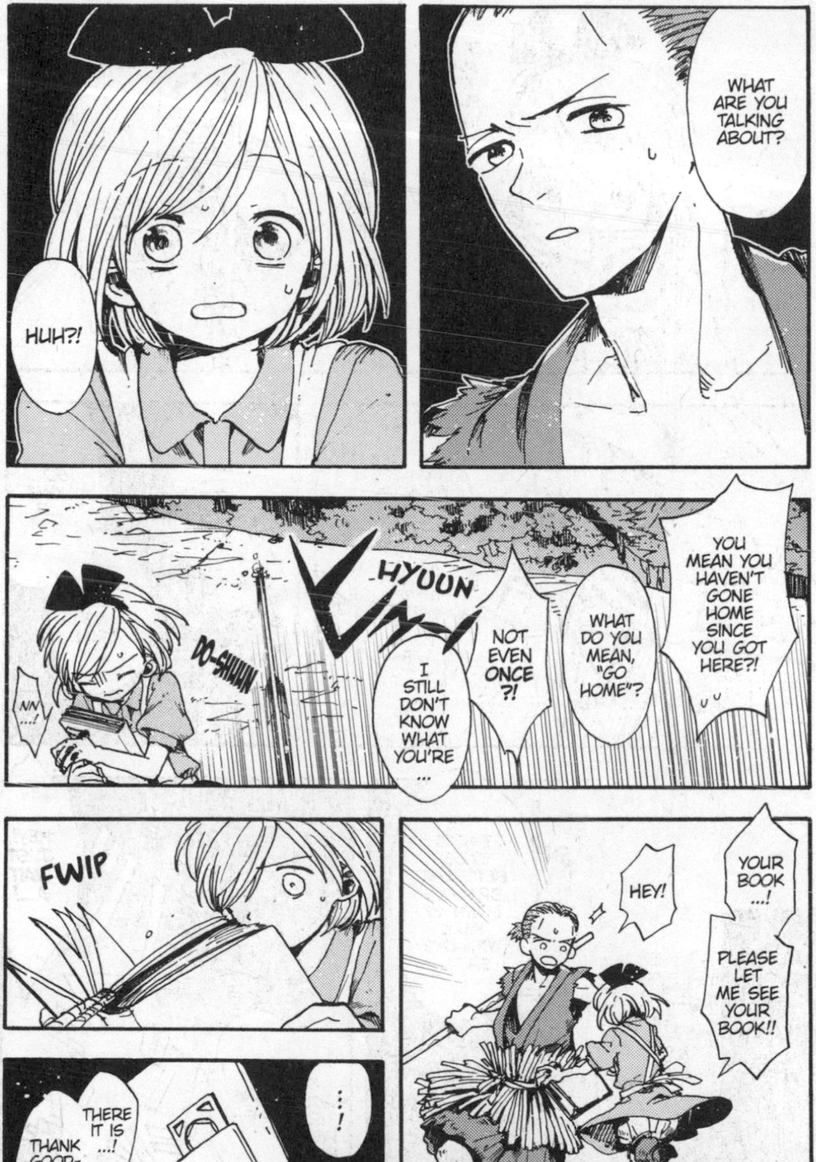
WHAT ARE YOU TALKING ABOUT?
HUH?!
YOU MEAN YOU HAVEN'T GONE HOME SINCE YOU GOT HERE?!
WHAT DO YOU MEAN, "GO HOME"?
NOT EVEN ONCE?!
HYUUN
I STILL DON'T KNOW WHAT YOU'RE ...
DO-SHUUN
NN ...!
YOUR BOOK ...!
PLEASE LET ME SEE YOUR BOOK!!
HEY!
FWIP
...!
THERE IT IS ...!
THANK GOOD-NESS ...!

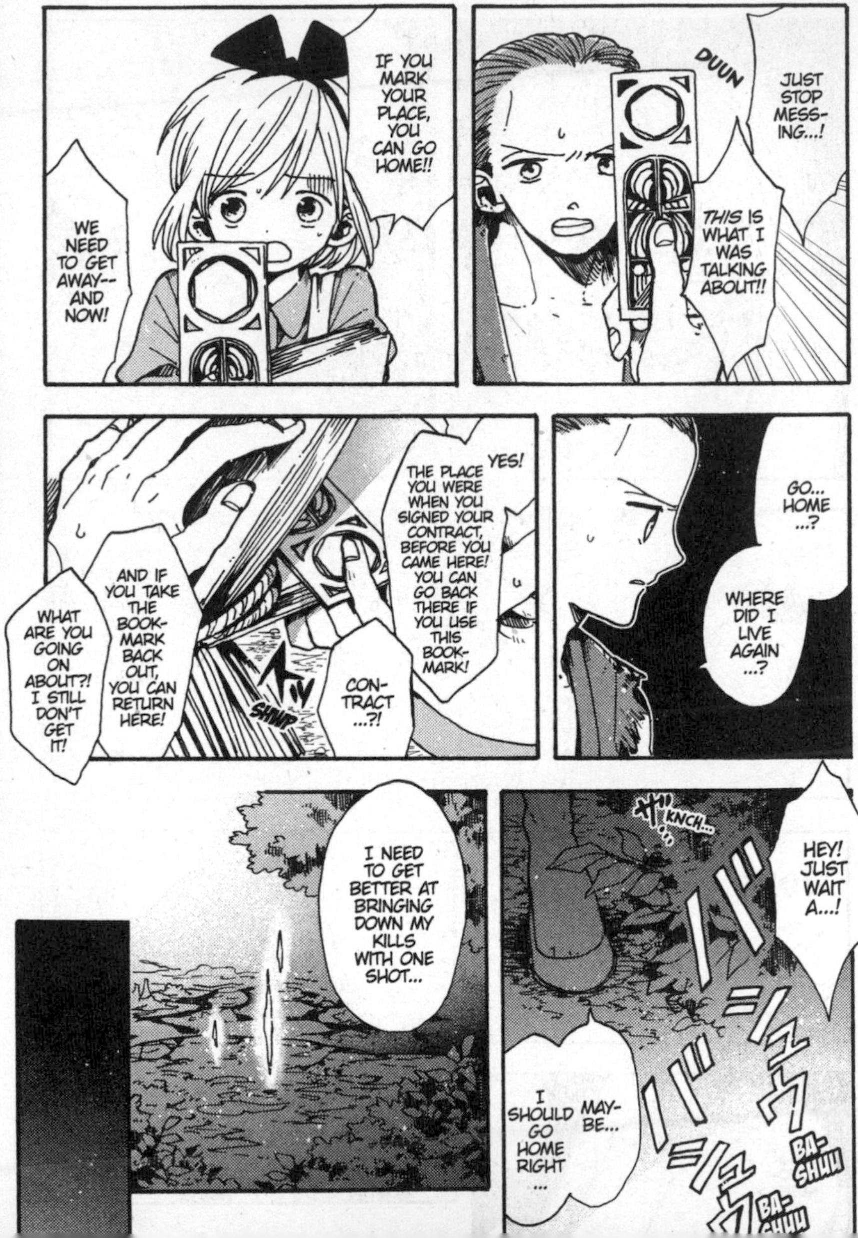
DUUN
JUST STOP MESSING...!
THIS IS WHAT I WAS TALKING ABOUT!!
IF YOU MARK YOUR PLACE, YOU CAN GO HOME!!
WE NEED TO GET AWAY--AND NOW!
GO... HOME ...?
WHERE DID I LIVE AGAIN ...?
YES!
THE PLACE YOU WERE WHEN YOU SIGNED YOUR CONTRACT, BEFORE YOU CAME HERE! YOU CAN GO BACK THERE IF YOU USE THIS BOOKMARK!
CONTRACT ...?!
AND IF YOU TAKE THE BOOKMARK BACK OUT, YOU CAN RETURN HERE!
SHWP
WHAT ARE YOU GOING ON ABOUT?! I STILL DON'T GET IT!
KNCH...
HEY! JUST WAIT A...!
MAYBE...
I SHOULD GO HOME RIGHT ...
BA-SHUU
BA-SHUU
I NEED TO GET BETTER AT BRINGING DOWN MY KILLS WITH ONE SHOT...

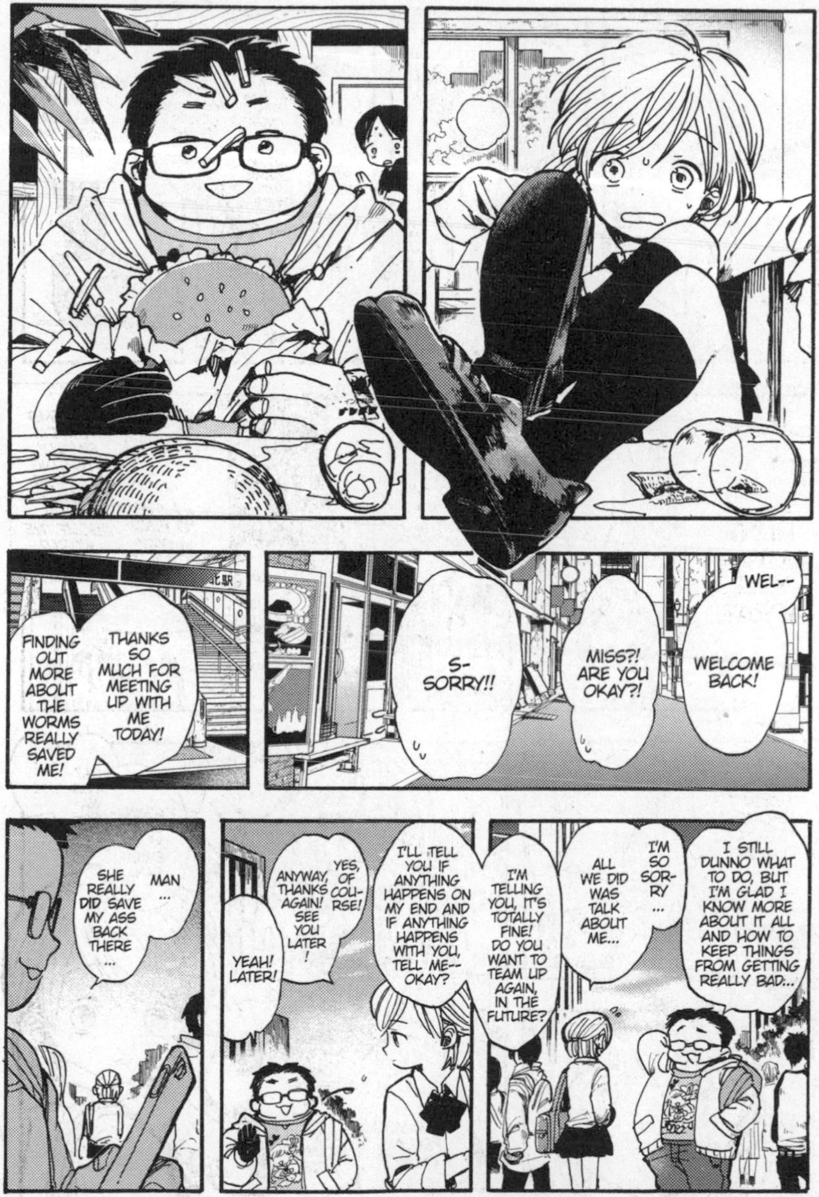
WEL-- WELCOME BACK!
MISS?! ARE YOU OKAY?!
S- SORRY!!
THANKS SO MUCH FOR MEETING UP WITH ME TODAY!
FINDING OUT MORE ABOUT THE WORMS REALLY SAVED ME!
I STILL DUNNO WHAT TO DO, BUT I'M GLAD I KNOW MORE ABOUT IT ALL AND HOW TO KEEP THINGS FROM GETTING REALLY BAD...
I'M SO SORRY ...
ALL WE DID WAS TALK ABOUT ME...
I'M TELLING YOU, IT'S TOTALLY FINE! DO YOU WANT TO TEAM UP AGAIN, IN THE FUTURE?
I'LL TELL YOU IF ANYTHING HAPPENS ON MY END AND IF ANYTHING HAPPENS WITH YOU, TELL ME-- OKAY?
YES, OF COURSE!
ANYWAY, THANKS AGAIN! SEE YOU LATER!
YEAH! LATER!
MAN ...
SHE REALLY DID SAVE MY ASS BACK THERE ...

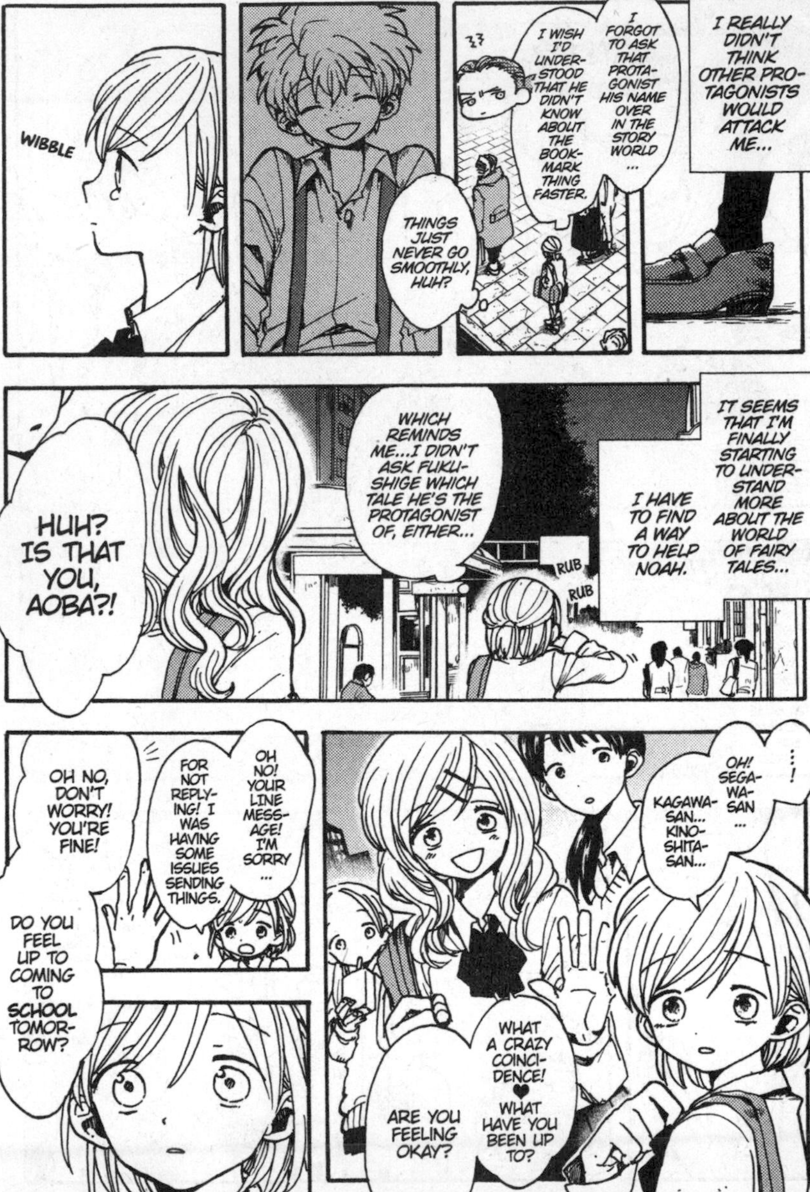
I REALLY DIDN'T THINK OTHER PROTAGONISTS WOULD ATTACK ME...
I FORGOT TO ASK THAT PROTAGONIST HIS NAME OVER IN THE STORY WORLD...
I WISH I'D UNDERSTOOD THAT HE DIDN'T KNOW ABOUT THE BOOKMARK THING FASTER.
THINGS JUST NEVER GO SMOOTHLY, HUH?
WIBBLE
IT SEEMS THAT I'M FINALLY STARTING TO UNDERSTAND MORE ABOUT THE WORLD OF FAIRY TALES...
I HAVE TO FIND A WAY TO HELP NOAH.
RUB
RUB
WHICH REMINDS ME...I DIDN'T ASK FUKUSHIGE WHICH TALE HE'S THE PROTAGONIST OF, EITHER...
HUH? IS THAT YOU, AOBA?!
...!
OH! SEGAWA-SAN...
KAGAWA-SAN... KINOSHITA-SAN...
WHAT A CRAZY COINCIDENCE! ♥ WHAT HAVE YOU BEEN UP TO?
ARE YOU FEELING OKAY?
OH NO! YOUR LINE MESSAGE! I'M SORRY...
FOR NOT REPLYING! I WAS HAVING SOME ISSUES SENDING THINGS.
OH NO, DON'T WORRY! YOU'RE FINE!
DO YOU FEEL UP TO COMING TO SCHOOL TOMORROW?

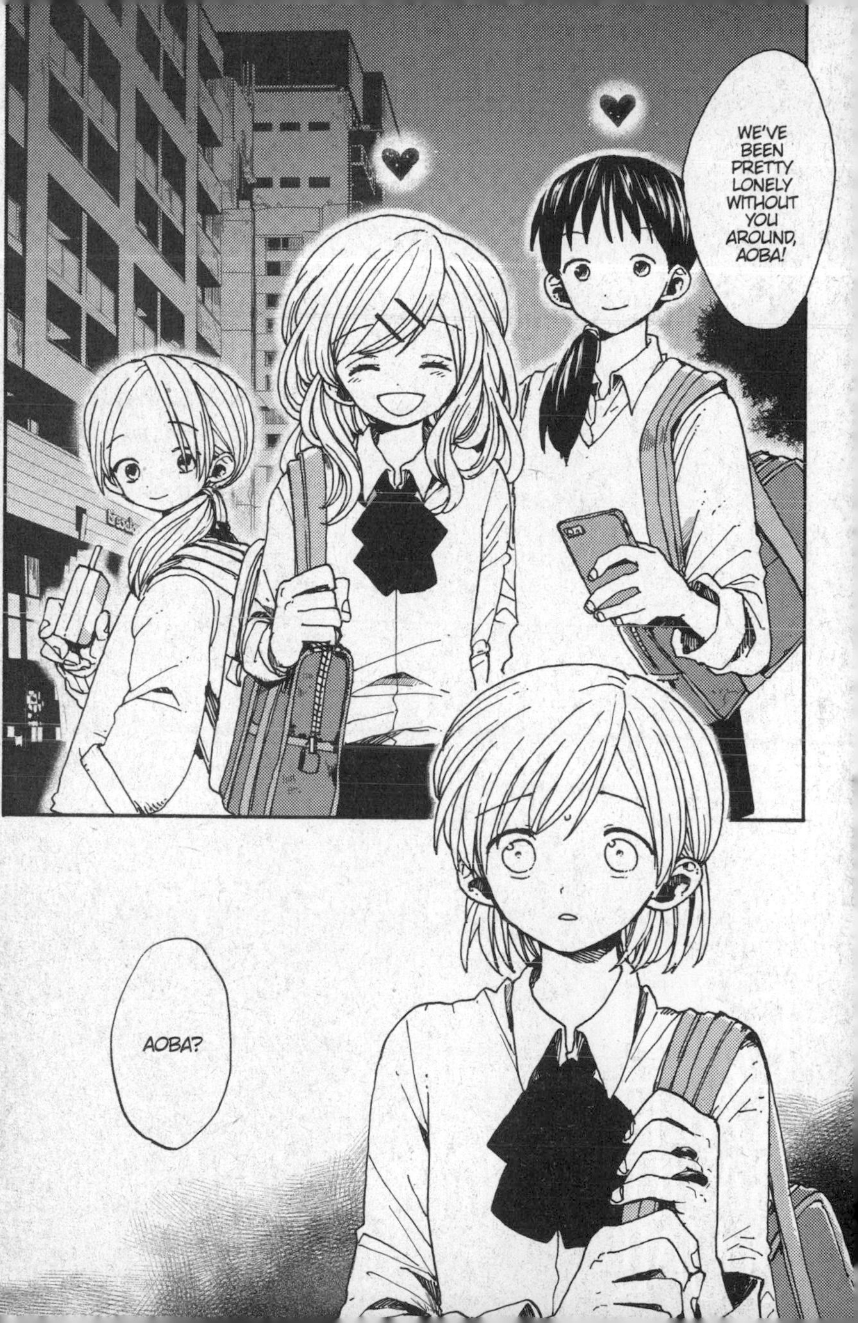
WE'VE BEEN PRETTY LONELY WITHOUT YOU AROUND, AOBA!
AOBA?

FAIRY
TALE
BATTLE
ROYALE

FAIRY TALE BATTLE ROYALE

Extra ~Side Story: Noah~

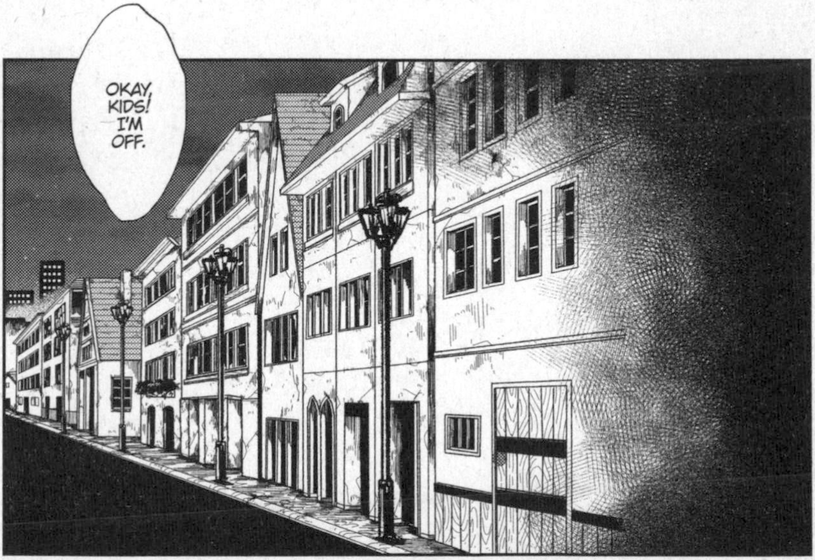
OKAY, KIDS! I'M OFF.

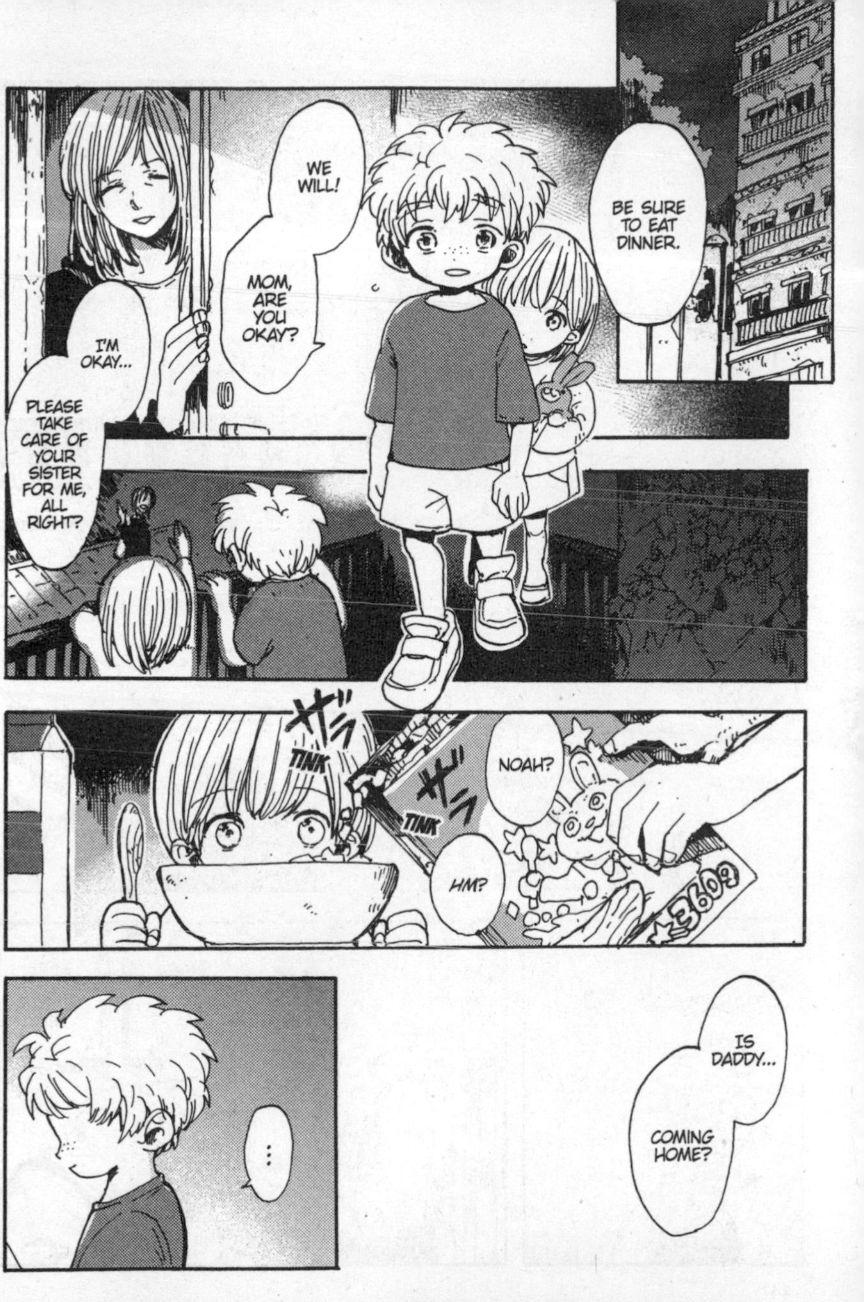
BE SURE TO EAT DINNER.
WE WILL!
MOM, ARE YOU OKAY?
I'M OKAY...
PLEASE TAKE CARE OF YOUR SISTER FOR ME, ALL RIGHT?
NOAH?
TINK
TINK
HM?
3609
IS DADDY...
COMING HOME?
...

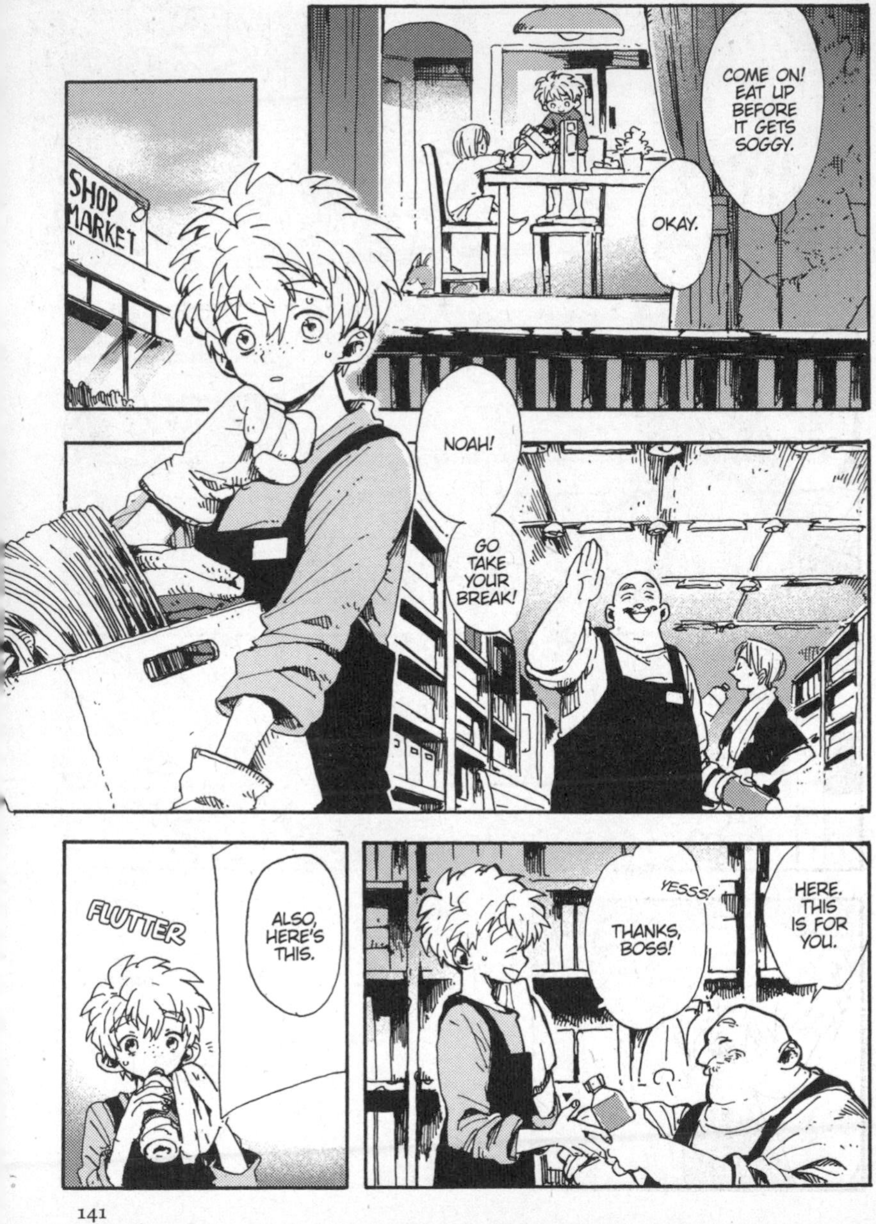
COME ON! EAT UP BEFORE IT GETS SOGGY.
OKAY.
SHOP MARKET
NOAH!
GO TAKE YOUR BREAK!
HERE. THIS IS FOR YOU.
YESSS!
THANKS, BOSS!
ALSO, HERE'S THIS.
FLUTTER

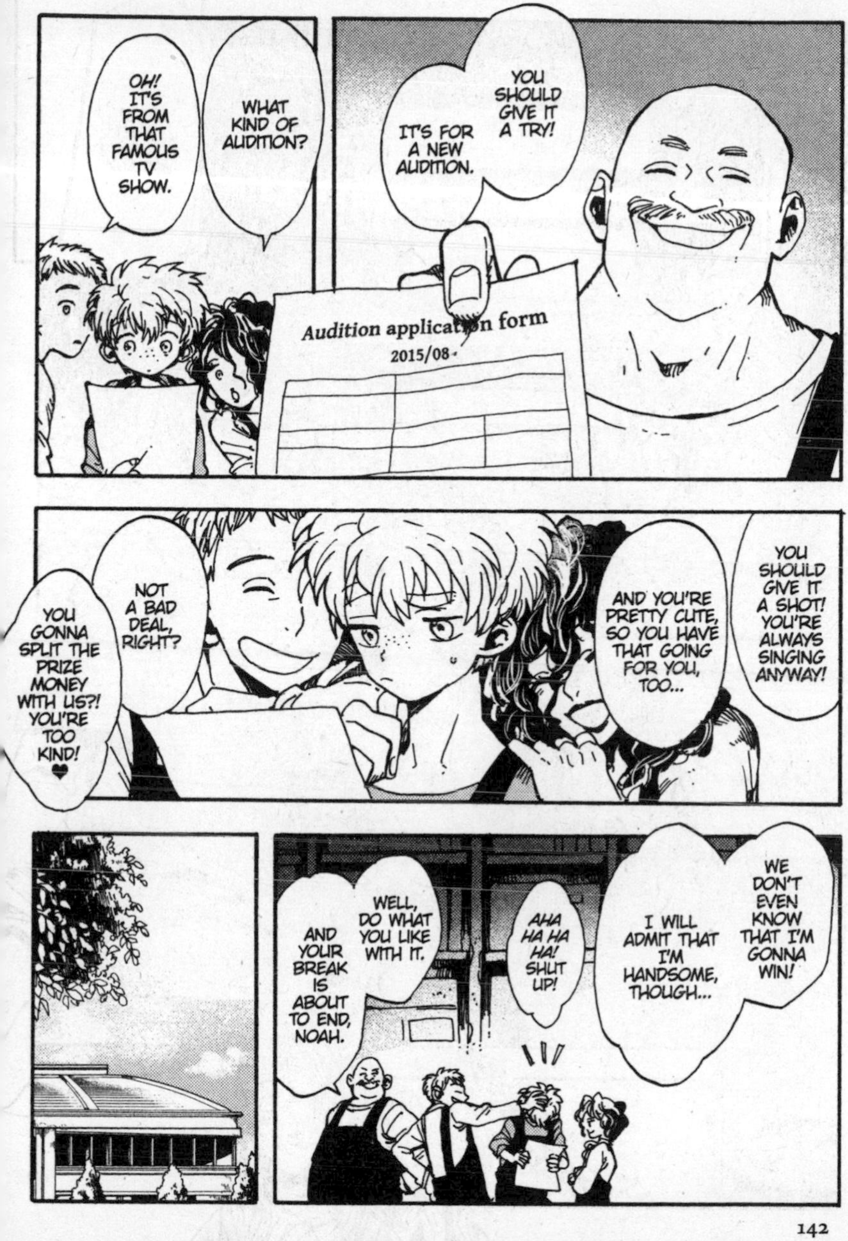
YOU SHOULD GIVE IT A TRY!
IT'S FOR A NEW AUDITION.
Audition application form
2015/08
WHAT KIND OF AUDITION?
OH! IT'S FROM THAT FAMOUS TV SHOW.
YOU SHOULD GIVE IT A SHOT! YOU'RE ALWAYS SINGING ANYWAY!
AND YOU'RE PRETTY CUTE, SO YOU HAVE THAT GOING FOR YOU, TOO...
NOT A BAD DEAL, RIGHT?
YOU GONNA SPLIT THE PRIZE MONEY WITH US?! YOU'RE TOO KIND! ♥
WE DON'T EVEN KNOW THAT I'M GONNA WIN!
I WILL ADMIT THAT I'M HANDSOME, THOUGH...
AHA HA HA HA! SHUT UP!
WELL, DO WHAT YOU LIKE WITH IT.
AND YOUR BREAK IS ABOUT TO END, NOAH.

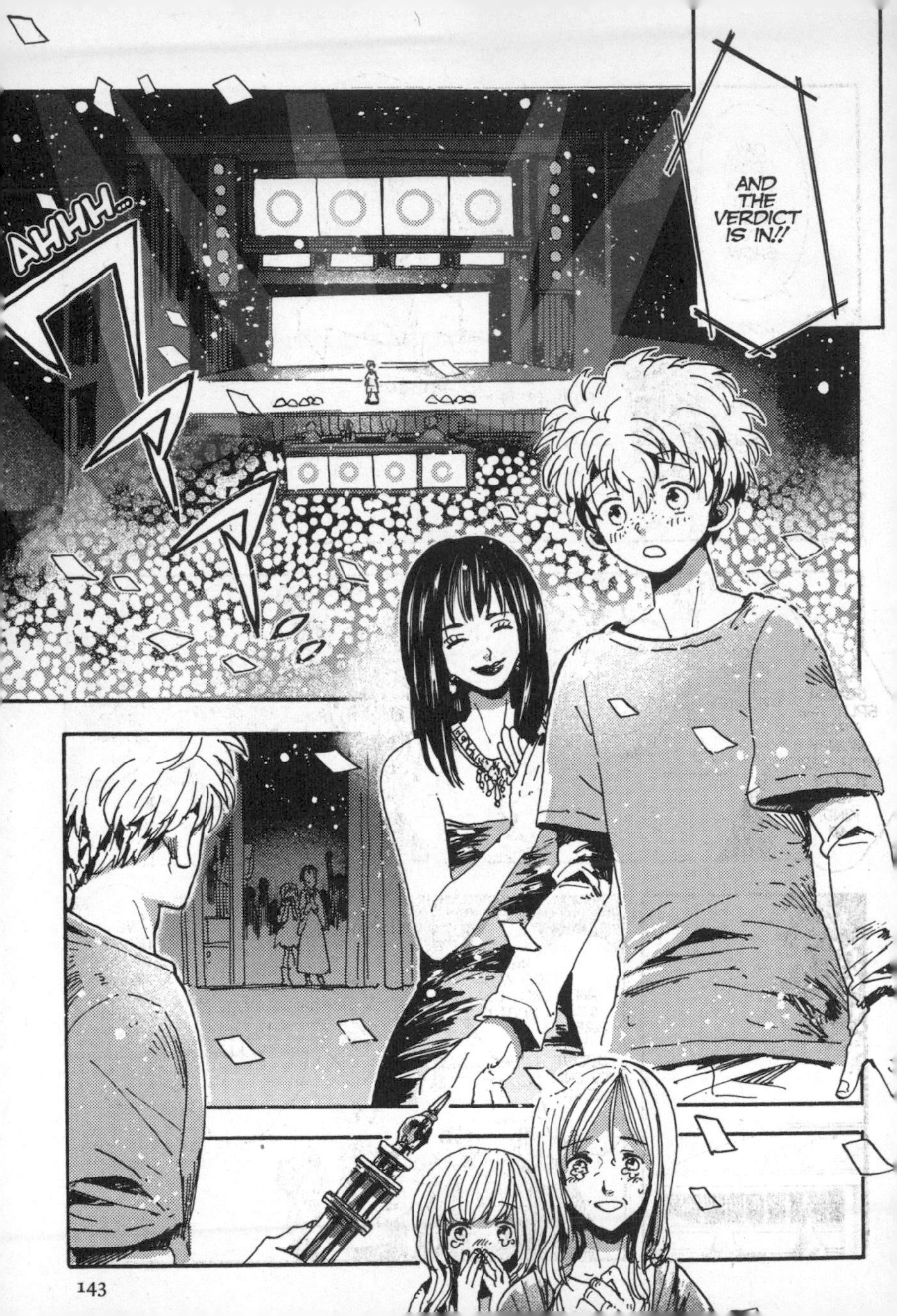
AND THE VERDICT IS IN!!
AHHH...

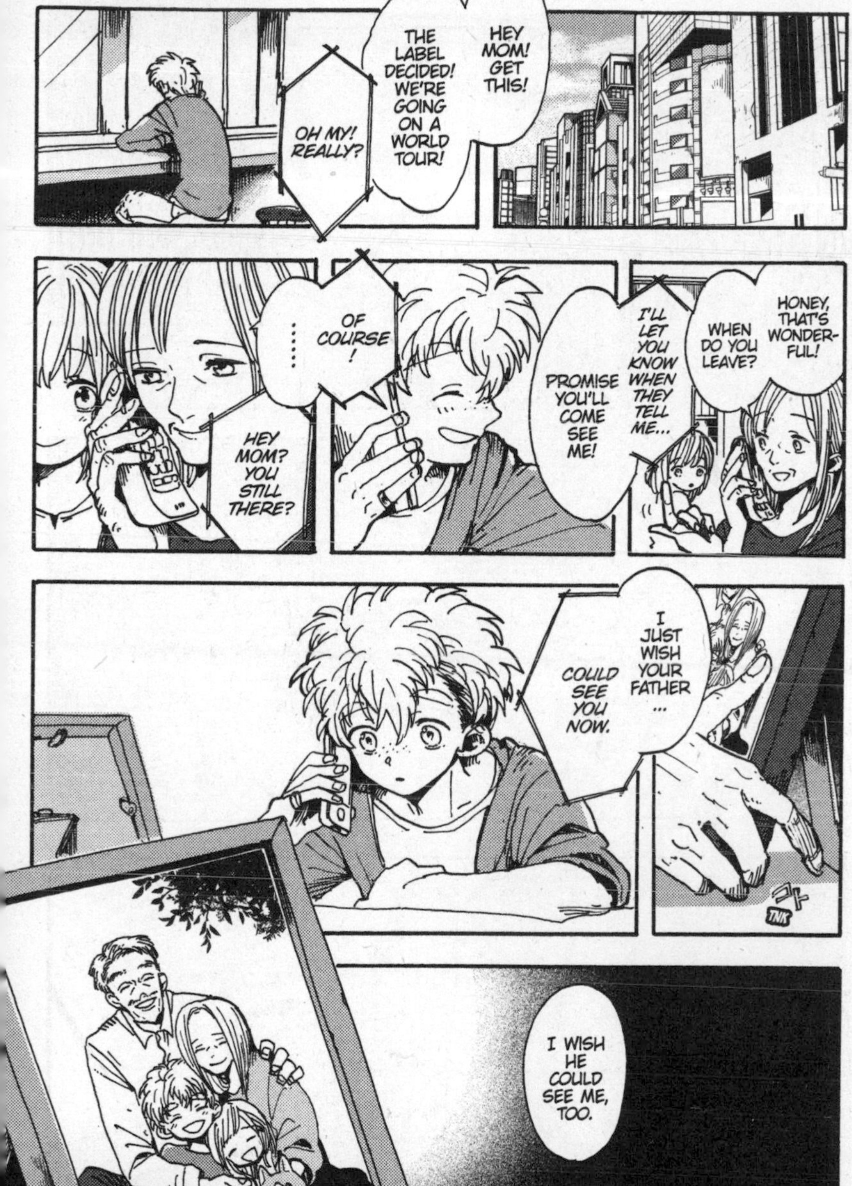
HEY MOM! GET THIS!
THE LABEL DECIDED! WE'RE GOING ON A WORLD TOUR!
OH MY! REALLY?
HONEY, THAT'S WONDERFUL!
WHEN DO YOU LEAVE?
I'LL LET YOU KNOW WHEN THEY TELL ME...
PROMISE YOU'LL COME SEE ME!
OF COURSE!
......
HEY MOM? YOU STILL THERE?
I JUST WISH YOUR FATHER ...
COULD SEE YOU NOW.
TNK
I WISH HE COULD SEE ME, TOO.

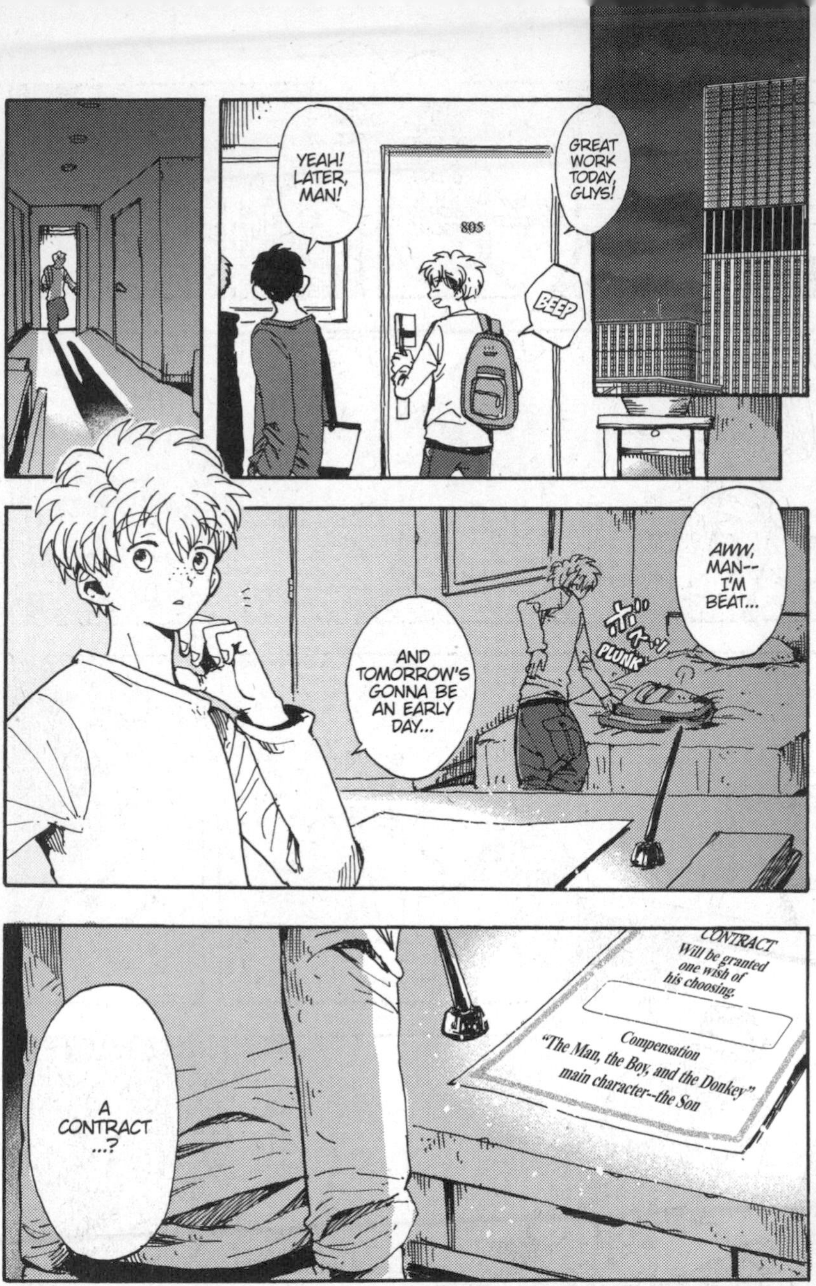
GREAT WORK TODAY, GUYS!
YEAH! LATER, MAN!
805
BEEP
AWW, MAN-- I'M BEAT...
PLUNK
AND TOMORROW'S GONNA BE AN EARLY DAY...
CONTRACT
Will be granted one wish of his choosing.
Compensation
"The Man, the Boy, and the Donkey" main character--the Son
A CONTRACT ...?

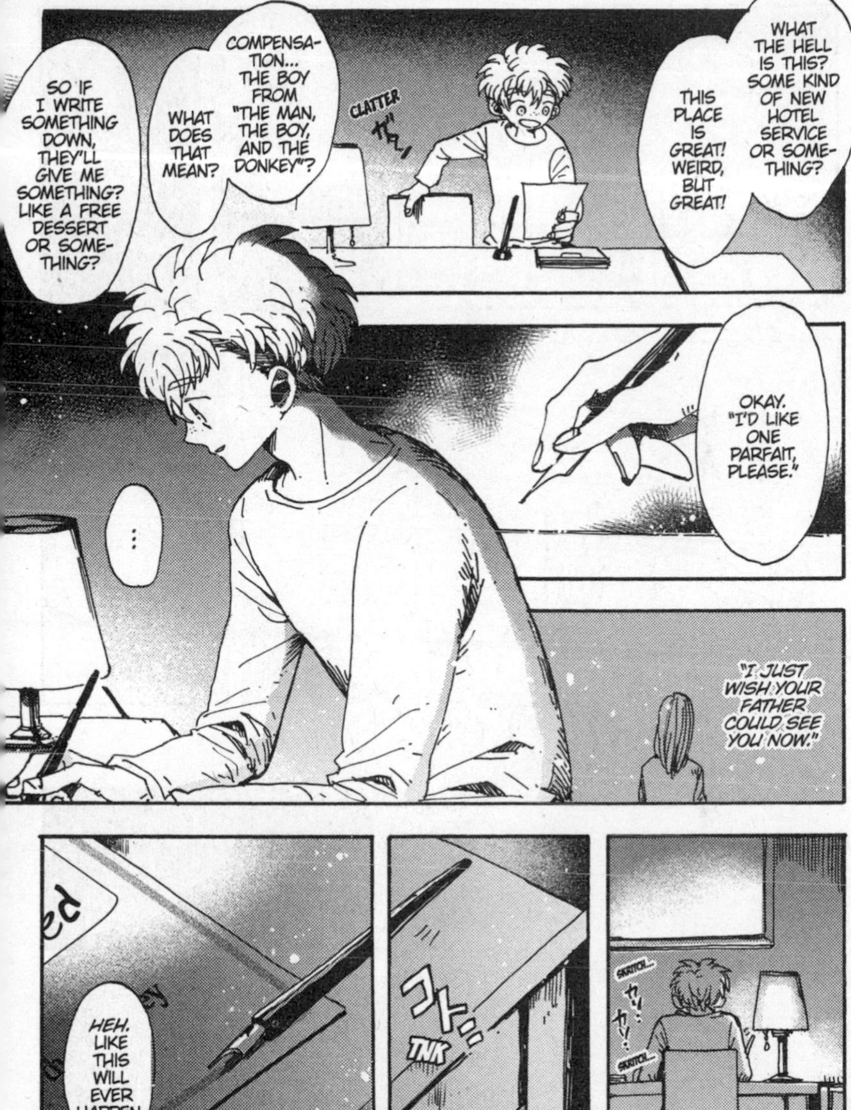
WHAT THE HELL IS THIS? SOME KIND OF NEW HOTEL SERVICE OR SOMETHING?
THIS PLACE IS GREAT! WEIRD, BUT GREAT!
CLATTER
COMPENSATION... THE BOY FROM "THE MAN, THE BOY, AND THE DONKEY"?
WHAT DOES THAT MEAN?
SO IF I WRITE SOMETHING DOWN, THEY'LL GIVE ME SOMETHING? LIKE A FREE DESSERT OR SOMETHING?
OKAY. "I'D LIKE ONE PARFAIT, PLEASE."
...
"I JUST WISH YOUR FATHER COULD SEE YOU NOW."
SKRITCH...
SKRITCH...
TNK
HEH. LIKE THIS WILL EVER HAPPEN.

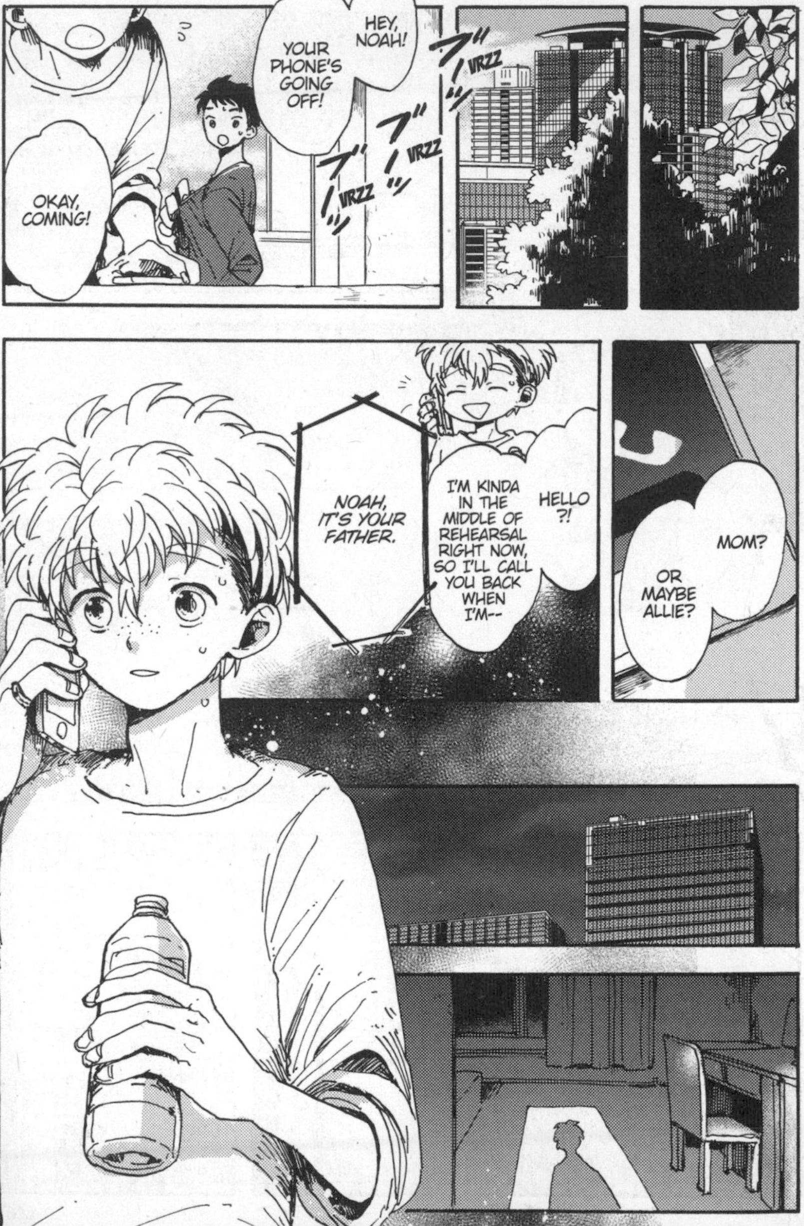
VRZZ
VRZZ
VRZZ
HEY, NOAH! YOUR PHONE'S GOING OFF!
OKAY, COMING!
MOM? OR MAYBE ALLIE?
HELLO ?!
I'M KINDA IN THE MIDDLE OF REHEARSAL RIGHT NOW, SO I'LL CALL YOU BACK WHEN I'M--
NOAH, IT'S YOUR FATHER.

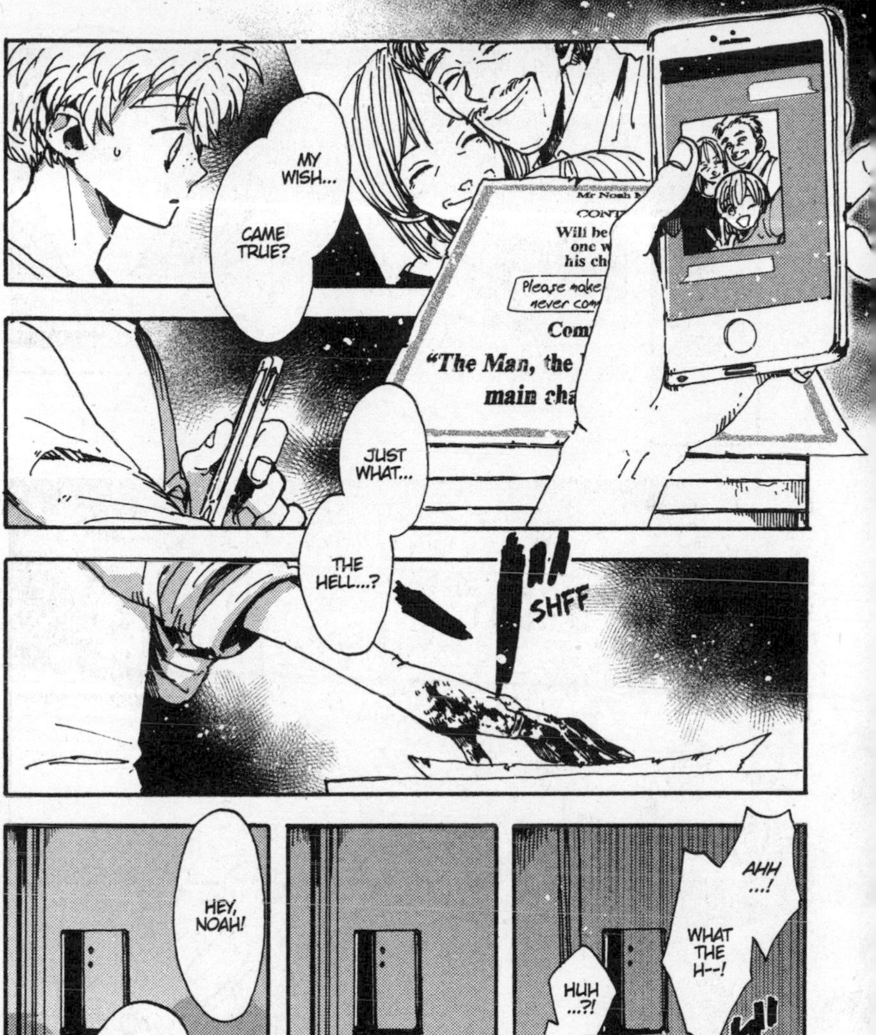
Mr Noah M
CONT
Will be
one w
his ch
Please make
never com
Com
"The Man, the
main cha
MY WISH...
CAME TRUE?
JUST WHAT...
THE HELL...?
SHFF
AHH ...!
WHAT THE H--!
CLATTER
HUH ...?!
AHHH ...!
...!!
HEY, NOAH!
WE'RE GOING OUT TO EAT! COME WITH US!

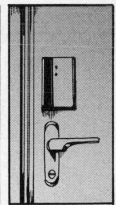

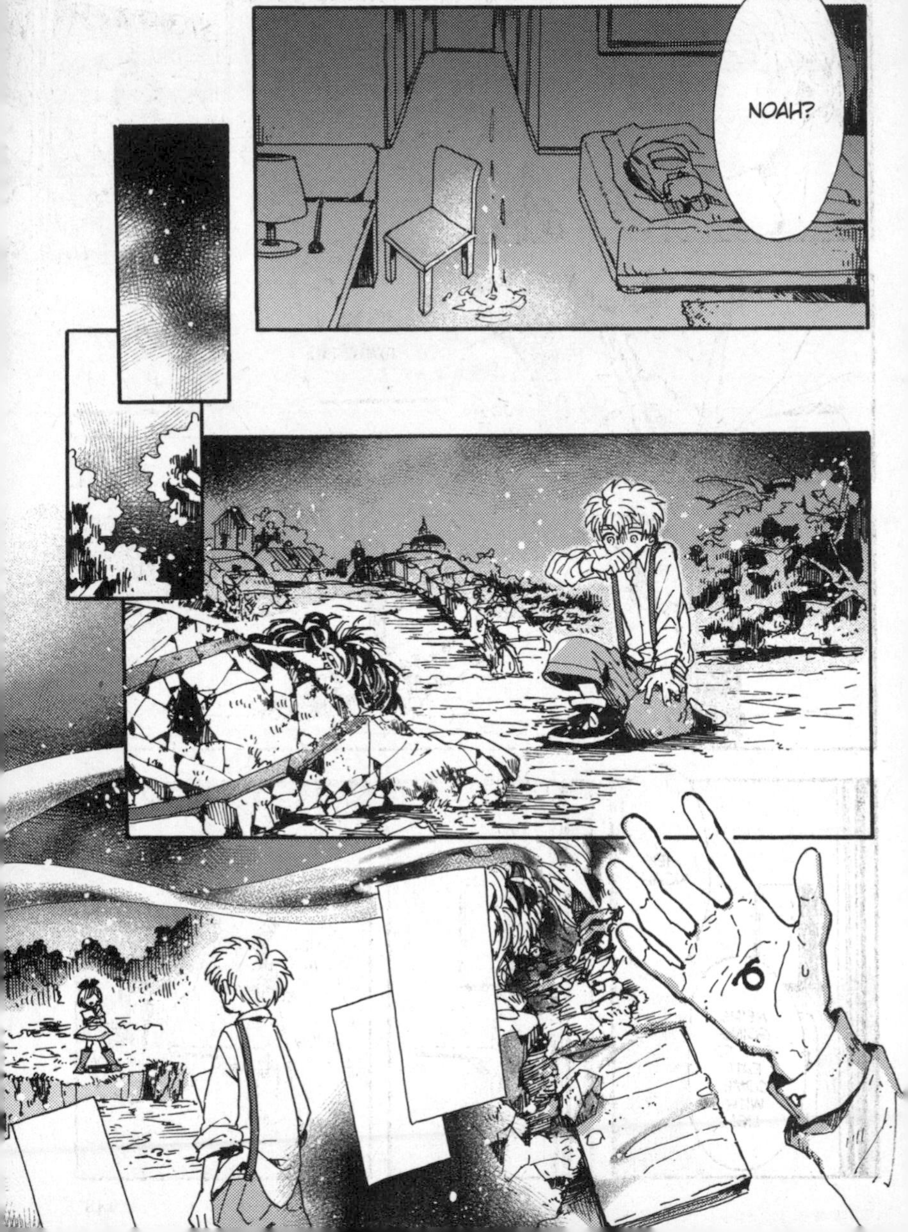
NOAH?

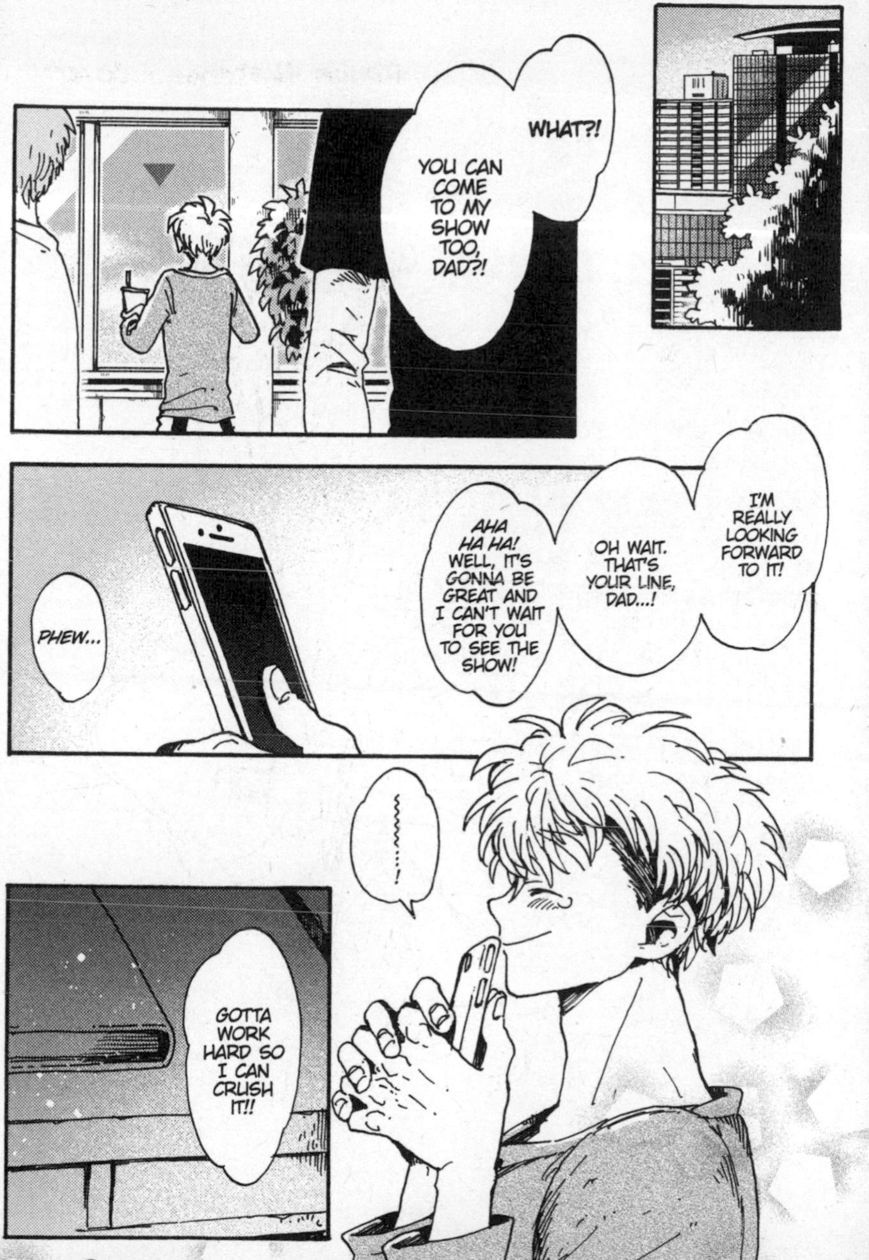
WHAT?!
YOU CAN COME TO MY SHOW TOO, DAD?!
I'M REALLY LOOKING FORWARD TO IT!
OH WAIT. THAT'S YOUR LINE, DAD...!
AHA HA HA! WELL, IT'S GONNA BE GREAT AND I CAN'T WAIT FOR YOU TO SEE THE SHOW!
PHEW...
...!
GOTTA WORK HARD SO I CAN CRUSH IT!!

Volume 2: END

Rough Sketches - Cover

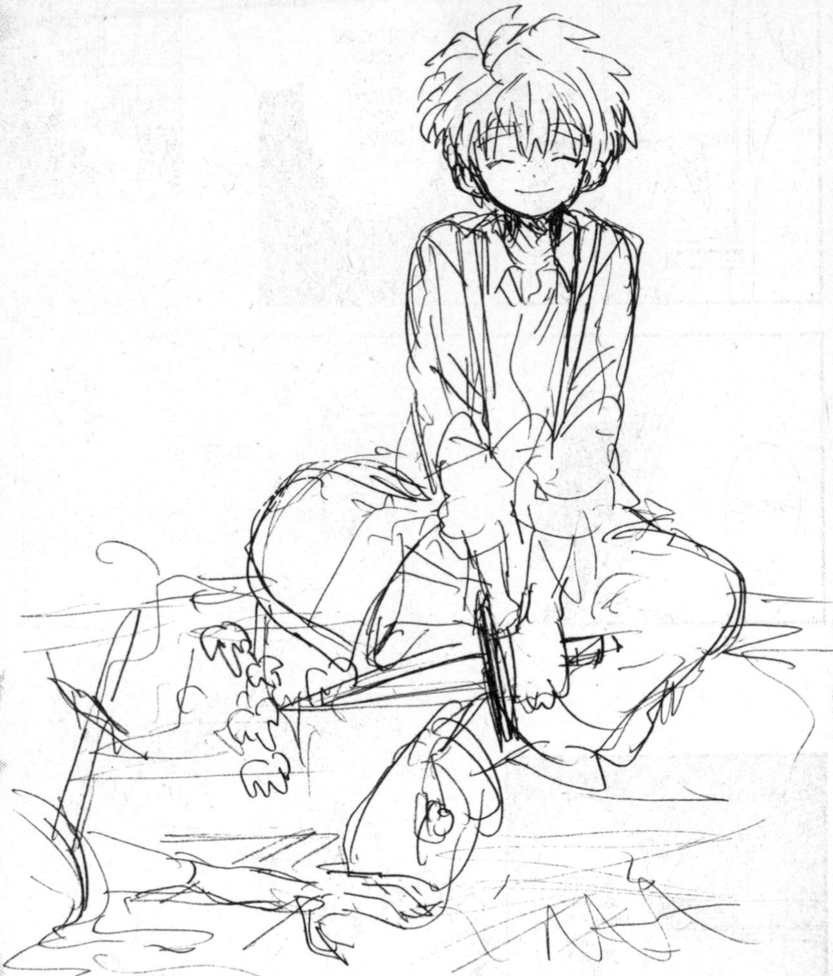

Rough Sketches - Cover

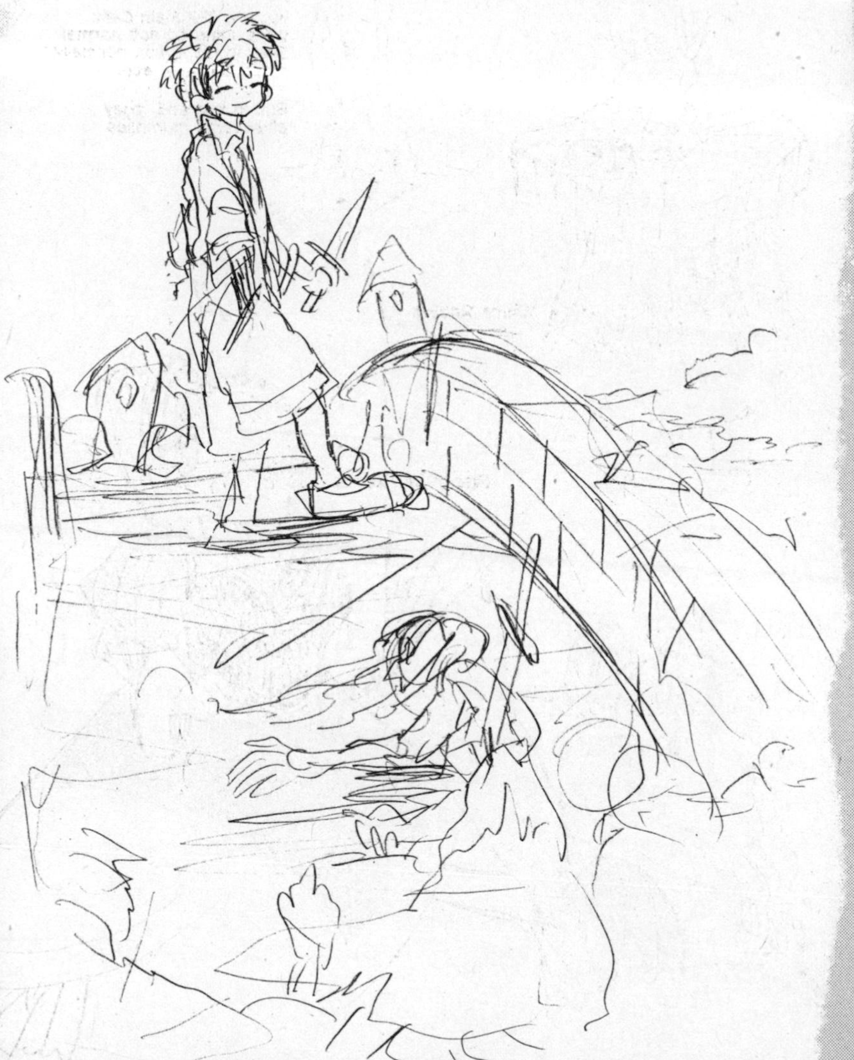

Alice in Wonderland Main Cast Rough Sketches

Initially, the Main Cast were going to act normal. They would speak normally, move normally, etc.

But in the end, they all became mummies.

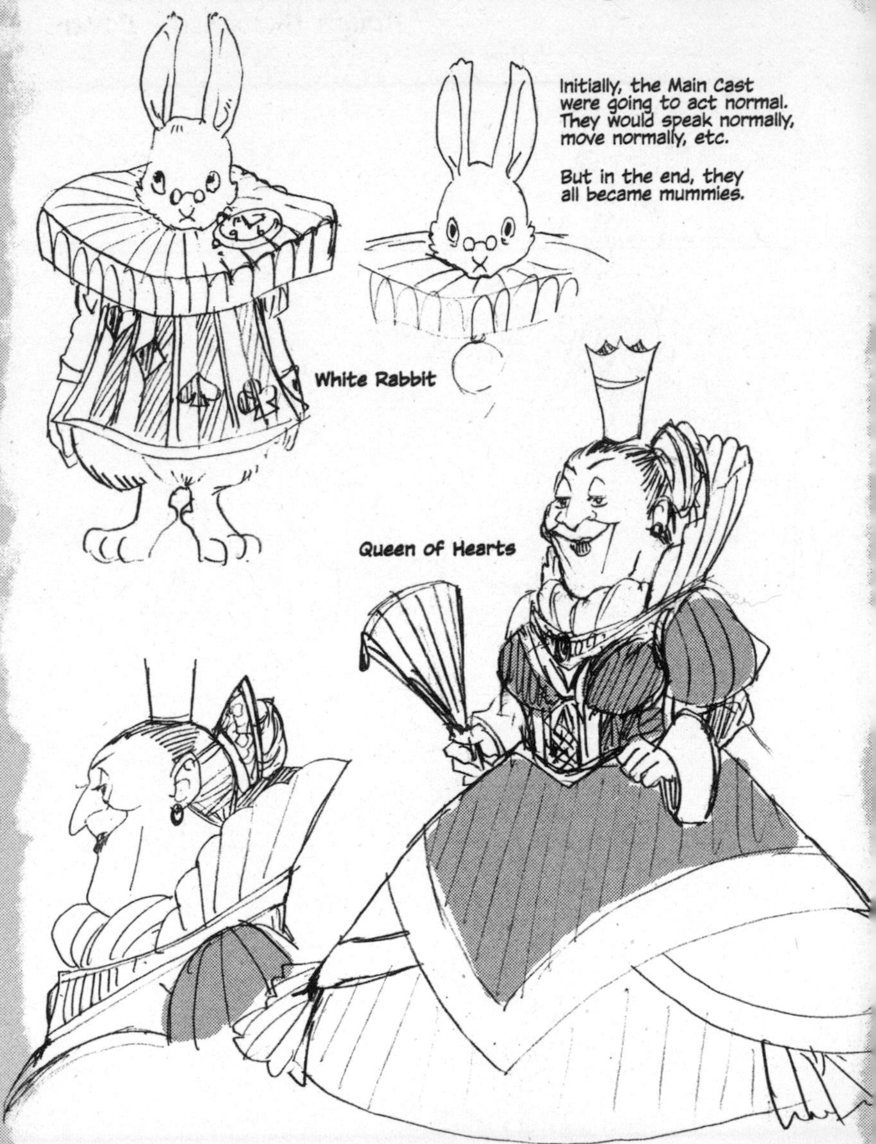
White Rabbit
Queen of Hearts

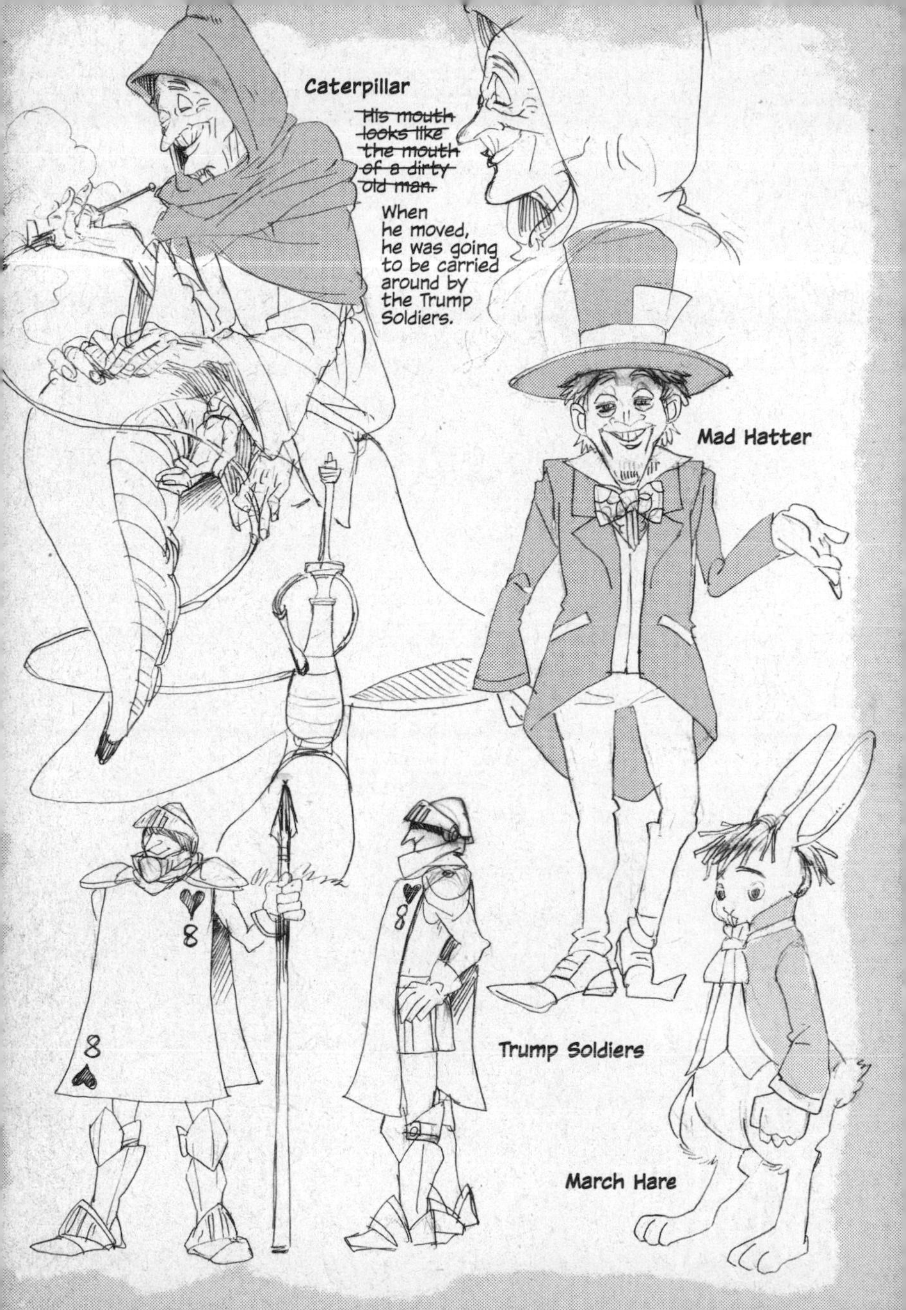
Caterpillar
His mouth looks like the mouth of a dirty old man.
When he moved, he was going to be carried around by the Trump Soldiers.
Mad Hatter
Trump Soldiers
March Hare

FAIRU
TALE
BATTLE
ROYALE

FAIRY
TALE
BATTLE
ROYALE

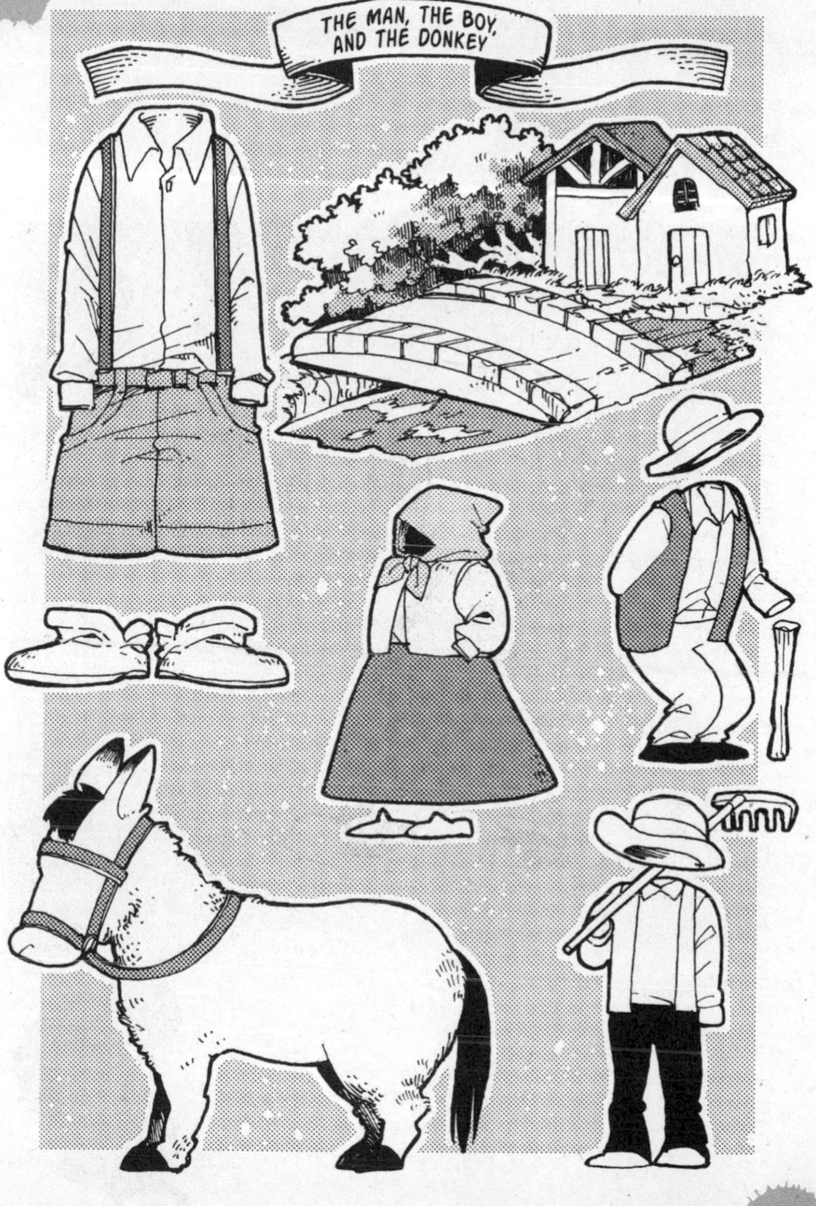
THE MAN, THE BOY, AND THE DONKEY

FAIRY
TALE
BATTLE
ROYALE